Beyond MFN

Beyond MFN

Trade with China and American Interests

Edited by James R. Lilley and
Wendell L. Willkie II

The AEI Press

Publisher for the American Enterprise Institute
WASHINGTON, D.C.

1994

Library of Congress Cataloging-in-Publication Data

Beyond MFN: trade with China and American interests / edited by James R. Lilley and Wendell L. Willkie II.

p. cm.

Includes bibliographical references (p.).

ISBN 0-8447-3856-5 (cloth). — ISBN 0-8447-3857-3 (pbk.)

1. United States—Foreign economic relations—China. 2. China—Foreign economic relations—United States. 3. United States—Commerce—China. 4. China—Commerce—United States. 5. Favored nation clause—United States. 6. Human rights—China. I. Lilley, James R. II. Willkie, Wendell Lewis, 1951- .

HF1456.5.C6B49 1994

337.51073—dc 20

94-8228

CIP

ISBN 0-8447-3856-5 (alk. paper)

ISBN 0-8447-3857-3 (pbk.: alk. paper)

The AEI Press

Publisher for the American Enterprise Institute

1150 17th Street, N.W., Washington, D.C. 20036

Contents

Preface

The relationship between the United States and China is of rapidly increasing importance to Americans. China is rising to preeminence in Asia—and Asia is acquiring central importance in world affairs. China is now defined by great expectations. By the year 2010, some experts say, China could have the world's biggest economy, with a large and prosperous middle class conducting business throughout East Asia and the world. *Beyond MFN* explores America's relationship with the world's most populous country and fastest-growing economy. Both addressing and looking beyond the annual debate on MFN, this book examines the complex economic, strategic, and philosophical issues confronting U.S. policy makers in this critical Pacific relationship.

The recent history of Taiwan, South Korea, and Japan demonstrates that political pluralism and the rule of law follow the development of a market economy in a society open to Western influence. How can the United States best encourage such trends in China? The volume explores the views of the Chinese people themselves, the evolving human rights policy of the Chinese government, the economic opportunities China presents, our continuing national security interests in the relationship with China, the legacy and political implications of the Jackson-Vanik amendment, and the internal deliberations within the Clinton administration on China policy. From diverse perspectives, the book addresses several other important issues in America's relationship with China.

If Chinese human rights practices were our sole concern, would not normal, indeed enhanced, trade relations still be the wisest policy for the United States? Is the growth of a substantial, well-educated, and increasingly independent middle class the single most powerful force in advancing political liberalization? Authors consider whether an energetic and economically liberated population with an enlarged appreciation and understanding of the outside world can erode the foundations of political repression. Indeed, it would appear this is already occurring.

Since the *dan-wei,* or work unit, is the most immediate instrument of Communist control over people's lives, creating a dynamic alternative sphere of economic activity outside the *dan-wei* has already expanded personal freedom. The appreciation the Chinese people have of Western values is still limited; yet the Chinese themselves are nonetheless absolutely convinced of the importance of American economic engagement, sensing, correctly, that a brighter future lies in greater openness to the West rather than isolation.

While Americans are, and should be, concerned with the rights and well-being of the Chinese people, it is clearly in the national interest of the United States to address other issues as well. Our strategic and economic interests in East Asia are of increasing importance to our nation's future. Strategic coordination with China is critical as we face the specter of a nuclear-armed North Korea prepared for war. Chinese cooperation in UN Security Council resolutions during the Persian Gulf War was essential to permit Allied forces to operate with the moral authority of the United Nations. Chinese cooperation is also necessary to prevent the global proliferation of dangerous technologies. America's national security, in short, clearly mandates a constructive working relationship with China.

With regard to our national economic interests, others have commented on the drastic consequences of withdrawing most-favored-nation status. The chairman of the International Trade Subcommittee of the U.S. Senate, Max Baucus, has said 180,000 high-paying American jobs could be lost.

But the true importance of American trade with China can best be measured by the staggering economic potential of that country. Highly competitive American products—aircraft, fertilizer, computers, and telecommunications and environmental technology—will be in intense demand in China in the next few years. China's market for some of these products could be the world's largest. The demand for aircraft and aerospace products will be enormous, while $30 billion worth of telecommunications could be sold in the next five years. Over the next three years, American auto parts sellers have extraordinary opportunities in a market valued at more than $29 billion.

When so many economists agree that the great untapped potential in the American economy in the 1990s lies in international trade, aggressive pursuit of this huge emerging market becomes a national imperative. Indeed, if the United States does not take the fullest advantage of the enormous business possibilities in China, American industries may suffer a long-term disability relative to their foreign competitors.

We would like to thank the fine staff of the AEI publications department, especially its director, Dana Lane, for her substantial assistance in the stylistic editing of the book. The interns who have volunteered their time to this project receive our gratitude as well. More than any other aide, our research assistant, Christopher Carson, has helped bring this project to its fruition. His assistance, both substantive and administrative, has been invaluable in producing this work expeditiously.

We are deeply grateful to Lee Hamilton, David Lampton, Claude Barfield, Andrew Nathan, Anne Thurston, Jerome Cohen, Matthew Bersani, and Karlyn Bowman for their superb contributions to this volume. They have each been a pleasure to work with in this endeavor. We are fortunate indeed to have had such busy and talented authors who were always willing to cooperate with our extraordinarily tight deadlines. It is our hope and belief that their chapters in *Beyond MFN* will make a useful contribution to the continuing debate over America's China policy.

Contributors

JAMES R. LILLEY is a resident fellow and the director of Asian Studies at the American Enterprise Institute. Before joining AEI in January 1993, Mr. Lilley served as assistant secretary of defense for international security affairs from November 1991 to January of 1993. He was ambassador to the People's Republic of China from April 1989 to May 1991 and was ambassador to the Republic of Korea from 1986 to 1989. He has also served as national intelligence officer for China, political coordinator and senior East Asian specialist on the National Security Council, and deputy assistant secretary of state for East Asian and Pacific Affairs.

WENDELL L. WILLKIE II is a visiting fellow at the American Enterprise Institute, where he is engaged in research, writing, and lecturing on legal policy and international trade. Mr. Willkie served as general counsel of the U.S. Department of Commerce from 1989 until 1993. During the last five months of the Bush administration, he also performed the duties of deputy secretary. From 1985 to 1988, Mr. Willkie was general counsel of the Department of Education and was associate counsel to the president, 1984–1985. Mr. Willkie is a graduate of Harvard College and the University of Chicago Law School. He also holds an M.A. from Oxford University, which he attended on a Rhodes scholarship.

CLAUDE E. BARFIELD is a resident fellow at the American Enterprise Institute and director of Trade and Technology Policy Studies. Mr. Barfield was a consultant with the Office of the U.S. Trade Representative, where he wrote the Reagan administration's "Statement of Trade Policy" in 1983. He was codirector of the staff of the President's Commission for a National Agenda for the Eighties. He served as the deputy assistant secretary for research and demonstration at the Department of Housing and Urban Development. He is the author of several books and articles on the subjects of trade, technology, and industrial policy, including, most recently, *Capital Markets and Trade: The United States Faces a United Europe* and *Industry, Services, and Agriculture: The United States Faces a United Europe.*

MATTHEW D. BERSANI has practiced law with the international law firm of Paul, Weiss, Rifkind, Wharton & Garrison since 1988. He was the resident representative of the firm's Beijing office during 1990 and 1991. Mr. Bersani has practiced in the areas of international securities offerings, joint ventures and foreign investment, transnational arbitration, and general corporate law. He received his undergraduate degree from Princeton University and his J.D. from Columbia University School of Law. Mr. Bersani has been an officer of the United States–China Business Council Legal Committee and the Asian Committee of the New York State Bar Association. He has published several articles on Chinese legal topics.

KARLYN H. BOWMAN is a resident fellow at the American Enterprise Institute and editor of *The American Enterprise* magazine. Ms. Bowman was research director for a public relations firm, and from 1971 to 1976 she worked for a U.S. senator. She has written on many public opinion topics, including the gender gap, foreign policy attitudes, and the federal government's role in society.

JEROME A. COHEN is professor of law at New York University School of Law and is of counsel to the international law firm of Paul, Weiss, Rifkind, Wharton & Garrison. He specializes in business law relating to Asia and has long represented foreign companies in contract negotiations and dispute resolution in mainland China, Hong Kong, Taiwan, Japan, and Korea. Mr. Cohen formerly served as professor, director of East Asian Legal Studies, and associate dean at Harvard Law School. He has published several books and many articles on Chinese law as well as a general book, *China Today,* cowritten with Joan Lebold Cohen. In 1990, he published *Investment Law and Practice in Vietnam,* with the cooperation of N. N. Bich and Ta Wan Tai.

LEE H. HAMILTON, a senior member of the Indiana congressional delegation, serves as chairman of the House Committee on Foreign Affairs. He is also the cochairman of the Joint Committee on the Organization of Congress and a member of the Joint Economic Committee. He has served, since 1965, as the U.S. representative from the Ninth District of Indiana. Congressman Hamilton obtained his B.A. from DePauw University and spent one year studying at Goethe University in Germany in 1952. He then attended Indiana University School of Law, where he obtained his J.D. in 1956.

DAVID M. LAMPTON is president of the National Committee on United States-China Relations in New York. He received his Ph.D. from Stanford University and is former director of China Policy Studies at the American Enterprise Institute. The author of numerous books and articles on Chinese foreign and domestic politics, Mr. Lampton has most recently published (with Barber B. Conable, Jr.) in *Foreign Affairs* and coedited a volume with Kenneth Lieberthal entitled, *Bureaucracy, Politics, and Decision Making in Post-Mao China.*

ANDREW J. NATHAN is professor of political science and director of the East Asian Institute at Columbia University. His publications include *Chinese Democracy* (1985), *Human Rights in Contemporary China* (cowritten with R. Randle Edwards and Louis Henkin, 1986) and *China's Crisis* (1990).

ANNE F. THURSTON, a writer and China specialist, is a peace fellow at the U.S. Institute of Peace. Most of her research is based on extensive interviews in China, where she has spent five years. She lived in Beijing from May 1989 through June 1990, during the student demonstrations and the crackdown that followed, and is on the board of directors of the New York–based Human Rights in China and works on China issues with Amnesty International. She is the author of several books, including *Enemies of the People; A Chinese Odyssey: The Life and Times of a Chinese Dissident;* and *The Private Life of Chairman Mao,* written with Mao's personal physician, Dr. Li Zhisui.

1

Introduction

Lee H. Hamilton

To write about the future of U.S.-China relations is as risky as predicting at half time what the score of a basketball game will be at the final buzzer. As this chapter was written, a deterioration of U.S.-China relations—the result of conflicts over trade, human rights, and proliferation of weapons of mass destruction—appeared likely. In particular, human rights conditions set forth in the president's executive order of May 28, 1993, by the Clinton administration for the renewal of China's most-favored-nation (MFN) status were, by the end of 1993, still unfulfilled, by the administration's own measure. Although the tone of the relationship has improved since then, it remains to be seen whether those conditions will be met.

Yet, given the high stakes involved in this relationship, there is merit in examining the U.S.-China relationship beyond MFN. A resumption of cold war tensions between China and the United States could cause major problems for the United States and strained relations with its allies. For China, a break with the United States would also be serious because of the importance of its economic and political relations with the West. Conditioning or ending China's MFN status has been no more than a means of exerting leverage to achieve U.S. foreign policy objectives. As circumstances change, policy makers and the public should ask whether U.S. foreign policy objectives *vis-à-vis* China have changed and whether the United States should continue to employ the MFN lever to achieve them.

So, as the fifth anniversary of the Tiananmen tragedy approaches, a new look at some old questions is in order:

- What is the current situation in China, and how is it likely to evolve?
- What are U.S. interests concerning this dynamic situation?
- Given those interests, and given the changing Chinese reality, what should be the objectives of U.S. policy toward China?
- How are those objectives best achieved? In particular, is the MFN level still useful?

The past five years have demonstrated that U.S. policy toward China is only viable if it has broad political support. The approach articulated by President Clinton in May 1993 facilitated a consensus on China policy between Congress and the White House and allowed Washington to speak to Beijing with a clear voice.

With his moves in 1993, President Clinton bought some time in dealing with China, but, as current controversies show, he has not solved the problem completely. China has still not responded substantively to the U.S. agenda. Clinton has tried to broaden and upgrade diplomatic contacts as a way of showing engagement and improving relations, but the risk is that China will regard this as a sign of weakness. In the end, U.S. China policy will be judged by results, and the results are not in yet.

China Today and Tomorrow

In pace and breadth, change is so rapid in most areas of Chinese life that both Chinese and Americans are hard pressed to understand it. Words do little justice to the complexity of the world's most populous political unit. We probably do not appreciate how far China has traveled from rigid communism and how difficult it is to force the tempo of change.

On the one hand, the Chinese economy, particularly on the coast, is growing at an unprecedented rate. A flood tide of entrepreneurship is sweeping the country. The state-owned sector, though still significant, is declining in importance. Foreign business is finding enormous opportunities to use China as an export-assembly platform, to sell to the increasingly prosperous domestic market, and to participate in a major program of infrastructure development. On the other hand, there are causes for concern about the Chinese economy. The central government, for example, has difficulty controlling the money supply and the pace of investment; efforts in 1993 to rein in inflation were only partly successful. Moreover, China's lack of modern infrastructure is a serious drag on further growth. Corruption, too, has become so widespread that businessmen complain about the absence of even basic rules of the economic game. And China has moved slowly to carry out commitments to protect intellectual property and to ensure greater market access to foreign business.

The social and cultural picture is also mixed. Traditional social institutions like the family and religion are reemerging after three decades of Communist suppression. Economic growth has begun to create an urban middle class that wants the good things in life, material and otherwise. Finally, Chinese who have long worried about their country's weakness and isolation now witness the initial achievements of a century-old aspiration for national wealth and power.

Increasing prosperity, though, has brought a host of social problems. Capitalism in China today is reminiscent of nineteenth-century England. Migration from the countryside to the city is straining social services already in short supply. China's higher-education system lacks the resources to train the next generation of scientists and engineers. Drug abuse and prostitution have returned, and traditional values have declined. Neither the Confucian nor the Communist visions of society have much appeal today. Nationalism and consumerism have partly replaced them, but these cannot answer all the questions facing contemporary Chinese civilization.

Politically, matters are even more problematic. The state's failure to control corruption is corroding its legitimacy, even as it maintains the will and means to suppress challenges to its rule. Chinese who want the government to leave them alone are free to make money. Chinese who overtly oppose the regime are treated harshly. Government does not account for its abuses of power and provides few channels for the expression of popular grievances.

Amid these difficulties, China has already begun a political transition of fundamental importance. With the passing of Deng Xiaoping and other Communist party elders, China's leadership will be in the hands of individuals who have no personal connection with their country's weakness in the early twentieth century, with the wars against the Japanese and the Chinese Nationalists, or with Mao Zedong. Nor will any of the potential successors have the political base that Mao or Deng did.

We cannot know who or what will follow Deng Xiaoping, who projected a vision of collective prosperity and national strength. The new leadership may continue a combination of economic liberalization and political authoritarianism as the best guarantee of the power of the Communist party. New leaders, however, may believe the party's future depends on significant political reform, if not democratization, despite the risks. Or the existing pressures for political decentralization may grow, leaving the central government with only modest ability to assert its authority nationwide.

Thus, China today is a massive developing country, with all the chaos and contradictions that implies. It is worth asking, at least in the abstract, whether a process of rapid change in a country of 1.2 billion people is simply too much for one government to administer in an efficient, honest, and humane way. Will it remain an authoritarian state? Will it collapse into chaos and civil war? Or will it, like Taiwan and South Korea, transform itself into a prosperous and pluralistic nation? As China specialist Michel Oksenberg has stated: "The United States . . . will have to deal with a sprawling, territorially amorphous, culturally nationalistic, socially undisciplined, economically vibrant and politically messy China."

Predicting China's future international role is similarly difficult. Will it convert the fruits of economic growth into military capabilities and become an East Asian Prussia of the late twentieth century? Why is it pouring more money into the military when its most serious military rival, the Soviet Union, has collapsed? Why is it exporting nuclear technology to Algeria and Iran? Will it become a source of instability and refugees? Will China have both the ability and the will to participate in multilateral regimes in arms control and economic relations? To cite one small example, will the central government of China, whose administrative reach is already receding, be able to prevent the pirating of tapes and compact discs by companies far from Beijing—as it is obligated to do under its commitments to protect intellectual property? The simple answer is that we do not yet know.

U.S. Interests concerning China

The United States needs to deal with China as it exists and is becoming, not as some imagine it or hope it to be. While that does not require abandoning the fundamental principles of American foreign policy, it does suggest applying those principles toward objectives that are both meaningful and achievable and employing policy tools appropriate to the circumstances. What are U.S. interests in China?

Political. China's stability is in the U.S. interest. It is not in the interest of the United States to bring down China's political regime or to seek the fragmentation of the country. To state the point more fully, it is in the U.S. interest that there be a Chinese government that is coherent, effective, and responsive to the needs of the Chinese people. The international community does not need the obligation of feeding, clothing, housing, educating, employing, and providing medical care to even a fraction of the 1.2 billion people of China.

It is also in the U.S. interest that the Chinese government restrain the arbitrary exercise of state power. Among abuses that need to be corrected are official corruption, the absence of due process, torture and other forms of inhumane treatment of prisoners, the use of criminal sanctions against dissenters, and politically biased "justice." Based on the experience of many Western and non-Western countries, the best way to reform those practices is to establish the rule of law, an independent judiciary, and some guarantee of political rights.

In addition, it works to the advantage of the United States if the Chinese government can address the profound alienation of peoples outside the core of the Chinese mainland, including Tibetans, Mongols, Uighurs, Muslims, citizens of Hong Kong, and citizens of Taiwan.

Economic. The U.S. interest is served by China's continuing economic development, for the sake of both improving the material welfare of the Chinese people and fostering political liberalization.

Moreover, the United States should both contribute to and benefit from China's economic modernization and reform. It is not politically sustainable for China to have open access to the U.S. economy and not provide similar access to American exporters and investors. The memoranda of understanding between the United States and China on market access and protection of intellectual property, plus the consideration of China's application to accede to the General Agreement on Tariffs and Trade, are useful tools for ensuring mutual economic benefit.

Security. It is in the U.S. interest that China not become militarily powerful in ways that threaten regional peace and security. It is possible, though, that China's military build-up will proceed in ways that lead others in East Asia to respond in kind. The best method of preventing tensions and a regional arms race is to convene a multilateral security dialogue designed to increase transparency, build confidence, and encourage arms restraint.

The United States should continue to urge the Chinese government to support strongly all key arms control regimes: the Nuclear Nonproliferation Treaty, the Chemical Weapons Convention, the Biological Weapons Convention, the Missile Technology Control Regime, and, for the future, restrictions on the number and testing of nuclear weapons.

Diplomatic. It is in the U.S. interest that China continue to work with the United States and others to solve the many complex problems of the post–cold war world, as it has done concerning Cambodia and North Korea. China is a permanent member of the UN Security Council, and a positive Chinese contribution is far better than no contribution or Chinese obstruction. The United States will need all the help it can get from China in promoting global peace and stability.

U.S. welfare is also enhanced if the Chinese government, working with other countries in the region, seeks solutions to a number of pressing transnational problems, including environmental degradation and the production and trafficking of narcotics.

Does China have the capacity and will to be a responsible power? If so, it could bring a resurgence of the best of Chinese civilization. But we do not know. A combination of Chinese chauvinism, protectionism, and brutality is certainly possible, in which case many American interests would be damaged or undercut. So, too, is a descent by China into weakness and division, again to the detriment of U.S. interests. But it is also possible that a new China will emerge committed to more humane government, upholding global norms, and facilitating international cooperation on economic and security issues. There are trends that favor this outcome, and a U.S. policy objective should be to find ways to strengthen them.

Toward a Policy of Realism

We must first be clear on what U.S. policy cannot achieve. Neither the United States nor any other country will be able to determine China's future—only the Chinese can. The task of policy will be to protect U.S. interests, whatever occurs. In the short term, however, it may be possible to work at the margin to encourage a positive direction for post-Deng China.

The first objective of the United States should be to maintain broad public support for its policy toward China. That has been the single most important achievement of President Clinton's approach, in contrast to four years of controversy during the Bush administration. Without unity of purpose, the United States cannot act with the skill and clarity needed to protect its interests.

The United States must also remain flexible in the succession to Deng Xiaoping, a process that is already under way. We should avoid undermining those groups and individuals in China who seek to move China in a direction that benefits the United States. Whatever the U.S. interest—China's international role; its military posture; its actions on proliferation of weapons, trade, and human rights—who and what succeed Deng are the most important factors shaping China's future. In the late 1970s, it made a great difference who—Deng Xiaoping or Jiang

Qing or Hua Guofeng—became the leader of China. It will be no less so in the mid-1990s.

In that same context, the United States must avoid creating the impression within China's elite that it intends to bring down the current system or divide the country. That, of course, is not the U.S. objective. Yet a combination of historical memory, paranoia, and misunderstanding about America's pluralistic political system has led some Chinese to weave together a theory that the United States is bent on such a mission. If the United States is indeed prepared, as I believe it should be, to treat China as an important partner if it meets its international obligations, then the United States should make its intentions crystal clear to Beijing.

Last, the United States should continue to encourage China's adherence to international norms and bilateral agreements in security, economics, and human rights. In all the disputes between the United States and China, the key issue is whether China is prepared to recognize the same rules of conduct as most other countries. That is the basis for a sound relationship and American political support for it. As a rule, however, the United States should not pursue any one interest in a way that works to the detriment of other U.S. interests.

While there is currently no reason for President Clinton to abandon or change his executive order of May 28, 1993, linking China's continued MFN status to progress in human rights, there are at least two circumstances under which a reassessment would be in order.

First, if there is heightened confrontation on the Korean peninsula over North Korea's nuclear program, China's cooperation will be fundamental to achievement of U.S. objectives. China, of course, has its own reasons for preventing Pyongyang from getting nuclear weapons. But it will have differences with the United States on how to achieve the shared objectives. Given the stakes in Korea, it is vital that China and the United States, along with South Korea and Japan, be in fundamental agreement on the course to pursue. No good would be served in a crisis by raising Chinese doubts about U.S. intentions.

Second, if Deng Xiaoping should die in the near future, there is some question whether his successors will be willing or able to take on tough policy issues while they jockey for political position. Such immobility of policy occurs in the United States during a transfer of power, and the Chinese system is far less institutionalized. It took Deng Xiaoping over two years to achieve a dominant position after the death of Mao Zedong.

Deng's death or political incapacitation before June 3, 1994, when President Clinton must decide whether China has met the conditions of his executive order, would create a difficult situation. In such a circumstance, each of the Chinese leaders competing to succeed Deng is likely to oppose meeting the president's conditions. They would be reluctant to do so not because each of them would necessarily regard those steps as bad for China but because each would fear criticism by his rivals for caving in to the "American hegemonists." In such a situation, U.S. insistence that conditions be met by the June deadline would make a termination of MFN for China all but inevitable. In response, China might pursue policies, both internal and external, contrary to American interests.

The United States, however, could bide its time and let the Chinese sort out the succession. Although there is no guarantee, restraint on the part of the United States could make more likely the emergence of a Chinese leadership more dedicated to the protection of civil and political rights and to foreign policies that are congruent with U.S. interests.

I emphasize that these scenarios are hypothetical. With some cooperation from Pyongyang, tensions on the Korean peninsula are probably manageable. The immediate post-Deng leadership may in fact be coherent enough to take initiatives toward the United States that would otherwise spark political controversy. It will be up to the president and his advisers to make a careful judgment as to whether U.S. objectives would best be served by insisting that conditions be met by the date certain. Whatever he decides, the president will also have to build political support for the course he chooses.

For the longer term, U.S. policy makers should not assume that the policy tools of the recent past—threatening the termination of MFN—will necessarily be appropriate for China's future. U.S. interests concerning China will remain constant, but how the United States pursues them will depend on circumstances that are likely to be fluid and uncertain. China may find it extremely difficult, if not impossible, to synchronize its political clock to America's MFN clock, where midnight comes on June 3 every year.

The Jackson-Vanik amendment and the concept of MFN conditionality were policy measures created during a different era to achieve a different policy purpose *vis-à-vis* a different government. Even those who conclude that Jackson-Vanik was effective in increasing emigration of Jews from the Soviet Union may legitimately question whether MFN conditionality is still a good way to achieve U.S. policy goals toward China today, including broad human rights objectives. The consensus answer may still be yes, but the question surely deserves to be asked. If the emerging answer from the expert community is no, then it is time for political leaders to think about moving beyond MFN, toward a better policy to protect and promote the U.S. national interest.

2

China Policy in Clinton's First Year

David M. Lampton

In a much earlier era of American policy toward China, Senator Kenneth S. Wherry of Nebraska said, "With God's help we will lift Shanghai up and ever up, until it is just like Kansas City."[1]

In the June 1993 debate over China policy, Representative Sam Gibbons of Florida, chairman of the Trade Subcommittee of the House Ways and Means Committee, said,

> I want to include China within the family of nations, at least on a probationary basis, to see what we can do to bring the way they treat their people up to the standards that we would like to think that we treat our people by: equality, freedom, justice—all of those things that we cherish so highly, and rightly so highly.[2]

The views expressed in this chapter are the author's alone, not those of the National Committee on United States–China Relations, its members, or its sponsors. The author would like to thank Debra Kam and Michael Spiro for their research assistance and Professor A. Doak Barnett for his trenchant comments on a previous draft. An earlier version of this chapter was delivered at the "Third Japan-U.S. Symposium on China," sponsored by the Japan Institute of International Affairs, Tokyo, Japan, July 15–16, 1993.

Introduction

On May 28, 1993, President Bill Clinton issued an executive order to extend most-favored-nation (MFN) tariff treatment (that is, normal tariff treatment) for China for an additional year (1993–1994) and established comparatively limited conditions for the next renewal decision in mid-1994. In so doing, the China policy he adopted seemed much more like the policy of his predecessor, George Bush, than his 1992 campaign rhetoric would have led one to expect. In August 1992 in Los Angeles and two months later in Milwaukee, candidate Clinton had excoriated President Bush for his "ambivalence about supporting democracy around the world in a manner worthy of our heritage, our ideals, and our name. . . . There is no more striking example of President Bush's indifference to democracy than his policy toward China."[3] Yet, the day before issuing his executive order on May 28, President Clinton said at a town hall meeting, "I've basically decided to extend MFN for a year because I want to support modernization in China, and it is a great opportunity for America there."[4] How, and why, did this decision come to pass, and what does this tell us about the Clinton administration's emerging decision-making style? What are the policy's consequences likely to be, and where is the U.S.-China relationship headed?

It is not enough to say that the 1992 campaign proclivity for hyperbole gave way to the sobriety induced by the exercise of power in May 1993, though such postcampaign conversions are not uncommon:

> Before taking office, decision-makers often claim they will introduce new policies. But these promises are often neglected. Eisenhower's foreign policy more closely resembled that of his predecessor than it did his campaign rhetoric. Gladstone pledged himself to avoid immoral and wasteful imperialism, and, although he successfully extricated Britain from some entanglements, he was eventually drawn into commitments similar to those made by Disraeli. And while in 1937 Clement Atlee said that "the foreign policy of a Government is the reflection of its internal policy," when his party took power the foreign secretary declared that "Revolutions do not change geography, and revolutions do not change geographical needs."[5]

In addition to the postelection conversion phenomenon, however, one must examine three sets of factors to begin to understand President Clinton's decision: first, the domestic and international political contexts in which President Clinton and his advisers perceived themselves, the links among issues at the top of their domestic and foreign policy agendas in the spring of 1993, and the bargains struck among the competing interests, bureaucracies, and branches of government; second, perceptions that Clinton and his principal advisers had of the People's Republic of China (PRC), its course of development, its global role, and Beijing's behavior during the period November 1992–May 1993; and third, the resources that the president and his advisers believed they had to pursue alternative policies.

Well before the executive order of May 28 was issued, a plan was in place for producing a policy by June 3, 1993. After that came another, and ultimately decisive, political phase: winning support in Congress and with influential interest groups so that the president could avoid conflict with members of his own party. The president would need every congressman and senator he could get in future battles over the budget, health care reform, and the administration's entire legislative agenda; he was unprepared to squander scarce resources in a fight over China policy. As Assistant Secretary of State Winston Lord said at the House Ways and Means Committee hearings on June 8, 1993,

> Only after extensive consultations with Congress, human rights organizations, business interests and others, did the President decide on the approach defined in his Executive Order. Such consultations will continue to be a hallmark of this administration's China policy.[6]

Policy process issues aside, the president's decision announced in the May 28 executive order has consequences, some of which can be foreseen and some of which cannot. By establishing standards, however vague, for his June 1994 decision on whether to renew MFN status for China again, President Clinton may have simply deferred a painful problem to a time when it could be even more painful. In 1994, Sino-American two-way trade will probably be much larger than the 1992 level of $33.2 billion, and therefore the costs to everyone of removing MFN status, even from "state enterprises,"[7] will be higher still. But if there are occurrences in China that are perceived to be untoward in America (an ever-present possibility, if not an inevitability), the president could have relatively little room to maneuver. In this sense, his policy is hostage to the vagaries of domestic developments in both China and America to a greater extent than before. In the colorful words of Peter Passell of the *New York Times*, "The President may be stuck with a weapon that looks more like a doomsday machine than a smart bomb."[8] More ominously, it might prove to be a blank, a bluff that if called would harm the administration's credibility.

Indeed, the decision of May 28 was not even three months old when the administration launched another "review" of policy toward China, sparked by "a rapid-fire series of controversies [that] exploded between the two nations [America and China]"[9] in August and September. Some feared that President Clinton, who had already made foreign policy missteps in the former Yugoslavia, Somalia, and Haiti, would now be called on to implement his threat to withdraw most-favored-nation treatment from China, thereby precipitating a dramatic downward spiral in relations with the world's most rapidly growing economy and alienating the United States from all its allies in the process. In contrast, to certify as acceptable what was being portrayed in Washington as "deteriorating Chinese human rights and other behavior" would seriously harm the president's credibility in America and abroad.

The other, more hopeful assessment of the consequences of the president's decision is that he accomplished two positive things with the executive order. First, in finding the middle ground, he achieved his minimal objective of loosely linking considerations of trade with the PRC to human rights on the mainland; and this link provides the Chinese some modest incentive to move in directions more compatible with American values (but which Beijing can perhaps live with).[10] And second, his decision *may* have helped restore an essential consensus on China policy between the legislative and the executive branches in Washington. If this possibility proves true, the administration may have set the stage for more stability in Sino-American relations than would have been the case had the struggle between Congress and the president over China policy continued, with the president losing ever more ground to an increasingly enraged legislature.

Even if the second scenario is the one that materializes, simply dodging the latest MFN bullet fired from our own weapon does not constitute a realistic, durable, and constructive China policy. Washington needs to develop a policy toward the PRC that makes sense in global and regional settings, as well as being consistent with American interests, capabilities, *and* values. The key elements of this policy would be:

• First, Americans need to acknowledge the tremendous social and political change that *is* occurring in China—a middle class is arising in the PRC and its creation is being driven by economic growth. If America wants to promote its values effectively, it should be fueling that engine, not trying to shut down the gas pump.[11]

• Second, American policy must recognize that *no* policy toward China can be successful if our allies and friends in Europe and Asia find it undesirable or unworkable, as they currently find the sanctions-based approach of Washington.

• Third, the Clinton administration's "enlargement strategy" is flawed, particularly in its application to relations with China. The United States cannot enlarge its immediate policy to promote democracy and free markets throughout the world at the very moment it reduces the physical, financial, and leadership resources devoted to achieving those expanded objectives.[12] Without a relationship between objectives and available means, we are left largely with empty rhetoric. Beyond that, the United States cannot use economic sanctions, which inevitably hit free markets, to promote the development of free markets.

• Fourth, Americans face a choice. We can set ourselves in opposition to Chinese nationalism, and thereby feed it in its most destructive form, or we can affirm through deed and action that we welcome a one-China that is peacefully achieved, strong, stable, and modernizing, a China with which America has a thick network of positive ties.

Clinton's Evolving China Policy

Between June 3, 1992, and May 28, 1993, candidate and later President Bill Clinton's views concerning MFN treatment for the PRC evolved through several stages. Some observers would say that this evolution is simply another example of a postelection policy conversion by the president. Careful analysis, however, indicates that the president's core idea remained consistent—to create a link between trade and human rights in the PRC—even as the means by which this was to be accomplished changed over time.

The phases in Clinton's views on the MFN issue were revealed by how his views on three subjects changed:

• Should legislation be the way in which conditionality is expressed?

• If MFN status is to be withdrawn upon failure to satisfy conditions, should it be withdrawn from the entire Chinese economy or only the state sector?

• Should conditionality include only human rights provisions, or should it embody concerns in other areas such as weapons sales and technology proliferation, China's trade practices, and policies toward Tibet and Hong Kong?

From June 1992 to May 1993, the president changed his publicly articulated position on nearly all these questions, while adhering to the core commitment to conditionality, or a link between trade and human rights.

In phase one, from just before he became the Democratic party's nominee in midsummer until September 1992, his rhetoric and the phraseology of the Democratic party's campaign platform were tough and broad. One apparent implication of his remarks and the platform's language was that he would move immediately to support the *legisla-*

tive imposition of a broad range of (human rights and other) conditions on the extension of MFN treatment for the PRC and that were withdrawal to occur, it would apply to the products of *all* PRC enterprises. On June 3, 1992, candidate Clinton said, "It is time to put America back on the side of democracy and freedom. I hope the Congress will move quickly to enact legislation [conditioning MFN treatment for China]."[13] The Democratic party platform called for conditions related to human rights and "greater access for US goods, and responsible conduct on weapons proliferation."[14]

In September, Clinton, following the earlier lead of Representative Nancy Pelosi of California and Senator George Mitchell of Maine, moved into phase two, trying to come to terms with the argument that taking the MFN status away from all enterprises in the PRC would retard the development of the private and cooperative sectors (as well as American joint ventures) in China, engines for change on the mainland. He modified his earlier position, now calling for removing MFN from only state enterprises if conditions were not met. More specifically, on September 14, 1992, Clinton embraced a revised form of conditionality legislation that had passed the Senate, saying, "MFN privileges would not be revoked for private enterprises in China or for US joint ventures."[15] Nonetheless, he continued to adhere to the position that conditionality was desirable, that it should be imposed legislatively, that it should be linked to a broad array of American dissatisfactions, and that such conditionality should be imposed immediately.

Within fifteen days of having defeated President Bush, President-elect Clinton entered phase three on November 19, a phase in which he seemed to back off a bit further while adhering to the notion of conditionality. This change may have reflected the prudence induced by the prospect of governing and knowing that a review of China policy would soon be under way. In his November 19 remarks after meeting with President Bush and congressional leaders, the president-elect said,

> As you know, I supported some restrictions on MFN status to China, pending some changes in the human rights and trade area. And I noted with satisfaction in the last several months, when the Bush Administration . . . took a tougher line on goods made with prison labor, on unfair trade practices, we began to have more moderation. . . . We have a big stake in not isolating China, in seeing that China continues to develop a market economy. But we also have to insist, I believe, on progress in human rights and human decency. And I think there are indications in the last few months that a firm hand by our government can help to achieve that.[16]

In this statement, his position on several issues was obscure, although his continued concern for human rights was unmistakable. It is this process of defining the dimensions of conditionality and the issues that the executive order (and the two other documents promulgated along with it)[17] raises for America's China policy in the future that are the principal subjects of the remainder of this chapter.

A Presidential Review Directive on China Policy

From 1990 on, Capitol Hill and the White House locked horns every spring over how, and whether, to renew China's MFN status. MFN had become the institutionalized vehicle by which China policy, in all of its dimensions, was discussed each year. By 1993, everyone in the process had become exhausted by it—Congress, the executive branch, and the Chinese. One Chinese academic captured the weariness on both shores of the Pacific when he said in April 1993, "Writers say love is the eternal theme. I feel MFN is our eternal theme."[18]

The argument over MFN provided the occasion for different groups in the United States to debate the rationale for the relationship with Beijing; the direction of China's economic and political development; American interests in the relationships with Beijing, Taiwan, and Hong Kong; and the importance of human rights relative to other strategic, regional, global, and economic interests.

Following the 1989 Tiananmen tragedy, President Bush had been through three such debates by late 1992, and Clinton was about to become the central player in the fourth: no later than June 3, 1993, the new chief executive would have to inform Congress of his decision on MFN renewal. That decision would need to be placed in a framework acceptable to a Democratic Congress, some members of which were quite publicly committed to a tough policy toward Beijing. Further, some of the highly charged rhetoric that candidate Clinton had used to characterize President Bush's China policy during the campaign had created expectations of significant policy change in several quarters, particularly among human rights organizations and many members of Congress who had been frustrated by President Bush's repeated rejection of legislative efforts to condition or withdraw MFN status from Beijing. Unlike the Bush period of divided government, the new president would not rely on his veto power to sustain a China policy unpopular with Congress.

The policy process consisted of four domains of negotiation and mutual influence:[19] (1) efforts to build a consensus within the administration itself and develop a strategy by which support in Congress could be achieved; (2) discussions (formal and informal, direct and indirect) with China to move ahead on key issues to justify as moderate a policy as possible; (3) efforts to ensure the support of Congress for the policy that was adopted; and (4) efforts to ensure that the policy that eventually was adopted did not elicit major negative responses from private sector organizations, particularly human rights groups or the business community. Assistant Secretary of State Lord described the process as follows:

> The President, consulting closely with the Congress, reached this decision . . . on extending MFN status. . . . This was not an easy decision for the President. It involved extensive consultations with the Congress, business interests, and Chinese cooperation on international issues. . . . We reached this decision after intensive dialogue with our Chinese friends both here in Washington . . . and also in Beijing. . . . Our purpose [in these negotiations] was through quiet dialogue to reach as much progress with our Chinese colleagues as we could.[20]

The policy process was kicked off within eleven days of the president's inauguration on January 20, when the National Security Council (NSC) issued a presidential review directive on China; this required creation of an interagency working group to draft a paper presenting policy options and recommendations to the president before June 3, 1993. How specific presidential guidance was to those involved in the policy review is unclear to outside observers, but most of the participants assumed that unless there was a significant Chinese reversal on human rights and in other policy areas, there were two irreducible presidential requirements: conditions on the extension of MFN status and solidarity with Congress.

Most such directives initiate the same general process: the working group prepares a draft paper, which is discussed collectively by deputy principals (or, in the case of very important issues, principals) representing each involved department. After discussion by the deputies or principals, there may well be revisions suggested, in which case the draft is sent back to the working group. This can go through several iterations. Eventually, the resulting document is submitted to the president, through the NSC, for his consideration. In this case, the Department of State was the lead agency in the working group, and the NSC, Central Intelligence Agency, Department of Defense, Office of the U.S. Trade Representative, Department of Treasury, Department of Commerce, and Office of the Vice President all participated. Because a new assistant secretary of state for East Asian and Pacific Affairs (Winston Lord) was not confirmed by the Senate until April 19, 1993, the holdover assistant secretary, William Clark, played a formal lead role in the process in February and March. Secretary of State Warren Christopher's testimony to Congress on March 30, however, nearly three weeks *before* Assistant Secretary-designate Lord was confirmed, makes it clear that Lord was the driving force behind policy: "The general approach that Winston Lord is recommending is the one that we'll be following. . . . That is to try to use MFN to encourage better performance, better conduct in China. . . . I must say for myself how pleased I am that Winston Lord is at the State Department, and we're able to be colleagues."[21]

During February, March, April, and May, China was by no means the most important foreign policy issue confronting the president or the agencies involved in the working group. At about the time the presidential review directive on China was issued, several sources report that there *may* have been ninety or more directives under consideration on most of the world's major foreign policy issues and geographic areas. For Asia alone, directives were issued on China, Japan, Korea, Vietnam, Cambodia, Taiwan, and Asia-wide issues. One executive branch respondent reports, "There was a two-foot-high stack and China was somewhere near the middle of the pile—it was not a top priority issue at the White House until a week or two before a decision had to be made." One informed congressional participant said there were three "time frames [for responding to the directives]—yesterday, today, and six to eight weeks." China was in the last category.

While many details of the directive-development process concerning China are not publicly available, three important things about it are clear: (1) the draft working paper from the working group went through several meetings at the deputy *and* the principal levels in March, April, and May;[22] this is important because common wisdom in the mass media and in Washington has it that the process was slow in moving along and that the executive order was the result of a crash program in the last two weeks before it was issued—that is not accurate; (2) various deputies and principals meetings were interspersed with discussions with China and key congressional personalities; and (3) an early draft of the working group's paper was completed by the third week in February; that document outlined many of the features of the process and the executive order that evolved over the next three months.

From the third week in February on, the road map to June 3 was fairly clear: human rights, weapons proliferation, and trade would be the principal concerns (as they had been for the Bush administration since 1990); there would be dialogue with the Chinese to seek as much progress as possible, with a hope that conditionality could be avoided (but with a widely shared premonition that it would not); and the administration would pursue a parallel track of discussion with Congress. This was an improvement on President Bush's tactics. From the earliest days of the process of the working group, it was consciously decided that developing a consensus between Congress and the executive branch on China policy was a central objective. And finally, a preference soon developed in the executive branch that if conditionality had to be imposed, the method by which to express it should be consistent with the president's authority over foreign policy. This created a disposition in favor of a presidential executive order.

Besides preserving presidential authority over foreign policy, a nonlegislative route provided for flexibility in policy, which was highly valued given the expectation that the succession to Deng Xiaoping could not be too far into the future; everyone wanted to have room to deal with contingencies. And finally, the lesson of Jackson-Vanik (1974) was staring everyone in the face—the Jackson-Vanik amendment had been adopted to foster Jewish emigration from the Soviet Union in the 1970s and had become a congressional lever to increase the Hill's power over a broad range of foreign policy issues two decades later. Few executive branch participants in the policy process wanted to build that kind of inflexibility into the conduct of foreign policy again.

The decision-making process within the White House executive offices (that is, the NSC, the National Economic Council, and the president's domestic policy advisers) is rather opaque to outsiders, though its contours can be discerned. First, beyond receiving periodic staff updates, the president was apparently not highly engaged in the process until his final approval was needed. Second, the president's national security adviser, Anthony Lake, was besieged with a host of issues, from Bosnia and Somalia to Haiti and North Korea. Consequently, while he had to approve policy (and he was a relatively forceful advocate for human rights concerns), he does not appear to have been much involved in the process throughout February, March, and April. Instead, his assistants, Sandy Berger, Nancy Soderberg (previously on Senator Kennedy's staff), and Kent Wiedemann (a foreign service officer with extensive China experience) were principally involved. Soderberg constituted a particularly strong voice for human rights issues within the deliberative process.

The National Economic Council (NEC), headed by former Goldman, Sachs & Company investment banker Robert Rubin, had a part in the process as well, though assessments of the NEC's role vary. The key people involved were Bowman ("Bo") Cutter and Michael Punke. Punke was formerly on Senator Max Baucus's staff (the senator who had nudged President Bush toward a more muscular policy on China in return for support for maintaining MFN treatment for China in 1991 and 1992). The NEC provided an important avenue for the articulation of business concerns in the executive branch, though business had comparatively more effect on Congress, with the White House more open to human rights and fair trade constituencies.[23]

Parenthetically, many of the people in the business community felt they did not have the access to the president that human rights constituencies were afforded. Business leaders failed in their attempts to meet directly with the president on the issue, though it is true that business had significant access to senior staff levels immediately below the president. It is this frustration that helps account for the public call on May 12, 1993, of more than 300 business firms and associations, urging Clinton's unconditional extension of MFN status for China.[24] With respect to the Office of the U.S. Trade Representative (USTR) as well, it appears that throughout the interagency process USTR was a force arguing for continuation of MFN treatment for China.

With respect to the intelligence community, it appears from both documentary and interview sources that the CIA and the Defense Intelligence Agency generally presented rather gloomy assessments of the PRC's behavior on weapons proliferation and at least implicitly argued for taking a tough line, while others in the intelligence community (particularly in the Department of State) challenged their conclusions. The CIA has devoted substantial effort to weapons proliferation concerns, while the DIA, because of reorganization, has relatively reduced area expertise on China and correspondingly has concentrated more on various functional concerns. As a result, the institutional forces in the intelligence community with knowledge of China are relatively weaker than those dedicated to specific issues such as proliferation and human rights. In turn, those on Capitol Hill on various committees (and the mass media) know where to turn in the intelligence community and the broader bureaucracy for views that will support their concerns.[25]

Because Winston Lord was one of the first assistant secretary–level foreign policy officials nominated by the new administration, the Department of State was appropriately the lead agency in the working group. Lord, who had briefed candidate Clinton during the campaign, was presumed to be fully acquainted with the president's orientation. Furthermore, because of his credibility in Congress on China-related human rights issues, he assumed the main role in calls on Capitol Hill, working very closely with the Department of State's Legislative Affairs Office. Lord's consultations with the Hill were extensive from February through May. The White House Congressional Liaison Office was not the focal point of contact with Congress on this issue, which, given the poor relations of the White House Congressional Liaison Office with the Hill at this time, was probably fortunate.

A policy process in which an assistant secretary and a few White House presidential aides play a key role has strengths and weaknesses.

A small group of people focused on a single issue can create a strategy and carry out a guided and sequential implementation. This modus operandi, however, means that the president is not closely involved, which can be interpreted as lack of commitment. In turn, a perceived lack of presidential commitment or interest reduces the degree to which a single foreign policy vision can be effectively articulated and pursued. The incentive for others to comply is diminished because the power of the presidency has not been brought fully into play.

This kind of policy process also excludes many in the bureaucracy and Congress who believe they ought to be involved, thereby generating morale problems. Predictably, therefore, some in the bureaucracy and Congress grumble that they were not consulted, at least not until rather late in the process. As one person put it, "President Bush had a bigger orchestra—this is a string quartet, not an orchestra." It may be worth remembering that Winston Lord studied bureaucratic politics and the making of foreign policy at the knee of Henry Kissinger.

One other observation stemming from the Nixon-Kissinger era is appropriate. It is now a cliche that only someone like Richard Nixon, with impeccable credentials on the right, could have effectively made the move toward China in the early 1970s because he was almost untouchable by the right wing in American politics. In the same way, more than twenty years later, it would take persons (Clinton and Lord) with strong credentials in the human rights community to forge a comparatively moderate policy acceptable to the liberal wing of the Democratic party. President Bush could not have won congressional acceptance of the policy that President Clinton implemented, even had he desired to do so.

The Chinese Track

Much of the interaction with the Chinese from late February until May 28 is veiled in secrecy and was characterized by a mixture of formal, informal, and indirect communications and negotiations. Although there are genuine uncertainties for the future, the resulting executive order did not precipitate an immediate and dramatic deterioration of bilateral relations, though in August and September 1993 a series of events created a well-concealed crisis in the two governments that led to the restoration of high-level dialogues in September.[26]

According to informed sources in several executive branch agencies and on Capitol Hill, as well as media reports, by late February one of the central aims of diplomacy was to induce the Chinese to make as much progress (on the American agenda of human rights, trade, and weapons and technology proliferation issues) as possible. Therefore, sometime in March the administration formally conveyed, through Ambassador Stapleton Roy in Beijing, a rather substantial list of fourteen items on which the United States would like to see progress;[27] the implication was that if progress were evident in these areas, Washington would be in a position to adopt a constructive, moderate policy. Even though Winston Lord was not confirmed as assistant secretary of state until April 19, he played a key role in formulating this communication to the Chinese. Although the specifics of this communication have not been made public, by all accounts it included issues such as amnesty for, and a full accounting of, political detainees, effectively halting the use of prison labor for exports to America and ending M-11 missile technology sales to Pakistan that the United States would consider in violation of the guidelines and parameters of the missile technology control regime. According to Hong Kong sources, the Chinese referred to it as a "coercive ultimatum,"[28] and it took Beijing some time to respond to this communication. When it did, it issued its own list of seven areas of dissatisfaction with the Americans.[29] The precise content and timing of Beijing's response are not publicly known, but they obviously were inadequate to convince the administration to eschew conditionality entirely.

In addition to the communication mentioned above, there was a steady stream of consultations in March, April, and May between Chinese and American policy makers that included Secretary Warren Christopher; the Chinese ambassador to Washington, Zhu Qizhen; Vice Foreign Minister Liu Huaqiu; Under Secretary Peter Tarnoff; the new Chinese ambassador, Li Daoyu; Assistant Secretary Winston Lord; and Ambassador Stapleton Roy in Beijing. A central moment in the process came when Assistant Secretary Lord traveled to Beijing (May 3–5, 1993) for eleventh-hour consultations with Vice Foreign Minister Liu Huaqiu. "A senior Western diplomat" in Beijing described Lord's purpose as follows: "What we are coming up to is the crunch. . . . The question is, when the president has to make his decision, whether the progress has been sufficient to convince Congress that they can work easily with the president on a positive China relationship."[30]

Although Assistant Secretary Lord did not clearly state his conclusions after the discussions in the Chinese capital, one businessman who heard the secretary's postdiscussion briefing for Americans in Beijing concluded, "Basically, it looked like they haven't made up their mind, but there was clearly no support for unconditional MFN. . . . Everybody came out of there very pessimistic."[31]

These formal discussions, however, were only part of the implicit negotiating and bargaining process. Indeed, this process had been going on ever since it was apparent that Bill Clinton was likely to become president. What Beijing *did* was more important than what it *said;* by their actions the Chinese demonstrated that they were highly committed to building constructive relations with the new administration in Washington. Beijing was willing to make concessions, up to a point.[32]

In these negotiations, Beijing had a three-pronged strategy: first, activating the American business community by holding out the lure of the China market, pointing to the danger that America's competitors might make gains through Washington's missteps, and underscoring the potential contradiction between the president's commitment to international economic competitiveness and the risks incurred by a zealous pursuit of human rights objectives. Second, well-known dissidents were selectively released, and the Chinese hinted that they would restart the human rights dialogue with Washington. And finally, the Chinese made it clear that continued cooperation in the UN Security Council would be influenced by the state of bilateral relations. Basically, the Chinese tried to make progress in the areas easiest for them (strategic and economic relations) hoping that this forward movement would moderate the American reaction stemming from continuing human rights frictions.

On the economic front, in the spring one senior Chinese official frankly laid out China's view:

> CAAC [Civil Aviation Administration of China] signed a contract for 20 Boeing aircraft worth $600 million. . . . China's civil aviation is growing 30 percent per year. If U.S.-China relations [stay] good, China may be one of the biggest buyers of aircraft. Also . . . the head of the natural gas corporation [in China] was in Texas to purchase oil equipment and talk about oil exploration . . . in China. The Tarim Basin is rich in oil, so if we can cooperate in oil and energy, there are rich opportunities for [both of us]. Also, the State Planning Commission Vice Chairman . . . is leading a delegation to the United States to purchase automobiles and the purchase will be quite big. The auto market in China is growing rapidly. . . . There will be more and more cars in China and [someday] it will be the biggest market. Also, AT&T is very interested in the telecommunications market here. If you [that is, the United States] come into the market too late, it will be occupied by others. The Chinese market is a big cake. Come early and you get a big piece. I hope our two countries have good relations, but it takes two to tango![33]

David Zhu reports, "In the nine-month period between July 1992 and April 1993, China made two big purchases of automobiles from General Motors, Ford, and Chrysler, [for] a total of $314 million. According to *Business Week,* China has recently concluded deals (worth

$4.6 billion) with six other U.S. companies (Wing-Merrill, Arco, AT&T, Coca-Cola, General Electric, and Motorola)."[34]

On the strategic front, considering that China historically has opposed big power intervention (particularly Western military intervention) in the third world and has opposed the imposition of economic sanctions, the degree of cooperation the Chinese have provided on the Security Council ever since the Gulf crisis of 1990–1991 has been remarkable. China has either voted in support of or abstained from crucial votes on Security Council actions against Iraq, Somali warlords, Libyan terrorism, and Serbian aggression. In the Bush administration, the Chinese role was crucial in getting both Koreas into the UN in 1991. In addition, there is every indication that Beijing sought to moderate the Cambodian civil war and the North Korean nuclear problem, though the Chinese have thus far opposed the imposition of sanctions against Pyongyang. In support of this view, both the Khmer Rouge in Cambodia and the North Koreans have apparently been involved in incidents that have inflicted casualties on Chinese military personnel,[35] something that presumably would not have happened had they been pleased with Chinese policy.

On the human rights front, the Chinese never openly said they were responding to U.S. entreaties, suggestions, or pressure, asserting that such issues were an internal affair. Nonetheless, selected releases of some political detainees occurred. The administration's May 28, 1993, "Report to Congress concerning Extension of Waiver Authority for the People's Republic of China" acknowledged these releases:

> The Chinese recently released, prior to completion of their sentences, several prominent dissidents whom we had identified on lists provided [the authorities in Beijing]. These included not only Tiananmen-era demonstrators but also Democracy Wall (circa 1979) activists. . . . A number of prominent dissidents, despite long delays, have been able to leave China. Some others have not. Those who have been able to obtain exit permits in the past year include labor leader Han Dongfang, writers Wang Ruowang and Bai Hua, scientist Wen Yuankai, journalists Wang Ruoshui, Zhang Weiguo, and Zhu Xingqing, and scholar Liu Qing. Others like Hou Xiaotian, Yu Haocheng, and Li Honglin, continue to face difficulties in obtaining exit permission. . . . Since then [November 1991], the Chinese have released additional political prisoners, including Han Dongfang, Wang Youcai, Luo Haixing, Xiong Yan, Yang Wei, Wang Zhixin, Zhang Weiguo, Wang Dan, Wang Xizhe, Gao Shan,

Bao Zunxin, and a number of Catholic clergy and lesser known activists.[36]

In addition, in early April, a senior Chinese leader made it clear to a visiting American group that if relations could be put on an equal footing, Beijing was willing to restart the human rights dialogue with Washington that had been curtailed in late 1992.[37]

In short, formal and informal, official and nonofficial dialogue with the Chinese achieved some successes in the economic and foreign policy areas. With respect to human rights, however, Beijing has generally been unwilling to make formal commitments or be seen either by the world or by its own citizenry as capitulating to foreign pressure, particularly American coercion.[38] On human rights issues, China's leadership made some movement, though not enough to satisfy either the administration or Congress. In the arms control area, the Bush administration's late 1992 agreement to sell 150 F-16 fighter aircraft to Taiwan, a move that China contends violates the August 17, 1982, Joint Communiqué agreed to by Washington and Beijing, demonstrably toughened Chinese attitudes in the weapons sales and technology transfer areas. Beijing, under heavy pressure from its military, seemingly believes that it has little reason to adhere to the letter of all understandings when it believes Washington feels no similar compunctions.

Consulting and Negotiating with Congress

Every administration, particularly since the reforms of Congress in 1974,[39] has felt that the legislative branch consists of 535 aspiring and undisciplined secretaries of state. In the legislative process, every bill has the potential to become a "Christmas tree" on which are hung the ornaments of every member's desires, frustrations, values, and ambitions.

As mentioned earlier, since shortly after the 1989 Tiananmen tragedy, Congress has debated whether to extend MFN for China, and how, if at all, it might be conditioned. In each debate, a torrent of complaints and outrage cascaded from the lofty heights of rostrums in congressional hearing rooms. This outrage has been directed toward human rights violations in Tibet, Beijing's opposition to unilateral political reform in Hong Kong, China's refusal to renounce the possible use of force against Taiwan, America's mounting trade deficit with China, Chinese weapons and technology transfers, Beijing's perceived lack of support in the United Nations, a wide variety of human rights issues, Chinese population policy, unfair Chinese trade practices, and even the Three Gorges Dam project. These frustrations mounted between 1990 and 1992 as congressional majorities persistently grew to take action against Beijing, only to have their will frustrated by two presidential vetoes.

With the inauguration of President Clinton, Democrats in Congress expected that things would be different. Representative Nancy Pelosi and Senate Majority Leader George Mitchell were particularly determined that things would be different. They were the coauthors of legislation that President Bush had vetoed.

Because MFN status is a tariff issue, it must originate in the House of Representatives. The committee of jurisdiction is Ways and Means, headed by Dan Rostenkowski of Illinois (and absolutely crucial to all President Clinton's budget, health reform, and investment initiatives), with the committee's Trade Subcommittee headed by Sam Gibbons of Florida, a free trader of long standing. Also of great importance is the House Committee on Foreign Affairs, led by Lee H. Hamilton of Indiana, a moderate who generally believes that Congress should not impinge on the president's prerogatives in the foreign policy domain unless absolutely necessary. He also tends to believe that wise foreign policy requires a careful balancing of "principle and pragmatism"[40] and that "the United States has a wide range of interests in China, interests that are both parallel and competing."[41] On February 8, 1993, Hamilton signed a consensus policy paper on China prepared for the new administration and the new Congress stating the importance of U.S.-China relations, a paper prepared by a broadly based citizens' group.[42]

To provide an overview of the period February 1993 through May 28, 1993, a centrist bloc began to emerge among congressional Democrats, particularly in the House. While this bloc was reluctant to sacrifice the mounting stakes America had in its ties with China, it was also reluctant to reject, outright, their new president's desire to create some link between trade with China and human rights practices on the mainland. This loose congressional assemblage, therefore, began reluctantly to support an executive order to establish such a tie, if the president was determined to link trade with human rights concerns. In the House, the leadership of the Ways and Means and Foreign Affairs Committees provided the core support for this approach.[43] The interaction between these leaders and Representative Pelosi is one of the important stories in the House, about which we know little.

By the end of February, the administration had determined that if Representative Pelosi and Senator Mitchell could support its eventual policy, then the administration's approach would be sustainable in the Congress as a whole. In making his initial calls on Capitol Hill, Winston Lord asked Pelosi and Mitchell to hold off introducing legislation until he was confirmed and until the administration had an opportunity to conduct its review of China policy. They reportedly agreed to do so; it is no accident that they introduced their bill ("To Extend to the People's Republic of China Renewal of Nondiscriminatory [Most-Favored-Nation] Treatment Provided Certain Conditions Are Met") on the heels of Winston Lord's April 19 confirmation.

In this same period, senior House Democrats from the centrist bloc made their views known to Pelosi and others.[44] One of the most articulate expressions of these views came from Representative Hamilton, who on April 1 spoke to the Business Coalition for U.S.-China Trade and said,

> As China's leaders face fundamental questions about the future of their country, we must decide how best to promote our ideals and interests. And we must understand that when and how we make those decisions will influence how the Chinese make their own.
>
> We should be resolute and realistic. We should recognize when our interests coincide with China's, and when they collide. We should neither seek to undermine the regime in China nor tolerate its every action. . . .
>
> But because Congress and the President can now work together in setting U.S. policy, we do not necessarily need to implement that policy by *legislating* [emphasis added] conditions on China's MFN status. . . .
>
> Deftness and flexibility are exactly what is called for in the case of China, where politics are already fluid and will become more so once Deng Xiaoping dies. Trying to write conditions into law in these circumstances would be unwise. The President needs flexibility to implement policy at such an uncertain time.[45]

In the period between February and Lord's April 19 confirmation, other leaders in the House (Representatives Gibbons and Rostenkowski, for instance) conveyed their concerns to Pelosi and others. They desired to find a way in which the president could demonstrate fidelity to his campaign statements without irretrievably damaging relations with Beijing. By early April, participants in the process were fairly confident that Pelosi would eventually agree to the executive order approach. Nevertheless, they did not want to see congressional momentum toward legislation build, thereby foreclosing the possibility of an executive order approach for the president when he and his closest aides finally focused on the issue.

Only after Lord's trip to Beijing did the administration finally determine to move ahead with an executive order. At this point, in early and mid-May, the issue then became how such conditionality would be defined and expressed, whether conditions would be limited to the human rights domain, and how the decision would be announced. Pelosi was a vigorous advocate for having as much specificity in the human rights conditions as possible. Through a process that is unclear, the decision was made to focus on human rights conditions, leaving nuclear proliferation and trade problems to be handled through already existing legislation and bilateral agreements. Upon hearing this, Senator Joseph Biden, who was concerned about Chinese nuclear and technology proliferation behavior (with good reason),[46] was displeased, to put it mildly.[47]

In this context, the administration subsequently asserted that hinging MFN conditionality on human rights considerations alone was a major achievement, thereby not coupling China's MFN status with every other friction in the relationship—frictions in non–human rights areas could be handled under existing legislation. The result, however, has been somewhat different from what was perhaps anticipated. To keep members of Congress convinced of its sincerity, the administration toughened its attitude in the weapons sales and trade domains, thereby leading it to impose sanctions on incomplete evidence and to demand the right to inspect the *Yin He* (the *Silver River*), the Chinese ship that was eventually found not to be carrying the suspected chemical weapons precursors. In some sense, therefore, separating trade and weapons proliferation issues from the MFN debate led to a tougher, though not necessarily more effective, policy in those areas. Moreover, it is not clear Congress will decouple considerations of MFN from trade and weapons issues, even if the president desires to do so.

The Wider Political and Foreign Policy Context

By simply focusing on the several tracks of negotiation, however, one misses a key aspect of the entire process—the wider domestic political, foreign policy, and economic contexts in which the president was deciding. To put it succinctly, the president had to make his final decision in May 1993, a period in which he did not need any more trouble. He was highly motivated to find a decision that would not further compound his problems and not ruin America's chances in what seemed to be the world's fastest-growing economy in an era when the competition for trade-generated jobs was fierce.

President Clinton faced serious problems in the former Yugoslavia (given his campaign statements about stopping the slaughter), the situation in Somalia was deteriorating, a June 12 deadline in negotiations with North Korea (over its impending pullout from the Non-Proliferation Treaty) was approaching, while on the domestic front he was being accused of having "lurched leftward" after the election and having squandered scarce political resources on peripheral issues. He was making no one happy, as his budget package moved agonizingly through the Congress, where, in the Senate, a single senator (Boren) had the legislative process tied in knots. In addition, his administration was trying to win Chinese cooperation on Cambodia and North Korea and in the UN Security Council, something that would be hard to achieve if the United States were threatening to impose new restrictions on China in the MFN area.

Indeed, the president was in such domestic difficulty that he was embroiled in public flaps over a haircut on the Los Angeles International Airport tarmac aboard Air Force One and the summary firing of individuals in the White House Travel Office.

In this context, the president brought in David Gergen (long-time adviser to three Republican presidents) on May 29 as White House counselor with a portfolio covering both foreign and domestic affairs. The president's appointment of Gergen and other moves in various policy domains (with respect to his budget package, for example) in the week following his executive order on China appeared aimed at reestablishing himself as the "new kind of Democrat."

Another aspect of the landscape is important to identify—the administration's perceptions of its capabilities to effect change. On May 25, three days before the president's announcement on MFN status, Under Secretary of State for Political Affairs Peter Tarnoff indicated that the United States needed to be judicious in choosing when to assume costly leadership roles in international crises. He emphasized the need for the United States to cooperate with allies and choose commitments carefully because of limited financial and political resources. When this briefing became public, it created controversy about whether America was relinquishing its post–World War II leadership role,[48] a twist that Secretary of State Christopher then sought to dispel by saying, "I think where we need to lead, where our vital interests are threatened, we will find the resources to accomplish that."[49] These statements taken together, however, made it clear that the administration had made America's "vital interests" and the availability of resources important reference points in its foreign policy decision-making process.

Finally, the image that decision makers and the public at large hold of China (or any target of a foreign policy decision) greatly influences the assessment of one's own capabilities to produce change and a sense of what one may lose if relations deteriorate.[50] In the months preceding the May 28 decision, the press and scholarly literature were full of discussions of China's 14 percent annual growth rate, exploding foreign investment in the PRC (from South Korea, Taiwan, Hong Kong, Japan, and the West), the opening of China's domestic market, and the entrance of American banks, insurance companies, and accounting firms into the PRC. And finally, about a week before the decision was made public, the International Monetary Fund announced (using the purchasing power parity methodology) that China's economy was four times bigger than previously estimated (using exchange rate conversion methodologies) and that it was the world's third largest economy, after those of the United States and Japan. Against this backdrop, one can understand what President Clinton meant when he said on May 27, the day before his executive order was issued, "It is a great opportunity for America there [China]."[51]

Looking at the Documents

Much of the bargaining that produced the executive order of May 28 can be inferred from the three documents released on May 28. Although the executive order is the legally binding instrument, the other two (the president's speech at the White House and the "Report to Congress") are politically important and revealing. Each document speaks to a somewhat different audience, but the three should be read and analyzed as a package. Herein lies one of the potential problems, though. Different audiences were encouraged to hear what they wanted to in the president's decision, thereby possibly setting the stage for conflict and misunderstanding in mid-1994.

The document with the most flexibility is the legally binding executive order itself. There are seven human rights–related conditioning factors mentioned, with the failure to meet two of the conditions (pertaining to emigration and prison labor exports) requiring the secretary of state to recommend to the president a noncontinuation of MFN waiver authority for the period beginning July 3, 1994. In the case of the other five considerations, however, substantial flexibility is built-in, with the operative wording being, "In making this recommendation the Secretary [of State] shall also determine whether China has made overall, significant progress." In the words of Asia Watch's Sidney Jones,

> The term significant progress can be interpreted loosely or very tightly. In our experience, this can be a loophole. There is only one mandatory item in the executive order (regarding prison labor) while the others are left open to interpretation, meaning China might be able to get away with only symbolic gestures. . . . [President Clinton and the administration] will

be under close scrutiny to see how the Administration interprets "significant progress."[52]

The second document, the "Report to Congress concerning Extension of Waiver Authority for the People's Republic of China," serves two purposes. First, it lays out the rationale for the executive order, identifying the areas where progress has been made with China and specifying the areas of continuing significant dissatisfaction. Second, it tries to reassure those in Congress that their concerns will weigh in the balance of future presidential and administration consideration even though those concerns were not mentioned (or not mentioned forcefully enough to suit some) in the executive order.

The report, for example, raises the issues of "forced abortion and sterilization" in the PRC and urges Beijing "to resume dialogue with the Dalai Lama or his representatives" on Tibet, two items not mentioned in the executive order itself. Tibet was a particular concern of Senator Daniel Patrick Moynihan, chairman of the Senate Committee on Finance and a major influence over the fate of the president's budget. On the proliferation problem, the report tries to meet the concerns of persons in Congress (particularly Senator Biden, chairman of the Judiciary Committee, whose support was critical to the president's success in getting key judicial appointments through the Senate), by saying that "the U.S. is prepared to employ the resources under U.S. law and executive determination—including the imposition of sanctions—if the PRC engages in irresponsible transfers." Indeed, the administration delivered on this promise when it imposed sanctions on Beijing in August 1993 for alleged M-11 missile component transfers to Pakistan.

The president's May 28 White House speech in which he announced his executive order was designed to demonstrate unity between the executive and the legislative branches, show the support (or at least acquiescence) of the human rights and business communities, and provide another opportunity to reassure those worried that the executive order did not adequately address their particular concerns, especially proliferation of weapons of mass destruction. On that occasion, those who had accepted something other than their initial preferences had their policies embraced symbolically even as the substance of their earlier positions was not fully adopted. For President Clinton, it provided a chance to demonstrate that "gridlock" was out and consensus was in.

The President's Policy and the Future of U.S.-China Relations

Within the constraints of the Washington milieu and the president's past commitments, the policy he adopted on May 28 was probably the least damaging course that could have been taken at the time. In the rough and tumble of politics, perhaps this is all that need be said. This policy, for that moment at least, restored an uneasy peace between the legislative and executive branches and did not immediately prove to be the straw that broke the back of U.S.-China relations.

There are several other vantage points, however, from which this decision can be assessed. First, this policy, which arose from the politics of Washington, D.C., is not rooted in widespread public outrage, nor is it grounded in a public understanding of what the president's policy really is. James MacGregor Burns in his book *Leadership* drew a distinction between "transactional" and "transformational" leadership styles.[53] One emphasizes adopting policies that conform to the balance of forces of the moment; the other is dedicated to changing that balance of forces through educating the public and leadership colleagues. What is notable about the China decision is that it was not grounded in a larger vision of America's role in the world, the resources available to accomplish our goals, a vision of Asia, or even a well-defined view of China. It was a policy explained by reference to American values and aspirations, rather than a vision of the world in which those values and aspirations must be realized. This problem was only somewhat improved by the president's subsequent July trip to Japan and South Korea. In short, this is a policy that is so shallowly rooted that the first storm may blow it over.

Second, outside observers do not know much about the president's role in this process, and so any judgments in this regard must be tentative. Nonetheless, the president had the two clearly articulated goals stated earlier—create some links between trade and human rights and craft a policy Congress could accept. Beyond that, it appears that he was largely disengaged until the endgame, though I am told that he was briefed periodically during the process.[54] He let subordinates, particularly Winston Lord, forge a consensus on policy that he eventually accepted. There is much to recommend this as a practical way to make decisions.

This style of decision making, however, has several potential drawbacks. Hedrick Smith, in his *Power Game*, provides some insight:[55]

> In managing foreign policy, a president has two main options: One model is to frame an overall strategy with one chief adviser and have this collaborator put policy into practice, forcing other senior officials to fall into line. . . . The other presidential option is to follow an essentially reactive policy, responding to world events, improvising policy strands as opportunities arise or as the public mood—or the president's own mood—changes, because there is no grand design.[56]

The second style Smith mentions is subject to several pathologies. First, when various advisers disagree, policy can become stalemated, with no sense of shared strategic vision to provide the basis for forging consensus and cooperation in the administration. Second, without an articulated vision, the foreign policy bureaucracy grinds away below, rudderless, with no sense that it contributes to a coherent policy. Third, there is a reduced expectation abroad that any American policy is any more durable than the last constellation of public and congressional opinion, or presidential mood swing, that produced it. Such a decision style tends to reward the last, most forceful advocate to see the president.

Finally, as we have seen in this case, it is difficult, time consuming, and resource intensive to forge a consensus (particularly with Congress) and maintain it. Any lapse of attention can prove very harmful. With consensus as the goal, there will have to be a continuous, resource-consuming process of executive-legislative consultation leading up to June 1994. And, given the fractious nature of the Congress and the heterogeneous nature of the Democratic party, one has to ask whether the president can, and will want to, spend the necessary resources, given the priority he attaches to his domestic agenda and the difficulty he may have in winning congressional cooperation.

Third, when we speak of the president's policy as expressed in the executive order, we have to take into account not only the ambiguities in that document but also the fact that the two other documents issued at the same time have somewhat different target audiences and somewhat different messages, to both internal audiences and the Chinese. In short, the policy is not as clear as it may appear at first blush, creating booby traps for the future.

With respect to the Chinese, the fact that the legally binding document is the one most flexible, along with the president's evolving position over the six months before his May 28 announcement, may convey a lack of serious presidential commitment. Beijing may see this as largely a face-saving exercise for a president who is trying to shed a position he took when he was a candidate. If so, Beijing's incentive to make the progress in meeting American concerns that the president will genuinely need to demonstrate in mid-1994 may be weak.

Furthermore, even if the Chinese and Americans continue to make progress in resolving issues in the bilateral relationship, members of Congress and human rights and other interest groups who want more change in Chinese policy may very well refer less to the president's executive order than to his speech at the White House and to his "Report to Congress" to bolster their contentions that there has not been "overall significant progress." So, for instance, whether one attaches importance to China's September 1993 release of Wei Jingsheng and the Chinese statement in

November that Beijing would permit the inspection of prisons by the International Committee of the Red Cross[57] is essentially a political or judgment call. As well, the very content of the term *overall significant progress* is subject to wide and varying interpretation. In short, the real meaning of the president's policy is, to some extent, in the eye of the beholder.

There is a fourth concern. One of the putative achievements of the May 28 executive order was to remove the trade and weapons and technology sales and proliferation disputes from the annual MFN debate, handling frictions in these areas by existing legislation, rather than making them germane to MFN's conditionality.

Two problems almost immediately arose, however. First, as a statement of political reality, Congress can take anything it wants into account in its annual assessment of MFN status for China. It is not clear that Congress will decouple these issues, even if the president so desires.[58] Indeed, speaking in October 1993, Secretary Christopher admitted as much when he told businesspeople that problems in the weapons and trade areas would affect MFN's prospects. Second, the need to handle disputes in trade and proliferation by existing legislation (such as the Helms amendment on missile technology transfers) has meant that sanctions, and the threat of sanctions, are employed frequently to try to win concessions from Beijing. So, for example, in August 1993, Washington prohibited approximately $1 billion (over two years) in high-tech exports to China because of evidence that Beijing had exported components for the M-11 missile to Pakistan. The result of this approach may well be that the environment created by repeated sanctions (or their threat) in the trade and weapons areas further erodes the willingness of Beijing to make progress on human rights or other areas.

Finally, the success of the administration's policy will depend on China's actions to a considerable extent. U.S. policy is close to eliciting a counterproductive nationalistic backlash, a backlash not only of China's military but also of the leadership and populace at large. As one young Chinese lawyer visiting America told me, "Why are you Americans pushing China so hard just at the time we are making the most progress we have ever made in our history?" It is a mistake to believe that reformers in China find tough and repeated American pressure across a broad range of issues to be either in their interest or to their liking.

A spate of articles with the ring of authenticity appeared in the Hong Kong press in May and June 1993. They point to the deep dissatisfaction in some quarters of the Chinese military with the continued pushing and the threat of sanctions by Washington. One forum where these dissatisfactions were aired was a Politburo meeting (on May 14, in the wake of Lord's trip to Beijing) that addressed the subject of relations with Washington.[59] Only on September 1, 1993, after Deng Xiaoping had put his personal prestige and imprimatur on a policy of forbearance toward the United States, was it decided by the Standing Committee of the Politburo to adopt the "four nots" policy (not desiring confrontation, not provoking confrontation, not dodging confrontation, and not being afraid of sanctions or of resisting them).[60]

From November 1992 to late 1993, the United States made a series of decisions that hit raw nationalistic nerves in the Chinese polity (particularly the military), actions such as President Bush's agreement to sell Taiwan F-16s; President Clinton's meeting with the Dalai Lama; House and Senate resolutions urging the International Olympic Committee to avoid selecting Beijing as the site for the year 2000 Olympics; and the effort of the Senate Foreign Relations Committee to have it made law that the 1979 Taiwan Relations Act "supersedes" the August 17, 1982, Joint Sino-American Communiqué pertaining to U.S. weapons sales to Taipei.[61] While American analysts might explain these acts as the idiosyncratic result of disjointed independent political processes, the Chinese saw them as a conspiracy.

Toward the Future

To summarize, the U.S.-China relationship remains in a difficult state. The administration, in trying to maintain fidelity to its commitments of the campaign while not destroying an economic and strategic relationship it has come increasingly to value, postponed an immediate crisis in mid-1993 by running the risk of painting itself into a corner in 1994. By establishing human rights standards that would be the principal basis for making its 1994 MFN decision, the administration has exposed itself to a potentially divisive debate over what constitutes "overall significant progress" in the human rights realm in China. Further, it has made it hard to argue that the value of the bilateral relationship in the trade and strategic domains offers compensating justifications for continuation of MFN treatment for Beijing. Given the mounting concerns about North Korea's apparent efforts to develop nuclear weapons, and the possibly transcending importance of Chinese cooperation if strong measures need to be taken against Pyongyang, it may be that a severe crisis on the Korean peninsula will serve to create a consensus behind a policy of not revoking MFN. Whatever the outcome in Korea, however, it is unwise for Washington to count implicitly on another crisis to save itself from the consequences of past policy.

The administration has not articulated a China policy so much as it has addressed one discrete (albeit very important) issue. If we fail to develop a larger vision of China and Asia to give meaning to our particular actions, fail to communicate this to Congress and the American people, and fail to develop further channels of cooperation with Beijing, the president may well be trapped by the ambiguities of a decision built on a very fragile consensus in Washington. This consensus could be swept away by onrushing events. Were this to happen under current circumstances, Washington would be going it alone, without support from America's friends in either Asia or Europe.

3

Trade and the Waking Giant—China, Asia, and American Engagement

James R. Lilley

Americans have always had a propensity for misunderstanding China. Our public's views of that nation have oscillated from romantic enthusiasm, as in the 1930s, to deep antipathy, as in the two decades from the 1949 revolution to the Nixon-Kissinger mission. There rarely seems to be a middle ground. Nor have our intellectuals displayed any special sophistication in their assessments of China. The China where, as one historian put it, "a film of the ninth National Congress of the CCP [Chinese Communist party] in 1969 showed delegates, holding the *Little Red Book* aloft, jigging up and down in frenzy, tears rolling down their cheeks, yelping and baying like animals, in the Great Hall of the People"[1] was the China one prominent American banker praised as containing a "sense of national harmony," the China Felix Greene lauded for the lack of "children born out of wedlock," and the China in which another noted American visitor discovered the changes since the revolution to be "miraculous." Britain's Hewlett Johnson noted in Mao "something no picture has ever caught, an inexpressible look of kindness and sympathy, an obvious preoccupation with the needs of others [which] formed the deep content of his thoughts."[2]

Nevertheless, the real Communist China played out a drama of sorts, with hundreds of millions of real people as its players, and the West did not truly watch. The annual American debate over China's most-favored-nation (MFN) designation is in line with this tradition. Those who oppose the renewal of MFN for moralistic reasons betray a lack of awareness of the forces at work in China. I intend to argue in several case studies that powerful currents of democracy and freedom are rippling throughout Asia today and that a major engine of their movement has been a sustained American economic and political engagement. Moreover, our failure to grant MFN would constitute a direct assault on the Chinese political system—a unilateral move by the United States with neither international nor Chinese public support. Denial of MFN will isolate us from China, if enforced. I also intend to show the direct harm to America's security, influence, and interests in Asia if we were to revoke MFN in response to China's human rights violations; stability in the Korean peninsula, the South China Sea, and the Taiwan Strait could be adversely affected as well.

Taiwan

The Republic of China (ROC) on Taiwan is a clear example of how human rights and democratization have evolved from a long-term U.S. military and economic presence. The ROC imposed martial law on the island on May 20, 1949, suspending major constitutional provisions guaranteeing the people's right to form political parties and engage in organized labor activity. For twenty years, no national parliamentary elections were held at all, although local elections were permitted from the beginning.[3] The lifting of martial law and the legitimation of opposition parties did not occur until the mid-1980s. During this time, Taiwan's regime was described most frequently as "soft authoritarianism" or "authoritarianism with developmental features."[4]

What is significant is that the United States has constructively engaged the ROC during these past decades, not abandoned or isolated it for its antidemocratic practices. The United States imposed its protective shield around Taiwan, which was critical to Taiwan's survival, only after North Korea invaded South Korea in 1950. After China intervened in the Korean War in October 1950, the United States formalized the security arrangement protecting Taiwan with a mutual defense treaty signed in 1954 and ratified by the Senate on February 9, 1955. Nor was this merely "paper protection." At the outset of the Korean War, President Truman ordered the Seventh Fleet to patrol the Taiwan Strait as a "neutralization" move, and General MacArthur subsequently declared that Taiwan was now part of the American "island chain" of air power bases.[5] Through the next decades, the United States has repeatedly demonstrated its military commitment to the security of the island, despite the government's authoritarian character. The American military presence was the major deterrent to an invasion by the People's Republic of China (PRC). Free-market forces and democracy on Taiwan grew behind this shield.

America has remained economically engaged with Taiwan as well. Indeed, American government policy has been instrumental in Taiwan's remarkable prosperity, in at least two areas: (1) substantial economic aid given in the first two decades of the ROC, which helped the nation survive its serious lack of raw materials and capital; and (2) an accommodating trade posture, despite the ROC's routinely large trade deficits with the United States at the time. Taiwan was not merely granted MFN status, but it also enjoyed until recently the special treatment afforded to developing nations under the general system of preferences. By the year of major political liberalization, 1987, exports constituted 55 percent of Taiwan's gross national product (GNP), with exports to America accounting for 44 percent of the total volume.[6] So American policy, in addition to a stable monetary and free-market ROC strategy, has led to a "miracle" of economic success. From 1952 through 1987, real GNP and national income per capita increased more than sixfold. Large-scale tax evasion and "creative accounting" by many Taiwanese businesses indicate the existence of a large underground economy that would add perhaps $2,000 to the per capita GNP, bringing it to $8,000 in 1988.[7]

As Taiwan has built up its middle-class prosperity through an engaged U.S. economic and military presence, it has steadily liberalized politically and is now a thriving pluralistic democracy. "Opposition movements in Taiwan," write Hung-Mao Tien and Chyuan-Jeng Shiau,

> have been steadily growing since the 1950s, albeit in a zigzag course of dialectic evolution. . . . The activists, drawn mainly from the newly-emerging middle-class intellectuals and professionals, utilized street actions, squabbles on legislative floors, third party (liberal scholars) mediation, foreign pressures (U.S. Congress), and working through the overseas lobbying by anti-KMT [the Kuomintang, the ruling party] elements to enhance their bargaining position vis-à-vis the KMT.[8]

In response to the demands of this emerging middle class, the KMT has gradually and progressively yielded to its pressures.

The early 1980s witnessed the flourishing of many social movements in Taiwan, and by 1987 the authorities endured over 1,800 street demonstrations. By 1981, much nationwide opposition had coalesced behind the label of *Tangwai* (literally meaning "outside the party"), which was recommending candidates and encouraging political activity. In December 1986, the government agreed to allow the national opposition group, now called the Democratic Progressive party (DPP) to participate formally in the parliamentary election. The DPP scored impressive gains then and also in 1989 and 1992, when the "aging deputies" to the National Assembly, the Legislative Yuan, and the Control Yuan (all elected on the mainland in the 1940s) retired.

All these moves coincided with an evolutionary series of government liberalization actions, including the removal of martial law, press restrictions, and the various national security provisions that had afforded the government extensive police powers.[9] Clearly, the ROC's political liberalization was intrinsically tied to its economic liberalization, which was itself abetted by an actively supportive U.S. posture. The prodemocracy forces unleashed in Taiwan seemed to come in large measure from the people themselves, who became steadily more politically active as they grew more prosperous, educated, and aware of their potential role. Thus it seems clear that the U.S. policy of engagement with Taiwan has met with striking success. Had America chosen economic disengagement or pulled back its security guarantees during this time—in the name of "human rights"—the outcome would have been violence and government repression, the opposite of that intended.

South Korea

In 1988, a long process of political pressure on the authoritarian regime of the Republic of Korea (ROK) culminated in impressive changes. South Korea's government had always been dominated by the military. Constitutional limits on police power, viable opposition parties, and the rule of law were present only in short-lived and ephemeral phases. Major-General Park Chung Hee overthrew the constitutionally established government of Chang Myon in 1961, accusing it of being corrupt and soft on communism. Responding to both internal pressure and external pressure from the United States, however, he called a presidential election for November 1963. He won it by a slim plurality and stood again in 1967, when his victory margin increased. Carefully instituted free-market policies led, though, to substantial growth and prosperity, and the ROK developed a sizable and increasing middle class.[10]

Indeed, by practically any indicator, Korea's long-term economic performance has been spectacular, with the GNP growing more than 8 percent per year over the past two-and-a-half decades. Inflation has been kept low, and savings and exports have risen dramatically.[11] There can be little doubt that Korea's progress has been made possible by a favorable U.S. trading environment, including MFN, which encouraged the growth of Korean exports. Today, the ROK is one of the most important economies in the world, and the seventh-largest trading partner of the United States.[12] President Bill Clinton's agreement to keep American troops on the peninsula emphasizes to the countries of the region (especially North Korea) that force is not an option in the diplomatic realm. The United States has nearly always had an important presence, in every sense of the word, in South Korean life.

This engagement has occurred despite certain distasteful qualities of the various governments in power. The ROK under Park was hardly liberal, for example, even with its semblance of electoral legitimacy. When the economy took a downturn in 1969 and large-scale demonstrations broke out, Park clamped down, suspending nearly all student political activity. Ultimately, a presidential decree even provided for the death penalty for certain student protest actions. Before 1972, though, the general population enjoyed relative freedom of the press and of opposition activities. After that year, things took a turn for the worse.[13] Martial law was declared at this time, and the "Yushin Constitution" was imposed with significant antidemocratic elements in its wording, including presidential power to curtail civil rights by decree. By 1974, all criticism of the Yushin Constitution was banned, and a 1975 revision of the criminal code imposed stiff jail terms on any citizen who criticized the government.[14]

The scholars Han Sung-joo (now foreign minister) and Park Yung Chul, after examining some common explanations, believe that the single most important reason for the turn to authoritarianism under Park was the growing power of the political opposition. The substantial middle class built up during the Park years was the mainstay of the increasing opposition and seemed to promise that Park and his party (the Reunification Democratic party—RDP) would not remain in power indefinitely, especially with an apparently mismanaged economy.[15] By the end of the 1970s, Korean society seemed to be sinking into disorder, with major riots in such cities as Pusan and Masan and Park's party turning in a disappointing performance (despite government manipulation) in the 1978 National Assembly election. In October 1979, President Park Chung Hee was assassinated by his chief intelligence aide.[16]

About two months later, General Chun Doo Hwan led an army coup, which ousted all the major army leaders then running the country. A brief period of political liberalization followed, when, it seemed, the entire Korean population enthusiastically clamored for democracy and political pluralism. The students demanded the reinstatement of ousted professors, opposition leaders who openly called for sweeping liberalization were freed, and the National Assembly set up a committee to draft a new constitution.[17]

This mood was not destined to last. South Korean students have always had a radical streak, intensely egalitarian, nationalistic, and uncompromising. By 1980, the tenor became Marxist-Leninist.[18] It would be misleading, therefore, to suggest that South Korea's student protests were motivated primarily by the tenets of classical liberalism and pluralistic democracy. But the students were not really representative of the country; radical sentiment was never seriously echoed in labor, the commercial circles, the intelligentsia, or the army. Still, the students were emblematic of at least two strains of democratic thinking: the distrust of existing elites and the urge for political self-expression. Whether there existed a genuine Communist security threat or not, the ruling group clearly feared the prospect of losing its monopoly on power. In any event, by the time of the crackdown, opposition to the government was spread across social groups. As Andrew Nagorski put it in an article in *Foreign Affairs* at the time,

> With the economy experiencing its first negative growth in 16 years and inflation running at about 30%, the country's normally docile workers staged successive strikes, culminating in a coal miners' riot. . . . By May, the students were pouring off the campuses by the thousands, staging massive rallies and fighting hit-and-run battles with the police.[19]

After a few days, a popular backlash was setting in against the protesters, and the noted opposition leader Kim Dae Jung asked them to call it off. The students did so. Then came the unexpected: a major crackdown was suddenly instituted, encompassing the entire nation. When the situation had calmed and the threat to the government had diminished, Chun imposed martial law over the whole country and arrested those engaged in student political meetings. Kim Dae Jung and other famous figures were detained. In May 1980, the city of Kwangju experienced a general insurrection and ferocious government counterattack that left some several hundred dead. The efficiency of Chun's crackdown, in addition to the rapid publication of extensive charges against Kim Dae Jung, indicates that Chun had planned his repression well in advance, with the uprising serving merely as the pretext.[20]

So it was that yet another movement for broader political participation in Korea came to grief, this time with a serious cost in lives. The U.S. response, however, was to continue strategic and economic engagement. The Carter administration publicly expressed grave "concern" over the events but privately allowed representatives to assure the Korean government of continued American support. The U.S. ambassador, for example, conveyed his "understanding" of the reasons for the crackdown, and General John Wickham, the U.S. commander in Korea, said the United States might support Chun if he eventually came to power "legitimately."[21] These statements resulted in some loss of American influence and leverage, for the Korean government had received mixed signals from Washington, resulting in the canceling out of the effect of each statement. The Clinton administration's policy toward China is, as we will see, in some ways analogous to Jimmy Carter's policy with South Korea. But the fundamental American response to Korea's "Tiananmen"—Kwangju—was to continue the American engagement and not use economic pressure.

The Reagan administration toned down the rhetoric and reaffirmed the American commitment to South Korea, pledging to keep 39,000 troops in the peninsula; it agreed to send the ROK a number of F-16s and to conduct joint military exercises. Perhaps in response to the posture of a new and more cooperative administration, Chun commuted the death penalty of Kim Dae Jung and partly lifted martial law.[22]

Over the next few years, as the opposition in the ROK grew in strength, a new party formed, the New Korea Democratic party (NKDP), led by Kim Dae Jung and Kim Young Sam. By 1985, it was the largest opposition bloc in the National Assembly, and its primary platform was constitutional reform allowing for the direct and popular election of the president. Petition campaigns and large rallies were held, finally causing Chun to announce on April 13, 1987, that he had decided to "put further constitutional change on hold."[23] After hundreds of thousands of students rioted, Chun realized that he would have to put the country under martial law again or concede to the opposition. This time, however, certain powerful military leaders weighed in on the side of the opposition behind the scenes. Moreover, the U.S. government, having learned from its experience in the aftermath of Kwangju, consistently and forcefully supported the evolving democratic process in the south, while maintaining a strong deterrent to any opportunistic military moves by North Korea.

The crucial move came on June 29, 1987, when ruling party leader Roh Tae Woo announced on television that the ruling party (the Democratic Justice party—DJP) had accepted virtually all the demands of the opposition. Chun ratified the decision a day later. In the presidential election on December 16, Roh Tae Woo captured the presidency with a plurality, as the opposition vote was split between Kim Dae Jung and Kim Young Sam. The next year's National Assembly election results broke down on similar lines, but the result this time was to oust the ruling party's majority control of the parliament. All press restrictions were lifted. As Daryl M. Plunk has written,

> After years of turmoil and false starts, democracy is on the move in the Republic of Korea. The year 1988 was pivotal for the ROK. It began with the country's first orderly transfer of power and the implementation of a new and democratic blueprint for government. The year ended with the Seoul Olympic Games.[24]

Today, South Korea under the former opposition leader Kim Young Sam is a thriving and energetic democracy and seems poised for a definitive role in all East Asian affairs in the years to come.

Two lessons emerge from the experience of Korea. First, the development of a prosperous and educated middle class engenders powerful democratic and constitutional forces. Second, the U.S. economic and military presence and support for democracy in Korean life have allowed this middle class and the general liberalizing trend to evolve. A moralistic disengagement from the ROK in the face of antidemocratic practices would almost certainly have hindered the progress of the politically active middle class, forfeited our moderating influence on the government, and substantially enhanced the position of the authoritarian elements in the south. North Korea would also have benefited from this mistaken U.S. policy.

Japan

No nation in Asia has achieved greater economic success than Japan—and no nation has experienced a more comprehensive American presence. After World War II, Japan placed itself under the American defense umbrella, resisting U.S. pressure to rearm itself. The policy of Prime Minister Yoshida, elaborated in June 1950 (called by some the "Yoshida Doctrine"), was described by Kenneth B. Pyle as follows:

> 1. Japan's economic rehabilitation must be the prime national goal. Political-economic cooperation with the United States was necessary for this purpose.
>
> 2. Japan should remain lightly armed and avoid involvement in international political-strategic issues. Not only would this low posture free the energies of its people for productive industrial development, it would avoid divisive internal struggles—what Yoshida called a "thirty-eighth parallel" in the hearts of the Japanese people.
>
> 3. To gain a long-term guarantee for its own security, Japan would provide bases for the U.S. army, navy, and air force.[25]

Over the past few decades, Japan has never really departed from the Yoshida Doctrine. American military bases on Japanese soil were granted in exchange for an American guarantee of Japanese security. The Soviet Union was kept out of Japan, and its attempts to acquire Hokkaido were repulsed. A host of constitutional restrictions on Japanese military power evolved over the years, including a ban on dispatching forces overseas, a limit on defense spending to 1 percent of GNP, and a standing refusal to enter into collective security arrangements.[26] As a result, the United States assumed a large measure of Japan's defense responsibility. But any potential aggressors knew that, as in Korea, force used against Japan would impose a very high cost—thanks to the American security presence.

It is a truism to say that Japan has achieved great prosperity from its close economic relationship with the United States. Initially, American technical advice was central to Japan's reconstruction after the war. As Kenneth Pyle has pointed out, however, U.S. assistance was much more than this:

> In the past, the United States exercised unchallenged leadership in the Pacific Basin. Through its support of international institutions such as the World Bank and the GATT, it created a favorable environment in which the economies of this region could flourish. The American government provided aid, and American multinationals made direct investment in the region. Technology was transferred, and American universities trained large numbers of Asians in science and engineering.[27]

The American market, despite recurring trade tensions stemming from Japan's very success, has proved a boon for Japanese firms over the past decades. The reverse is true as well. Notwithstanding continuing import barriers, Japan is the second-largest foreign market—trailing only Canada—for American goods and services, totaling tens of billions of dollars in annual sales. Indeed, U.S.-Japanese bilateral trade is the largest overseas commercial relationship in the world.[28]

The overwhelming fact about Japanese political life, in all its long history, has been the dominance of elites. While occasionally this dominance has led to tyranny and war and sometimes to a placid prosperity, Japan has always seemed unable to act as a thriving and active pluralistic democracy with a strong emphasis on the individual. The sociological reasons for this inability are complex, but the relevant fact is simply that postwar Japan has not been a model of Western-style democratic constitutionalism.

"For over a quarter of a century," Karel van Wolferen writes in a recent issue of *Foreign Affairs*,

> informed Japanese and foreigners alike have readily expressed doubts about the authenticity of Japanese democracy. A vote in the countryside could be worth up to four times as much as one in the cities. The Supreme Court, although recognizing that this system violated the constitution, has refused to endorse corrective action that might "cause confusion."[29]

The ruling party elites have bribed the electorate outside the cities, especially the farmers, to keep themselves in power. Government largesse has been doled out to the rural districts in increasing amounts over the past quarter-century.[30] The Diet has not, in the main, been a forum for real debate on public issues, because the socialistic opposition simply has boycotted Diet meetings as its preferred method of communicating displeasure.[31]

More problematic than this, perhaps, is that Japanese politicians themselves have very little power. The semiautonomous bureaucracies such as the Ministry of Finance wield almost all power to make decisions and are effectively beyond the rule of law. The Constitution is regularly ignored.[32] The press in Japan is not censored by the government; it self-censors, with commentary on the day's news almost identical from newspaper to newspaper. Karel van Wolferen notes the bizarre sociological phenomenon that

> senior Japanese newspaper editors view themselves as public guardians, entrusted to maintain a disciplined society with a maximum of order and a minimum of conflict. Since politicians cause political disturbance, and cannot hide the fact that they want power—as opposed to bureaucrats, who are thought to be selfless and dedicated servants of the people—editors protect the bureaucrats and wage regular campaign against the politicians.[33]

It is interesting to note that U.S. criticism of Japan has focused completely on allegedly unfair Japanese trading practices and not at all on the monopolistic entrenchment of the Liberal Democratic party (LDP) and its implications for Japanese civil society.

What must be described as a sea change occurred in Japan in 1993. Public anger set in motion a chain of events that promised to open up the system permanently. In June 1993, when former finance minister Tsutomu Hata led a group of disaffected LDP members from the parliament, the government fell. Maverick politician Morihiro Hosokawa's New party then rose to prominence at the subsequent election. Hosokawa organized a coalition of the opposition parties, which constituted a majority in the parliament. The opposition parties that soared to prominence in the election were not the traditional fare of the hard-left Social Democrats and their allies; the election dealt them what seems to be a death blow. Hosokawa and his allies are reformist but also center-right.[34]

In August 1993, Hosokawa, the new prime minister, delivered a sharp and passionate inaugural speech, signaling a break with the past and a desire to move ahead with political reform.[35] In fact, the opposition-Hosokawa victory was a victory against the ministries even more than the politicians. With Hosokawa's election, perhaps the Japanese have finally confronted the underlying malaise in their society: Hosokawa's speeches focused on this phenomenon; very few of his followers are former bureaucrats.[36] On September 17, Hosokawa outlined his plan for parliamentary reform, which promises to be as much an energetic effort as the tackling of the ministries.[37] Spurred by purely internal forces, Japan seems to have finally embarked (though serious problems remain) on a journey to constitutionalism, something to which it has never previously aspired. The economic prosperity resulting from Japan's trade and military relationship with the United States has thus built up a sizable and educated middle class, which has gradually become dissatisfied enough to throw off the shackles of an entrenched and closed system. Without this exposure to the outside world provided by contacts with the United States, however, the Japanese public would almost certainly not have been aware of the civil deficits associated with the absence of political accountability.

Vietnam

The case of Vietnam is one of the most tragic in Asia: although nearly every country in the region has undergone suffering in our time, after all its travails Vietnam is still firmly under the domination of communism. Vietnam teaches the U.S. policy maker at least two lessons. First, a Western trade embargo will not necessarily result in political concessions and an improvement in human rights. Second, no matter what the political climate, strong internal pressures in a nation will eventually bring about a market democracy. On a "continuum of freedom" with the other nations discussed here, Vietnam is certainly by far the lowest on the scale. It demonstrates the misery resulting from a closed system but also the inherent instability and eventual doom of any such system. The only real difference between, say, South Korea and Vietnam is timing. In other words, Vietnam will have to liberalize its economy to avert mass famine and civil breakdown, and the middle class that ultimately emerges from this liberalization will eventually demand more and more political freedom.

Since the war, Vietnam has been effectively isolated from all but the Communist bloc countries. At the outset of large-scale hostilities, the United States classified North Vietnam as a "designated" country under section 5B of foreign assets control regulations, which prohibited Americans from doing any business at all with the North Vietnamese. After the Communist victory in South Vietnam, President Ford extended these sanctions throughout the country and froze some $70–75 million in Vietnamese assets in the United States.[38]

The subsequent misery of Vietnam cannot, of course, be attributed to these sanctions; in any event, the U.S. actions were not of great commercial importance to the United States.[39] The suffering of the population was almost entirely the doing of the Communist government and the prolonged war. In economic terms, the result was clear; the United Nations classified Vietnam as one of the twenty poorest countries in the world in the mid-1980s.[40] The recent legacy of "boat people" and "reeducation camps" is grim testimony to the state of civil liberties in that nation.

After decades of sanctions, Vietnam's political regime is not substantially more liberal today than it was during the 1950s. Indeed, it seems far away from constitutional pluralism. The Politburo was not pressured to allow greater human rights or democracy by the punitive U.S. posture. Nor did Hanoi's foreign policy seem substantially moderated, as its invasion and occupation of Kampuchea, among other things, seemed to demonstrate.

This is not to say that sanctions were unjustified. Trade with a totalitarian Vietnam could conceivably have aided only the government, as there were no economic reforms to have allowed a middle class to emerge, prosper, and ultimately demand change. Devotees of the moderating influence of sanctions against Communist governments, however, will find no support at all in the example of Vietnam. In addition, the plight of this country exemplifies the sheer human cost of isolation from the world. As we have argued, U.S. sanctions did not inflict this suffering on Vietnam: after all, Vietnam would not have allowed large-scale business investment and trade with the public anyway. The nation does provide, though, an interesting test case of the effects of such isolation on a whole people. Advocates of an effective cutoff of a large portion of our trade with China would do well to keep in mind the human price these sanctions can exact.

Many of us have heard the joke: "Communism is the longest and most expensive route from capitalism to capitalism." Vietnam provides yet more support for the notion. By the mid-1980s, the country was plagued by worsening inflation, debts, and material shortages, all due to the inherent inefficiencies of central planning.[41] Gorbachev's USSR was less and less willing to bail out the country, and calamity seemed at hand. The Vietnamese Politburo must have been especially dismayed at the dynamic performance of the neighboring free-market states of Southeast Asia, such as Thailand, Malaysia, and Indonesia.

In any event, necessity forced Vietnam to begin to marketize. In 1988, it began to move away from collective farming and started allowing more family farms. Small-scale private enterprise began to flourish unhindered in the cities, with 3,000 shops opening up in the first six months of 1987 alone. In addition, the government encouraged an investment law that allowed both joint and wholly owned foreign enterprises.[42]

The currency was devalued to reflect more accurately its market value, and by the close of 1989 price controls were lifted on most goods. Hyperinflation was brought down, interest rates were allowed to reflect market forces, and foreign goods flooded into Vietnam. By the end of 1991, the government stated that it would try to improve the climate of investment for foreigners, including signing agreements on the protection of investment. By 1992, Prime Minister Kiet announced that the creation of special enterprise zones for foreign investment was a possibility. In November of that year, the Central Committee stated that the remaining subsidies to state enterprises would be "entirely scrapped."[43] President Clinton, incidentally, has expressed a willingness to move forward the process of political and economic normalization with Vietnam, based in large measure on the cooperation of the Vietnamese with the issue of prisoners of war and those missing in action.

It seems that the economic opening of Vietnam to the outside world is only a matter of time, and all from necessity—created by the failure of socialism to succeed on even its own terms. If we look at the example of the first three nations in our survey, it is certain that Vietnam must respond to the same historical forces: once economic liberty is granted, a propertied and educated middle class exposed to the outside world inevitably rises and expands to demand greater civil freedom. As one of the last great utopian experiments on earth, Vietnam's experiment is, in the last resort, pathetic—both because of the immense harm it has caused its citizens and neighbors and because of its political fragility.

China

Communist China has not been an edifying spectacle. The scale of the oppression, mass cruelty, and violence in its history has had few equals, rivaled in modern times by Hitler's Germany and Stalin's Russia. Concerning Mao's reign, Paul Johnson writes:

> [Mao] seems to have believed all his life that the true dynamic of history was not so much the maturation of classes (that

> might be the outward expression) as heroic determination. He saw himself as the Nietzschean superman made flesh. In his artistic longings, in his romanticism and in his belief that will is the key not only to power but to accomplishment, Mao was an oriental Hitler.[44]

Soon after the accession of the regime, during the Korean War, the CCP launched the "Three Anti," "Five Anti," and "socialist remolding" campaigns, whose goal was the destruction of private enterprise and agriculture and even, to some extent, individuals who were engaged in them. The concentrated brutality of this period may well have caused as many as 15 million deaths.[45] In ways reminiscent of the Inquisition, people made public and "voluntary" confessions of "crimes," expressing remorse and seeking atonement. Cadres were organized, parades with drums and banners were held, loudspeakers were set up at key street junctions all over Shanghai and other cities, and everyone was encouraged to denounce his neighbor. As Jonathan Spence writes,

> The owner of the Dahua copper company provides an example of how a prominent industrialist could be brought to heel. He initially tried to duck further criticism by confessing to illegally obtaining 50 million yuan, but his employees kept after him to confess to greater crimes. At home, his mother-in-law and daughter also urged him to confess, as did a number of prominent capitalists who had recently had their own confessions accepted. After falling ill with worry, he finally "reconfessed," more contritely acknowledging graft totalling over 2 billion yuan.[46]

The newspapers published lengthy lists of the executed "counterrevolutionaries" every day; Chou Enlai himself estimated a figure of 22,500 deaths a month for the first several months of the program, and its total may well have been between 1 million and 3 million deaths. The Five Anti campaign also marked Mao's introduction of brainwashing techniques, which he called "thought reform," which in the end had touched every sector of society—not just the property-holding class.[47]

These kinds of activities have been carried out, in varying degrees, throughout the tenure of the CCP in China and are not limited merely to the initial postrevolutionary turmoil. The "Let a Hundred Flowers Bloom" campaign in 1956, which allowed some intellectual freedom, was later abruptly and violently suppressed, with professors sent to the camps or transferred to jobs involving latrine cleaning.[48] It seems reasonable that the Hundred Flowers episode was intended from the beginning to expose and crush the possible harbingers of dissent. But other imposed tragedies soon followed.

The infamous Great Leap Forward of 1958–1959 was a grandiose, incredibly ambitious experiment in human engineering, with over 700 million people's lives immediately and radically transformed. In transforming small and mid-size cooperative farms into huge communes, the Great Leap was an attempt to create socialism "ahead of time" by the sheer power of muscle and will.[49] Needless to say, it was a failure and resulted in a mass famine with some 20 million deaths: the social engineering had ruined food production and caused the amount of grain available to each person to fall from 205 kilos in 1957 to an appalling 154 kilos in 1961. In 1963, half of those who died were under ten years old. Mao himself admitted some "responsibility," saying that Confucius, Lenin, and Marx had also made mistakes.[50] Shortly after, in 1966, Mao devised another monstrous effort at human engineering in the name of abstract principles and his own Promethean will.

This enterprise, known as the Cultural Revolution, was a lurid, melodramatic spectacle that lasted ten years. It was certainly not about true culture. As Paul Johnson writes,

> It was a revolution of illiterates and semiliterates against intellectuals, the "spectacle-wearers," as they were called. It was xenophobic, aimed at those who "think the moon is rounder abroad." The Red Guards had a great deal in common with Roehm's Brownshirts, and the entire movement with Hitler's campaign against "cosmopolitan civilization." It was the greatest witch-hunt in history.[51]

The destruction during the Cultural Revolution was so vast and touched so many aspects of human life that one wonders why a general civil war did not break out in revolt against it. In a sense, the Red Guards acted spontaneously but nevertheless operated under the general rubric of a Central Committee directive issued in August 1966, which called for "vigilance" in supporting the "revolution" and prevented the police from responding to the random but widespread violence.[52] In any event, the nationwide attempt to destroy the "Four Olds"—"old customs, old habits, old culture, and old thinking"—led, in Spence's words, to "countless acts of calculated sadism."[53] The Cultural Revolution was an act of state.

The same basic governmental system is in power today, even though the scale of violence and repression has been significantly curtailed. The West should not have been surprised at Tiananmen Square; suppression of threats to the regime by force has been the norm for Communist China. There is a crucial phenomenon to be noted, however, about the past fifteen years in this nation. The power of the state, politically and economically, has eroded dramatically. And private enterprise has contributed substantially to the weakening of the power of the Communist system.

With the reaccession of Deng Xiaoping came an economic turn rightward. It had been clear for some time that the Chinese economy was a central-planning disaster and that marketization was desperately needed. In brief, the idea has been to move away from state control in economics while preserving the status quo in politics.[54] Agriculture has seen the most striking changes. As Thomas Bernstein writes, the apparatus of Communist party control over production has retreated, leaving only the village committee, which instead of making all decisions, now

> contracts land out to families, collects a tax and a payment to finance collective undertakings such as irrigation, and administers sales to the state, which were compulsory until 1985 and have since been based on contracts. Peasants are free to market their surpluses, to develop sidelines, and to engage in a range of economic activities previously forbidden.[55]

Prices for most foodstuffs were freed early on. At the start of Deng's reforms in 1978, farming output per capita had not risen since the mid-1950s. In the first half of the 1980s, however, real value-added output in agriculture rose by 7 percent per year while the number of farmers declined.[56] Total agricultural output during this time increased by 67 percent, a startling improvement in efficiency.[57]

Rural businesses have experienced a similar renaissance. In 1978, nonstate firms in the countryside were only 1.5 million in number, employing 28 million people. By the early 1990s, 40 percent of China's industrial employment was in rural areas, and rural industry contributed more than a quarter of China's industrial output and a quarter of its exports.[58] Total industrial output will have risen 20 percent or more in 1993, with the economy growing an estimated 12–14 percent in the first half of 1993, making China the fastest-growing economy in the world.[59] According to the International Monetary Fund, China is the world's third-largest economy; some estimates even predict that China will be the world's largest economy by the year 2010.[60]

A major aspect of local Communist party control has been the *dan-wei*, or work unit. The *dan-wei*, for example, determined "where an individual would be employed, whether he or she could change residence, and what ideological and political training a man or woman would have to undergo," as Seth Cropsey writes. It controlled nearly all aspects of a person's life.[61] Frequently, the state would not need to throw a recalcitrant citizen in jail, the *dan-wei* could be used to punish them: for a simple wage cut or job demotion would be sufficient to remedy any nascent political or personal problem. And reporting on one's neighbor would be *de rigueur*, for this itself could provide more leverage for the *dan-wei* to control its employees.[62] With the buildup of a private economic sphere, this system of state micromanagement and control has been greatly eroded, not so much by privatization as by the development of an alternative economic structure outside the auspices of the CCP. And the government has encouraged this. As Elizabeth Perry writes,

> The provision, via one's work or residential unit, of everything from grain rations to theater tickets afforded the state enormous leverage over the personal and political lives of city dwellers. These days, however, withdrawal of many of the state-subsidized perquisites for urbanites has undoubtedly loosened their bonds of loyalty.[63]

The economic alternatives now available to the Chinese in the nonstate sphere have effectively destroyed the monopoly of the *dan-wei*. A whole zone of human affairs has been removed from the control of the state and the Communist party, and it is steadily widening.

Ten years ago, state enterprises produced 78 percent of China's industrial output, with collectives constituting 21 percent and private firms only 1 percent. Near the end of 1992, the state made up 53 percent of industrial output, the collectives 36 percent, and private firms 11 percent. By the year 2000, the state is expected to produce only one-third of the output.[64] These figures are based on official statistics, which almost certainly underestimate the private sector's industrial growth because of the incomplete reporting of large profits by businessmen.[65] Consumer goods now flood the stores in China, most urban households have color televisions and washing machines, nearly half have refrigerators, and there is a booming market for consumer and designer stores.[66]

Because of this extraordinary economic growth, China is experiencing the rise of a new layer of professional people with certain economic means with knowledge of the outside world. These may well form a prosperous middle class in the near future. In addition to the thrifty and industrious nature of the Chinese people and the Deng reforms, the major explanation for the rapidity of China's growth has been its openness to foreign trade, especially American trade. U.S. exports to China were $7.5 billion in 1992, up 19 percent from 1991. U.S. imports from China were $25.7 billion in 1992, up by an enormous 35 percent from the previous year. China's share of total U.S. imports was 5 percent in 1992. Utilized direct investment in China exceeded $11 billion in 1992, a 160 percent increase over the year before, of which the U.S. contribution was over $500 million. The United States is China's fourth-largest direct investor, and China sends more than a quarter of its exports to the United States.[67] It seems certain, then, that, at the very least, the 1980 American extension of the MFN aided and abetted the reform process begun by Deng Xiaoping by providing a more generous climate for business.

The United States, then, has already been an enormous force for economic freedom in China—indeed, for freedom in general, in the cracking of the *dan-wei* monopoly. Any substantial reduction in the U.S. economic presence in China, as in the case of MFN revocation, would almost certainly do great harm to the Chinese economy and the booming private sector that is powering it. But most important, revoking MFN would weaken the one mechanism proven in Asia to remove illiberal and authoritarian regimes: a prosperous, educated, cosmopolitan middle class that gradually demands political concessions. The Tiananmen Square incident was, tragically, a symptom of this very phenomenon, for the students would never have entered the square if liberalization were not already so advanced. It is illustrative that the regime could finally use only the Twenty-seventh Army, a unit known for its provincial and uneducated troops, to crush the students. Indeed, as long as the United States remains economically engaged with the Chinese, it is only a matter of time before China's rapid progress toward a full-fledged market economy induces substantial political reform as well.

Security Implications of MFN Revocation

If one constant endures in international relations, it is the importance of credibility. Commentators and pundits, discussing the Clinton administration's performance in foreign policy, all recognize a basic problem: President Clinton does not seem entirely credible to foreign leaders because he has made threats without following up on them. There are many examples of this, most notably his threat to use air power against the Serbs in the conflict in Bosnia and his statement that there would be no European Community "veto" on his decision. The subsequent mission of Secretary of State Warren Christopher to Europe, during which the secretary acceded and finally succumbed to the opposition of the European leaders, was a loss for American resolve. The immediate Serbian response was to launch a major artillery assault on Sarajevo.

Somalia is another example of this phenomenon: after General Aidid killed Americans and dragged them through the streets, the United States decided to "suspend" its search for him, recognizing him as a legitimate negotiating partner (ultimately escorting him to the peace conference in Addis Ababa on a U.S. military aircraft). What was the immediate effect? Whipped up into a frenzy of anti-Americanism by incessant government reports exalting the American "defeat" in Somalia, the Haitian mobs prevented the October landing of U.S. troops on the island—creating still another American credibility problem. The long-term ramifications of this vacillation by the Clinton administration have yet to be played out. The Chinese are watching.

The president's China policy has already suffered from this problem. The negative rhetoric directed toward China from the start of his campaign, for example, turned out to be counterproductive. Why? He was not seriously interested in revoking MFN or taking other forceful action against the Chinese. When the president, in the spring of 1993, finally had to decide whether to revoke MFN, he chose to retain it—with more threats of action "next year." The response of the Chinese was, of course, to harden their position: after a series of threats in the summer by Secretary Christopher and Assistant Secretary Shattuck to revoke MFN in 1994, China has done less to improve human rights than it did for President Bush, who used tough yet private diplomacy. It is not that Clinton should have acted on his threats, but that threats must be credible and not, as the Chinese say, simply a firing of empty cannons. The fundamental issue for China policy makers is that if the United States is to brandish MFN as a weapon, we must be prepared to use it or our opponents will treat us with contempt. If we are not ready to revoke MFN for China, and clearly we are not, the president should cease his administration's verbal broadsides and deemphasize the issue.

The obvious question, then, is, Should we be willing to revoke MFN for China? Few actions would have a more damaging effect for all of East Asia. In the first place, we would poison the diplomatic relationship with the Chinese and forfeit the intangible benefits that it entails. What are these benefits? As in many Asian countries, the Chinese leadership places much store on personal relationships: Deng is the senior leader of China not because of his official positions (he has none to speak of these days) but from his *guanxi* or connections. In the same way, the Bush and Nixon administrations were able to exercise influence over the Chinese rulers by cultivating personal relationships that fostered respect and cooperation.

Everyone knows how President Bush's Rolodex and personal relationships with foreign leaders helped him form the coalition that defeated Saddam Hussein, but the Chinese cooperation he received during his presidency is less well known. One major benefit was Chinese support for or at least abstention from UN Security Council resolutions, especially during the Gulf War. Were China so disposed, as it would be if it felt that nothing would be gained from continued signs of good faith, the United States would rarely be able to give its initiatives the imprimatur of the United Nations.

This cooperation applies to many other issues. The most relevant case has been Cambodia. Previously, China had armed and backed the notorious Khmer Rouge for both ideological and balance-of-power reasons. But by the early 1990s, China believed it was time to support the peace accord and cease its backing of the revolutionary aims of this brutal organization. It would be too much to state that the positive U.S.-China relationship caused this turnaround. After all, the Chinese had an interest in anything that got the Vietnamese troops out of Cambodia, but it is certain that the important American relationship contributed to a deemphasis of the ideological attachment to Pol Pot.

Any long-term peaceful solution to the conflicting territorial claims in the South China Sea will require China's active cooperation. China is currently using a combination of carrot (good relations with the Southeast Asian nations) and stick (military buildup and power projection) to increase its influence in the area. The U.S. role is critical in precluding the exercise of force by China—not only through a continued forward deployed U.S. military presence but also through positive, mutually dependent political relations with the government. Revoking MFN would shatter this, render relations unstable, and possibly lead to a greater emphasis on military means in China's dispute resolution.

Perhaps most important of all is the benefit America has received from China's cooperation on the Korean peninsula, the most dangerous flash point in Asia, if not the world. Indeed, China has been transformed from a combatant (1950–1953) against America to an actual peacemaking influence on the peninsula. In the first place, China has informed North Korean leader Kim Il Sung that it would not come to his aid if he attacked the south. In the second and perhaps more striking change, China has now formally recognized the South Korean government, with all that implies, despite China's longstanding cultural and ideological support for the North Korean regime. Third, China has facilitated joint entry of the two Koreas into the UN, enhancing chances for a peaceful solution in the area. Significantly, President Roh Tae Woo personally intervened with President Bush not to revoke the MFN for China. Indeed, he said revocation of MFN would be nothing less than a disaster for Korea.

This fact brings us to another point. As we have seen, the revocation of MFN would seriously damage our position with the Chinese. What would it do to our influence in the rest of East Asia? Many countries look to our relations with China to see how we treat our friends: if we were to allow relations to substantially deteriorate with China, considered our friend by the world, how could we not affect the confidence many countries (such as Thailand, Indonesia, Peru, or Russia) have in the durability of our assurances?

East Asia in particular presents a more direct problem. The entire region is economically integrating as never before. The phenomenon known as Greater China is becoming evident to nearly everyone familiar with Asia. Many people have remarked facetiously that China will not swallow Hong Kong in 1997 because Hong Kong will swallow south China—but they might also add Taiwan, Macao, and Singapore to this phenomenon. As Murray Weidenbaum writes,

> This "bamboo network," which transcends national boundaries, also includes other key locations where business executives, traders, and financiers of Chinese background make important economic contributions. According to some estimates, Chinese companies in Malaysia, Thailand, Indonesia, and the Philippines make up about 70% of the private sector in those countries.[68]

The vast engine that is East Asia's growth is powered by this pool of talent, often centered on the transnational extensions of traditional Chinese clans.[69] Sadly, MFN revocation would harm these overseas networks of Chinese the most (dampening the "East Asian miracle") because they depend largely on trade and serve as conduits to America and elsewhere. But the larger security issue is even more important: the very economic interconnectedness of East Asia implies a political interconnectedness. The Association of South East Asian Nations (ASEAN) is evolving into a political forum as well as an economic arrangement. The United States must therefore work within a regional context to have any influence at all in Asia's future. Decisions cannot be taken in isolation.

A word about Taiwan in this context is in order. Taiwan needs the means to defend its democracy and way of life, and the United States has wisely supplied defensive weapons, including F-16s, to counterbalance the PRC military buildup and modernization program. The United States has no choice but to do this, given the fact that the PRC military still publicly discusses the use of force against the island. The way to deal with the PRC is to rule out its option to use force by a continued strong American military presence in Asia and, at the same time, encourage Taiwan and China in an active rapprochement. A key ingredient is constructive relations between the United States and China. These relations have centered on powerful economic forces—which necessarily diminish any military role. To attack and unravel this arrangement by unilateral punitive action on MFN would undermine the basis of peaceful cooperation and competition. Governor Chris Patten of Hong Kong has argued forcefully for keeping China's MFN status but at the same time has pushed for greater democracy and human rights in Hong Kong. Revoking MFN would shatter his efforts and set back the cause of democracy in the Crown Colony.

Why would American revocation of MFN affect our Asian influence? Realistically, no other nation will withdraw its favorable trading privileges with China. The United States, if it does so, will most certainly be doing so alone. Japan, for example, would be appalled by our action. As the lone actor in an extraordinarily unpopular decision throughout Asia, the United States would clearly suffer greatly reduced influence in the region. Thirty-eight of thirty-nine Asian nations supported the China-Indonesian version of human rights against the United States in Bangkok in March 1993. This does not in itself make those nations right and the United States wrong, but it indicates how strong the regional forces are arrayed against us on this issue of how best to advance human rights. The United States has long been deeply involved in the affairs of Asia, to the great benefit of Asia's peace and security. Indeed, it would be tragic if we were to forfeit the fruits of our long-term diplomatic accomplishments by forcing the rest of Asia to lean toward China and against us. More important, morality itself should compel us to respect the historical forces leading to pluralism and democracy that are now evolving vigorously throughout the Waking Giant and East Asia as well, from an increasingly propertied and prosperous people.

4

U.S.-China Trade and Investment in the 1990s

Claude E. Barfield

Relations between the United States and China are an important part of broader, evolving relations between the United States and East Asia, the most dynamic and the fastest-growing economic region in the world. Thus, although this chapter is devoted to the issues that will affect U.S.-China relations during the 1990s, these issues can best be understood in the larger regional context.

China in the East Asian Context

East Asia—the Four Tigers (Taiwan, Singapore, South Korea, and Hong Kong), the Association of Southeast Asian Nations (Malaysia, Indonesia, the Philippines, Thailand, and Singapore), and the People's Republic of China—has set the pace for world economic growth for the past decade. Omitting China for the moment, while each of the countries has exhibited individual growth characteristics and policies, they also have common elements, including high rates of saving, sustained human and physical capital investment, realistic currency valuation, and successful debt management.

As table 4–1 illustrates, these macroeconomic policies have produced extraordinary economic growth for East Asian nations. Indeed,

TABLE 4–1
GROWTH OF GROSS DOMESTIC PRODUCT IN EAST ASIA, 1970–1992
(percent)

	1970–1980[a]	*1980–1990*[a]	*1990*	*1991*	*1992*
Japan	5.21	4.19	3.5	4.5	1.3
People's Republic of China	7.90	10.10	5.2	7.0	12.8
South Korea	9.00	9.90	9.0	8.3	7.3
Taiwan	10.26	8.25	5.0	7.3	6.7
Indonesia	7.70	5.50	7.4	6.4	6.7
Thailand	7.90	7.80	10.0	7.5	8.0
Hong Kong	9.30	7.10	2.8	4.0	5.8
Singapore	7.90	6.30	8.3	7.0	6.1
Malaysia	7.30	6.10	9.8	8.6	8.5

a. Average.
SOURCE: Cited in Thomas Duesterberg, "Trade, Investment and Engagement in the U.S.-Asian Relationship."

in the current situation, with recession in the European Union (EU) and a slow-growth recovery in the United States, it is the Asian nations (along with South America) that have exerted a strong upward pull on world economic growth.

Rapid economic growth since the 1960s has also given the East Asian countries the highest increases in standard of living in the world, as measured by the change in gross domestic product (GDP) per capita. As figure 4–1 shows, nine of the top twenty countries in per capita income growth since 1965 have come from this region. They have attained these absolute increases while at the same time improving income distribution (although it should be noted that South Korea, Taiwan, and China started the period with a narrow range of income distributions). Today, the most dynamic economies of East Asia have achieved impressive results, placing them among the most advanced developing countries as measured in per capita income (see table 4–2).

Outward-looking policies, which have fostered huge gains from trade, have also been an abiding characteristic of economic policies of the East Asian economies. Total merchandise trade volume between the United States and Asia exceeded U.S.-EC trade by the late 1970s, and in 1992 total trade between the United States and Asia stood at $344 billion, 51 percent higher than total merchandise trade between the United States and Europe.[1] For the first six months of 1993, U.S. exports to East Asia and the Pacific constituted 28.5 percent of total U.S. exports, as compared with a European total of 21.5 percent. In addition, imports from East Asia and the Pacific made up 39.6 percent of total U.S. imports, as against 16.9 percent of the total that came from Europe (see figure 4–2).

FIGURE 4–1
CHANGE IN GROSS DOMESTIC PRODUCT PER CAPITA, SELECTED COUNTRIES, 1960–1985

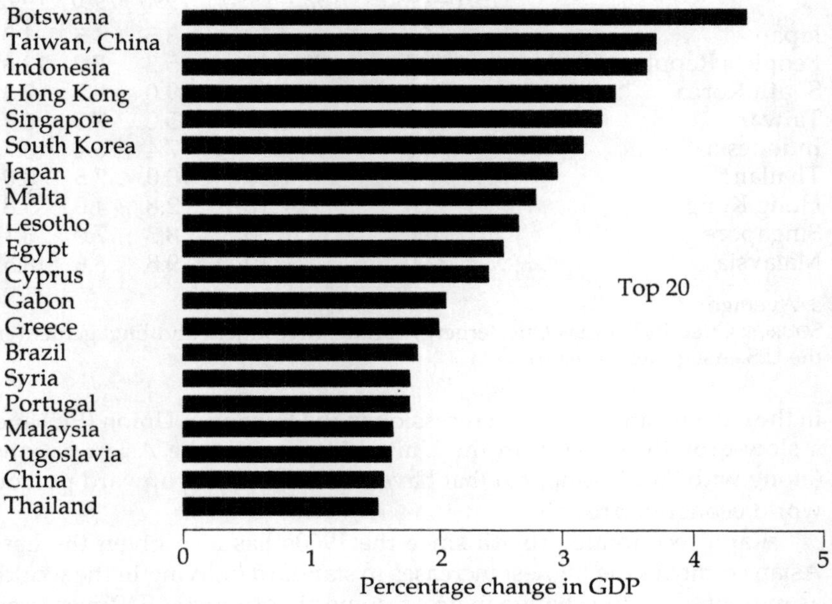

SOURCE: Cited in *The East Asian Miracle* (World Bank, 1993).

Moreover, although for much of the period U.S.-Japanese trade predominated, it has not kept pace with trade with other nations in the East Asian region in recent years. While U.S. exports to Japan have remained more or less constant since 1990, U.S. exports to China have risen by 55 percent, to Taiwan 32 percent, to Singapore 20 percent, to Indonesia 46 percent, and to Hong Kong and Thailand 33 percent.[2]

Two other trends regarding Asian trading patterns are important in explaining future U.S.-Asian relations. First, although Asia is still much more dependent on extraregional trade for its prosperity than other regions around the world, in recent years Asian intraregional trade has grown much faster than trade outside the region. Since 1980, intraregional Asian trade has grown from 19.7 percent of total Asian trade to 30 percent of that trade.[3] A second trend has been the diminishing dependence on the United States as the major purchaser of Asian products. As table 4–3 indicates, over the past decade dependence on the United States declined for the most dynamic trading countries in East Asia.

TABLE 4–2
POPULATION AND GROSS DOMESTIC PRODUCT PER CAPITA FOR EAST ASIAN COUNTRIES, 1990 AND 1991

	Population, 1991 (in millions)	*GDP per Capita, 1990*[a] *(1990 U.S. $)*
Thailand	57.2	3,990
China	1,149.5	1,990
Hong Kong	5.8	15,600
Taiwan	20.6	12,670[b]
South Korea	43.3	6,730
Japan	123.9	17,620
Malaysia	18.2	6,140
Singapore	2.8	15,880
Philippines	62.9	2,300
Indonesia	181.3	2,180

a. Purchasing power and parity.
b. Estimate.
SOURCE: United Nations Development Project.

The Chinese Miracle

China is a late bloomer. Only after 1978 did China gradually begin to introduce the market reforms that by the mid-1980s were producing bursts of economic growth. Decentralized economic decision making and competition among individual provinces were the driving forces behind China's economic dynamism. Step-by-step liberalization, first in agriculture and then in banking and industry, permitted the central government to experiment as it went along.[4] A pool of savings from the quickly profitable agricultural sector allowed local governments to invest in manufacturing and infrastructure. At the same time, the central government speeded the process by selecting certain provinces, particularly those along the coast, as development zones with special tax and tariff concessions.

While China is an extraordinary success, its development formula also has built-in problems. One is a growing disparity in wealth between the richer and the poorer provinces, which the central government is ill equipped to redress because of reduced tax revenues and a loss of power to the provinces. Although the central Chinese government announced a major overhaul of tax laws, aimed at substantially increasing its share of national tax revenue, these plans are expected to encounter fierce opposition from the individual provinces.[5]

A second problem has been the boom-and-bust nature of China's development over the past decade. What the central government most

FIGURE 4–2
TOTAL U.S. EXPORTS AND TOTAL U.S. IMPORTS, JANUARY–JUNE 1993

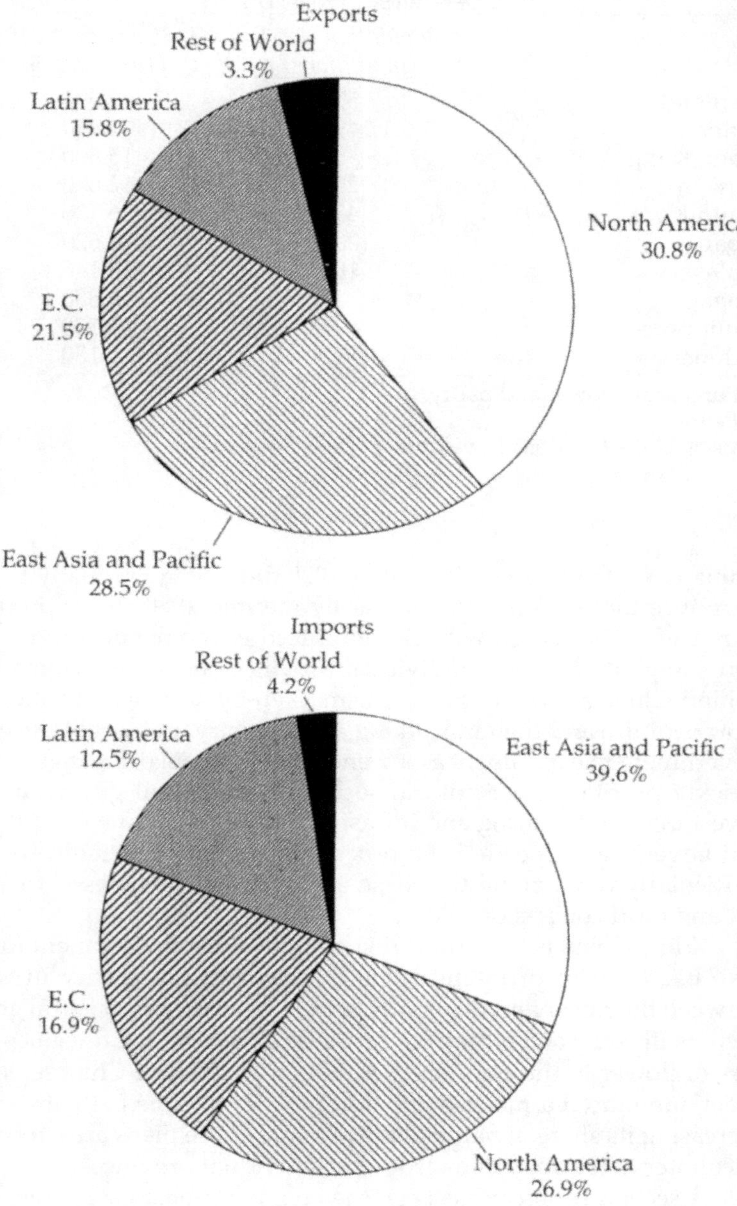

SOURCE: U.S. Department of Commerce, Bureau of the Census.

TABLE 4–3
EAST ASIAN EXPORTS TO THE UNITED STATES AS A PERCENTAGE OF TOTAL EXPORTS, 1975, 1985, AND 1992

	1975	*1985*	*1992*
Japan	20.16	37.92	28.27
People's Republic of China	2.08	15.37	34.46
South Korea	30.29	35.63	22.98
Taiwan	31.12	57.93	29.15
Indonesia	26.17	21.74	12.33
Thailand	11.29	19.87	22.59
Hong Kong	34.41	30.82	23.54
Singapore	13.87	21.17	17.80
Malaysia	15.97	12.76	18.72

SOURCE: Thomas Duesterberg, "Trade, Investment and Engagement in the U.S.-Asian Relationship."

needs now is to reassert some control over macroeconomic policy, particularly with regard to monetary and fiscal affairs. Specifically, the government needs to set up a strong central bank that will work with regional banks to curb monetary and fiscal excesses. (On December 5, 1993, China announced plans to create a modern banking system, including an independent central bank. It remains to be seen whether these ambitious plans will come to successful fruition.)[6]

All banks must begin to use competitive markets forces, but in China banks cannot truly enter into market competition until they are freed from the necessity of supporting money-losing state enterprises. Unfortunately, these enterprises form the main source of welfare services—health, pensions, and housing—and, until an alternative social safety net is devised, Chinese leaders are loath to confront the social unrest that the wholesale demise of these enterprises would generate. Thus, Chinese leaders face a delicate balancing act in bringing order to their unruly economy over the next decade.

Whatever the immediate future, from the mid-1980s the Chinese economy took off. Between 1987 and 1992, average real growth of GDP was just under 9 percent, and industrial output averaged just under 15 percent (these averages, as figures 4–3 and 4–4 show, masked peaks at the beginning and end of the period). And since early 1992, the pace of economic change has quickened, with both positive and negative results for the Chinese economy and its trade relations with other nations. The central event that produced the change was Deng Xiaoping's visit to southern China in January 1992, where he gave an unequivocal blessing to economic reforms, particularly to the plans of regional reformers to proceed rapidly with their own developmental initiatives.

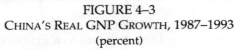

FIGURE 4–3
CHINA'S REAL GNP GROWTH, 1987–1993
(percent)

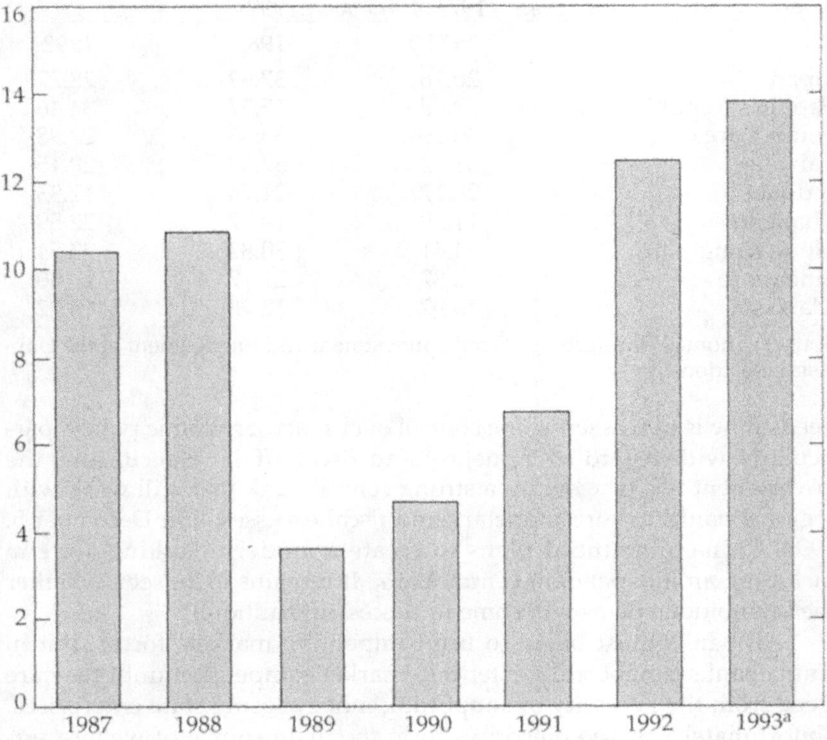

a. Based on half-year statistics, in comparison with same period in 1992.
SOURCE: Official Chinese statistics. Cited in CIA (Paper prepared for House Subcommittee on Technology and National Security of the Joint Economic Committee, July 30, 1993).

After Deng's trip, Chinese leaders took a series of steps to implement his vision. In central party meetings in October 1992 and March 1993, a new economic policy team was installed to direct Deng's call for a "social market economy." Furthermore, in March 1993, the government announced a major reorganization of the economic bureaucracy, the stated aim of which was to reduce government intervention in the economy. As a result of the clear signal that growth was the first priority, local and regional entrepreneurs unleashed a fury of activity that produced an increase in GDP of almost 13 percent in 1992 and an increase of investment spending on fixed assets of an astounding 37.6 percent. Total bank lending rose about 20 percent, which in turn produced an increase in the money supply of over 30 percent.[7]

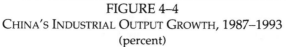

FIGURE 4–4
CHINA'S INDUSTRIAL OUTPUT GROWTH, 1987–1993
(percent)

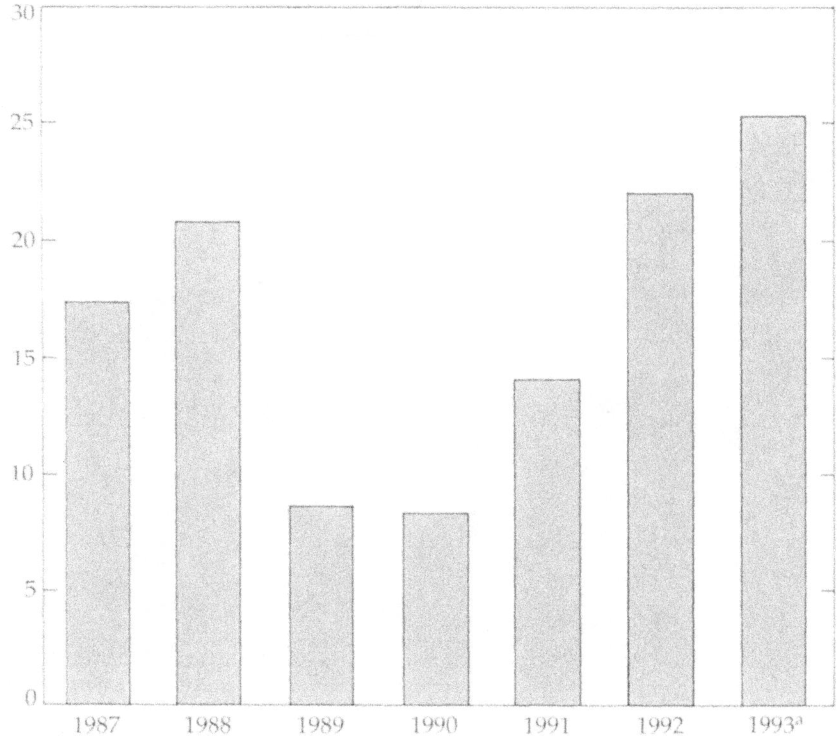

NOTE: Gross value of industrial output calculated using constant prices.
a. 1993 first six months compared with same period in 1992.
SOURCE: Same as source for figure 4–3.

By early 1993, the danger signs of an overheating economy were everywhere. In 1992, industrial sector output had surged almost 22 percent, and the sales volume of capital goods increased by more than 40 percent. This demand surge in turn produced shortages and a sharply rising inflation rate—steel prices increased 40 percent in one year, and cement prices jumped almost 50 percent.[8] A further danger sign has been the increasing strains on China's inefficient transportation and energy production sectors, both of which contributed bottlenecks that heightened inflationary pressures. In the fourth quarter of 1992, China briefly became a net importer of oil, for the first time in fifteen years.

Finally, state-owned companies, which account for just over 50 percent of industrial production but contain more than two-thirds of

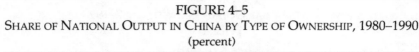

FIGURE 4–5
SHARE OF NATIONAL OUTPUT IN CHINA BY TYPE OF OWNERSHIP, 1980–1990
(percent)

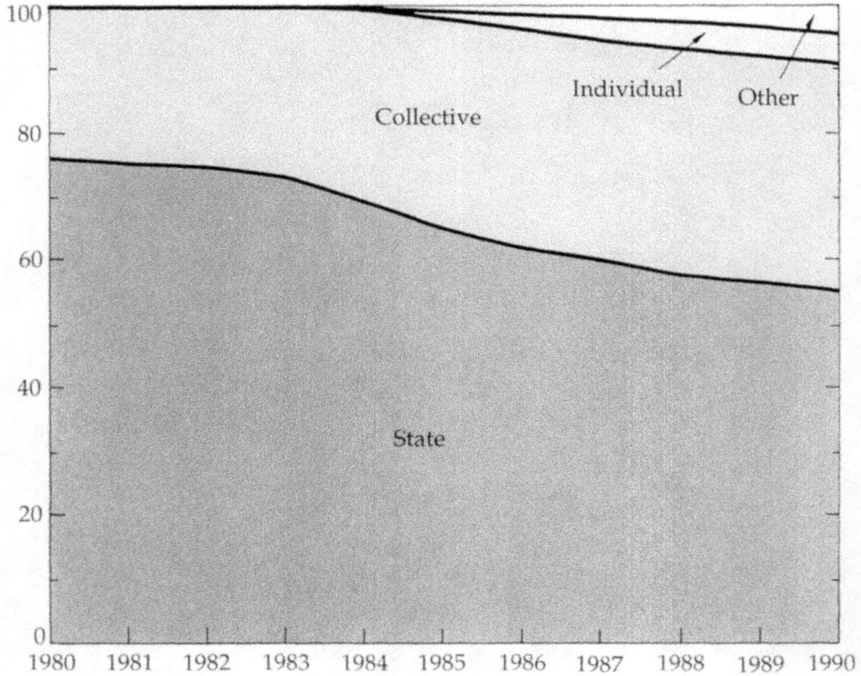

SOURCE: China Statistical Yearbook, as quoted in *The Economist,* November 28, 1992.

industrial workers, are being transformed only slowly (see figure 4–5). Only a third are estimated to be economically viable, and the other two-thirds constitute a heavy weight on the rest of the economy. Most are both overstaffed and technologically retrograde, but fearing social unrest, the government has moved slowly to force them to downsize and go into bankruptcy. Their continuing need for sustaining bank loans (many of which are disguised through accounting gimmicks) has also contributed to the inflationary pressures.

During the last six months of 1993, the Chinese government gave mixed signals regarding a policy to slow the economy. In June, it announced steps to recapture control of growth, including a freeze on new development zones, a clampdown on unauthorized local development bonds, increased pressure on local banks to restrict credit, and plans for a new tax on real estate appreciation. In November, however, top Chinese officials seemed to reverse course when they adopted a more benign approach toward the nation's still burgeoning growth and eased somewhat earlier credit restrictions. Although this may have been the result of lessening inflationary pressures, it was by no means certain in early 1994 that China had escaped the possibility of a painful, market-driven retrenchment.[9]

China's Trade and Investment Patterns

Until the early 1980s, China was virtually closed off to foreign trade and investment; but a major element of the reforms after 1978 was the decentralization of trade and investment decisions to local and regional officials. Today, trade is largely handled not by a Beijing bureaucracy but by 3,700 trading companies located throughout the country.

Since 1980, the dollar value of China's trade has grown by more than 12 percent annually, and exports have gone up fivefold. In 1992, China became the world's eleventh-largest trading nation (total trade of $165 billion), up from fifteenth in 1991.[10]

Total Chinese imports grew by 26.4 percent in 1992, fueled by the rapid internal growth that boosted imports of industrial and infrastructure goods, such as machinery and transportation equipment, and by raw materials such as steel. China's exports also increased substantially by over 18 percent. Low-technology goods like toys and textiles continue to dominate China's exports, but electrical and mechanical equipment and products have risen to almost one-quarter of China's exports in recent years.

Foreign investment in China has also grown rapidly (see figure 4–6). In 1992, utilized direct investment exceeded $11 billion, and contracted future investment reached almost $58 billion. Asian countries continued to be the leading investors in China, with 70 percent of this outside investment coming from Hong Kong or from third-country investors channeled through Hong Kong. Taiwan was the second largest investor in China, with about 10 percent of both utilized and contracted investment. Japan ranked third behind Taiwan, and the United States ranked fourth.[11]

U.S.-China Trade and Investment. China's trade surplus with the rest of the world is eroding, while at the same time its surplus with the United States has surged upward over the past several years. That surplus jumped 43 percent in 1992, to reach $18.2 billion. Both exports and imports between the two countries increased, but exports to the United States jumped 35 percent (to $25.7 billion), while imports increased only 19 percent (to $7.5 billion).[12]

Much of the large increase in U.S. imports from China has come as a result of other Asian nations—particularly Hong Kong and Taiwan—

FIGURE 4–6

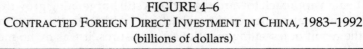

CONTRACTED FOREIGN DIRECT INVESTMENT IN CHINA, 1983–1992
(billions of dollars)

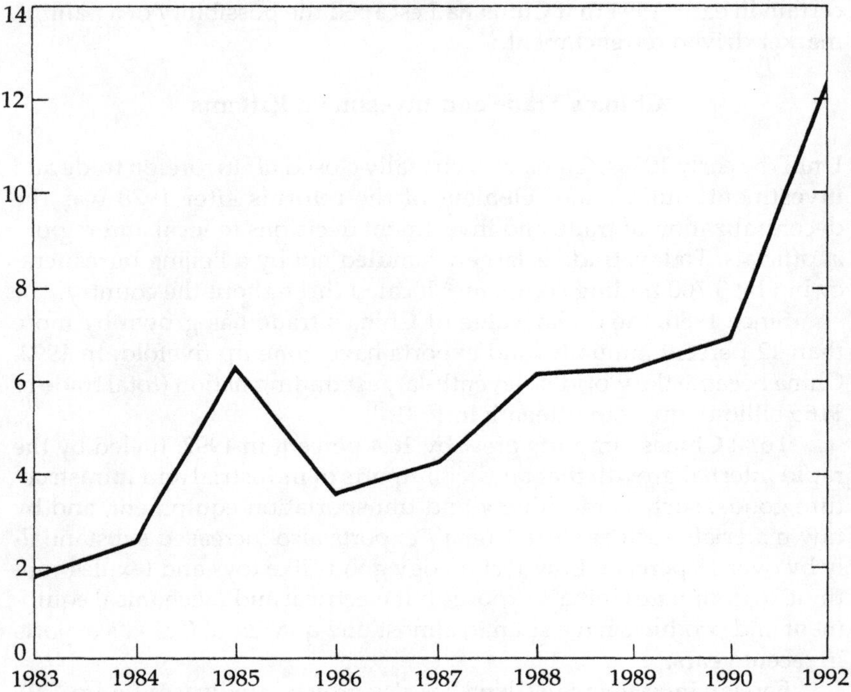

SOURCE: China Statistical Yearbook, as quoted in *The Economist*, October 30, 1993.

shifting labor-intensive, low-technology manufacturing to China. Over half of Chinese footwear exports to the United States, for instance, are produced in firms owned partly or wholly by Taiwanese.

U.S. exports to China exhibited mixed results in 1992. There were some notable increases: in transportation equipment, for example, against a total decline of 20 percent in Chinese transportation imports, U.S. firms more than doubled their share of this market to 40 percent ($2 billion in aircraft and equipment). In addition, U.S. sales of computers far outstripped the increases in total Chinese purchases of these products. The United States now supplies over 40 percent of all computers sold in China.[13]

In other industrial sectors, however, including industrial machinery, leather and textile goods, plastics, and chemicals, U.S. sales declined against a total increase in Chinese imports or did not keep up with the increases of foreign competitors in the Chinese market.

As figure 4–7 indicates, by value, the top U.S. exports to China are aircraft and related equipment, power-generating equipment, fertilizer, electric machinery, medical instruments, grain, chemicals, cotton yarn, and fabrics. Top U.S. imports (figure 4–8) include apparel, toys, games and sporting goods, electronics, footwear, leather goods, power-generating machinery, plastics, and petroleum.

Greater China

Up until now, three-quarters of outside investment in China has come from overseas Chinese around the Asian rim. This fact underscores a phenomenon that will play an increasingly important role in Asian development: the evolution of a greater China as a new economic colossus. When observers such as Murray Weidenbaum use the term *Greater China,* they are referring to China's regional neighbors where the Chinese population plays a predominant economic role.[14] The Chinese families who constitute the economic leadership in these countries have also taken the lead—through family ties as well as familiarity with mainland Chinese customs and business practices—in investment and trade with their homeland.

As an indication of the dimension of this phenomenon, some estimate the percentage of Chinese-controlled companies in Malaysia, Thailand, Indonesia, and the Philippines as high as 70 percent. Ethnic Chinese, for instance, account for only 10 percent of Thailand's population, but Chinese businessmen control nine of the ten largest business groups. In Indonesia only 4 percent of the population is Chinese, but all of the ten largest business groups are owned by Chinese entrepreneurs. Likewise, in Malaysia, the local Chinese business class occupies a predominant position in trade and investment (so much so that the government has instituted an affirmative action program for other ethnic groups).

Taiwan, Hong Kong, and the overseas Chinese in these countries have taken the lead in outside trade and investment in mainland China. This Chinese-based economy, according to Weidenbaum and others, consists largely of mid-sized, family-run firms that specialize in light manufacture and of services such as shipping and retailing. They are highly flexible and accustomed, among themselves and in relations with mainland China, to informal agreements and transactions to move goods, services, information, and investment.

Often relations are forged with families from the province from whence the Chinese entrepreneurs came. Thus, Hong Kong has account-

FIGURE 4–7
U.S. EXPORTS TO CHINA, 1992

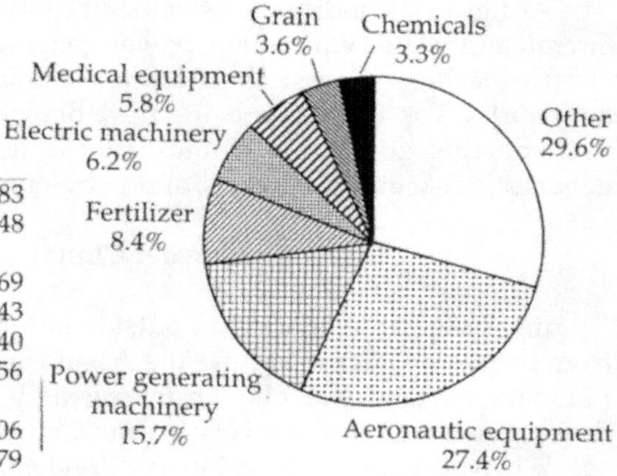

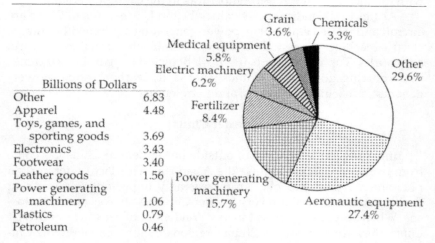

Billions of Dollars	
Other	6.83
Apparel	4.48
Toys, games, and sporting goods	3.69
Electronics	3.43
Footwear	3.40
Leather goods	1.56
Power generating machinery	1.06
Plastics	0.79
Petroleum	0.46

SOURCE: *China Business Review*, May–June, 1993; Department of Commerce; Heritage Foundation.

FIGURE 4–8
U.S. IMPORTS FROM CHINA, 1992

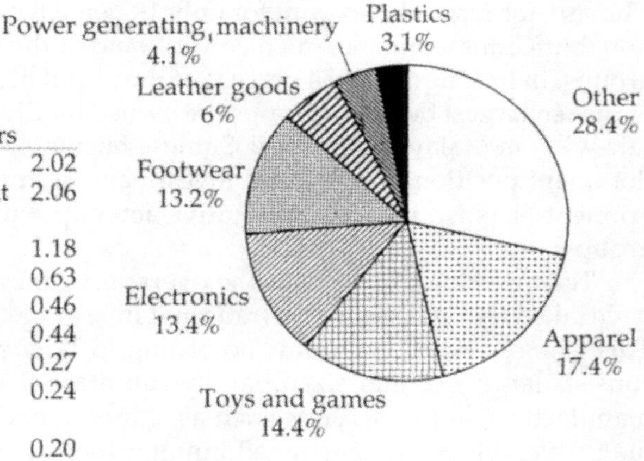

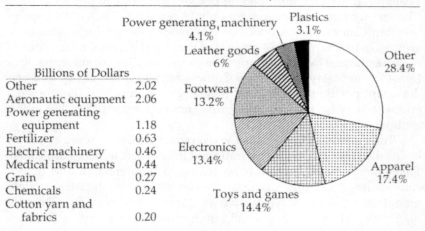

Billions of Dollars	
Other	2.02
Aeronautic equipment	2.06
Power generating equipment	1.18
Fertilizer	0.63
Electric machinery	0.46
Medical instruments	0.44
Grain	0.27
Chemicals	0.24
Cotton yarn and fabrics	0.20

SOURCE: *China Business Review*, May–June, 1993; Department of Commerce; Heritage Foundation.

FIGURE 4–9
TRADE WITHIN THE CHINESE ECONOMIC AREA, 1987–1991
(billions of dollars)

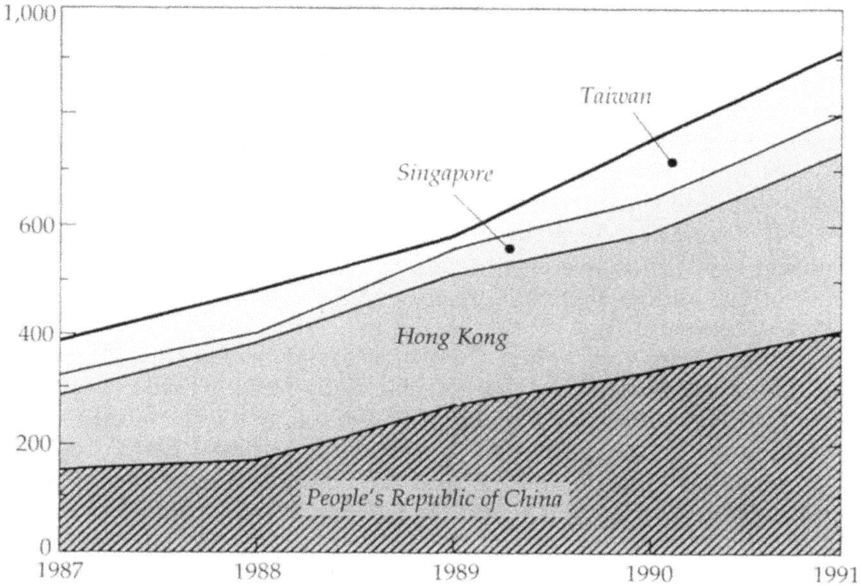

SOURCE: International Monetary Fund, International Financial Statistics. Cited in Murray Weidenbaum, "Greater China," *Washington Quarterly* (August 1993).

ed for 90 percent of the investment in adjacent Guangdong Province, while Taiwan has underwritten the expansion of Fujian Province, its nearest neighbor on the mainland. These cross-investments are not taking place only in China. In 1991, Taiwan was the single largest investor in Malaysia; and Taiwan, Hong Kong, and Singapore are catching up with Japan and the United States as major investors in Indonesia, Malaysia, and Thailand. As figure 4–9 shows, internal trade among the leading developing Asian economies has grown dramatically since the mid-1980s, as these overseas connections have deepened and widened.

In the future, mainland China will certainly be the center of a web of investment and trade relations because of its vast population and market potential. Thus, for the United States and other non-Asian nations, relations with China will become inextricably entwined with those of other nations of East Asia. These nations, in turn, will increasingly view their relations with the United States through a central prism of their economic and political ties to mainland China.

U.S.-China Trade and Investment Issues

Trade and investment issues between the United States and China fall into two categories: those that flow from human rights and political disagreements and from the linking of reform in China to the continuation of most-favored-nation (MFN) status by the United States; and those purely commercial trade and investment issues that are standard negotiating areas in the bilateral economic relations between all nations.

In May 1993, President Clinton renewed MFN for China for one year and based further renewal on certain conditions, including no export of goods produced by prison labor and "significant progress" in human rights, humane treatment and release of political prisoners, more freedom for Tibet, and greater access to international radio and television broadcasts.

Progress since the spring of 1993 has been mixed at best. China has promised, for example, to stop the shipping of goods made by prison labor. In November, the Chinese government also announced that it would enter into negotiations with the International Red Cross for inspections of its prison camps. It has, however, continued to detain some dissidents and has shown no signs of relaxing its tight control of Tibet.

At the crucial meeting of the APEC (Asia Pacific Economic Cooperation Forum) nations in mid-November, a standoff occurred between the United States and China on these issues. President Clinton warned that the United States expected real changes before next year, and President Jiang Zemin reiterated China's position that human rights and political issues were domestic matters not subject to international negotiations.[15] It is likely that this mixed pattern will continue until June 3, 1994, when President Clinton must make another determination. At that time—as in 1993—he will face a difficult trade-off, particularly in regard to U.S. trade and investment opportunities.

Both sides have a great deal at stake. For China, the United States represents the single most important market export and, of equal importance, the best avenue for technological upgrading through investment and joint venturing. As noted, Chinese exports to the United States reached $27 billion in 1992 and are predicted to continue growing steadily throughout the rest of the decade. For the United States, the Chinese market represents an equally promising future. Although China is running a substantial trade deficit at the moment, its huge development and infrastructure needs will produce enormous export and investment opportunities for U.S. firms in coming years. According to the U.S.-China Business Council, China plans to spend $200 billion in imports over the next two years, with longer-range markets (twenty years) worth $40 billion in aerospace, $30 billion in telecommunications equipment, up to $100 billion in power-generating equipment, and $40 billion in computers.[16]

While eliminating MFN in 1994 would cause the greater hardship for China, U.S. producers and consumers would also be harmed. In effect, eliminating MFN would cause goods from China to be assessed at the high tariff rates of the 1930s imposed under the Smoot-Hawley tariff, which would raise average tariff rates from about 7 percent to more than 40 percent. As a result, U.S. consumers, who now buy about $27 billion worth of goods from China, would then, by some estimates, pay $7–10 billion more for these products.[17] Moreover, removal of MFN would jeopardize the jobs and profits in companies that provide the goods for the $7.5 billion in U.S. exports to China.

At base, the issue of MFN comes down to a judgment call regarding means and ends. The strongest argument of those who favor avoiding a break with China is the historical record of the past fifteen years. As Zhiling Lin, a research associate at the American Enterprise Institute, has written:

> There are . . . two important factors that have been fundamental to China's evolution: the economic development based on economic reform, and the various connections with the outside world based on the opening-up policy. So long as China continues moving along this track, its economy can continue to be prosperous, its economic marketization and decentralization can continue to increase, and its society can continue to develop in a more modern and pluralistic direction. All these eventually will lead China to political pluralism, and that is the time when democracy will triumph. . . .
>
> MFN is still the most important . . . foreign support for China's economic development, especially in those coastal areas which are the driving force of the economy. Without MFN . . . the final goal of democracy could be farther to reach.[18]

Commercial Trade and Investment Issues. As with many developing countries, particularly the newly industrialized countries in Asia, the key to successful market-opening negotiations with China is doggedness, persistence, and a shrewd combination of the carrot and the stick. In this case, the ever-present carrot is the huge U.S. market. Although the Clinton administration has often dismissed the policies and tactics of the predecessor Bush administration, in truth the Clintonites are building on the successful commercial diplomacy of the Bush years. Indeed, for the short term, the main goal of the Clinton administration is to get the Chinese to live up to agreements signed under Bush.

In January 1992, China concluded a memorandum of understanding (MOU) with the United States on intellectual property. During his historic trip to south China in early 1992, Deng Xiaoping placed his personal stamp on this protocol, proclaiming, according to the *People's Daily*, that Chinese enterprises "must abide by international rules on intellectual property."[19] U.S. negotiators consider this agreement central to future success for U.S. exports, which will be centered on pharmaceuticals, chemicals, and electronics such as information and telecommunications equipment and services and computer software.

So far, the Chinese have made a good-faith effort to live up to the agreement and have published regulations for copyright protection of existing literary works, computer software, and sound recordings. China also joined the Berne Convention on Copyrights in April 1993. In addition, China has made extensive changes in its patenting system, including amending its law to extend protection to agricultural, chemical, and pharmaceutical products and processes. What remains to be seen is whether entrepreneurs and bureaucrats at all levels will live up to the laws and regulations that have come down from the top in Beijing. Intellectual property piracy remains a major problem in China. The International Intellectual Property Alliance estimates that in 1992 alone, U.S. companies lost over $400 million from piracy of American software, books, records, and movies.[20]

The same question—rigorous implementation—hangs over the far more sweeping MOU on market access, which China signed with the United States in October 1992, in one of the last negotiating triumphs of the Bush administration. In this document, China agreed to open its markets over the next five years in many of the sectors considered high priority by the United States. Licensing requirements, administrative barriers, and quotas will be phased out for computers, telecommunications equipment, heavy machinery, cameras, electronics, agricultural goods, wood products, and steel products, among others.

In December 1992, China reduced some of its prohibitively high tariffs. In mid-November 1993, China added to this list with further reductions of up to 8.8 percent on some 2,900 items, including gasoline and other petrochemicals, vegetable oils, color film, refrigerators, textile machinery, minicomputers, bicycles, watches, and cosmetics. These reductions will lower the average Chinese tariff rate from 39.9 percent to 36.4 percent.[21]

Of equal importance, China acknowledged the existence of secret, internal *neibu* (trade regulations or directives), including certifications and standards, which were used to keep out foreign goods. Chinese leaders promised to make its trade rules and regulations transparent in the future and to publish all such regulations and forbid enforcement of secret regulations. In that regard, China also promised that safety and health standards would no longer be used to keep out U.S. agricultural and food products. In its totality, the market access agreement constituted on paper a sweeping revolution in trade relations between the United States and China.

Services. One area of particular importance is the service sector. In no other sector of its economy is China so underdeveloped and in need of outside investment and technical support and advice. U.S. companies, with productivity and skills that exceed those of other industrial nations in most service sectors, have much to gain from an opening up of the Chinese service sector to trade and investment. In general, however, foreign companies still face major obstacles to conducting basic business services in China, including an inability to offer after-sales services for products, limited access to sales and distribution networks, inability to own or manage retail sales outlets, and prohibitions against foreign-owned leasing operations.

As with goods, a top priority of U.S. commercial negotiations with China must be the creation of a framework for a more stable business environment in China—and that means a framework for the services industries based on international principles and laws. China itself has much to gain from creating clear rules for investment and ownership in the service sectors. From insurance and banking to telecommunications and computer software, U.S. companies can help China lay down the foundations of a modern economy.

The Future

Regarding the crucial issue of MFN, the Clinton administration must continue to apply steady pressure with a minimum of heavy-handed rhetoric. It is essential that in coming months the president keep his vision focused on the ineluctable pressures that economic liberalization is placing on China's authoritarian central political system. Small gestures—in emigration, in increased access to outside information and media, in inspection of alleged political prisoner camps—should be encouraged and applauded. While all bets would, and should, be off if another incident like the one in Tiananmen Square occurred, the administration must be prepared to act with skill and patience on Deng's inevitable death and the ensuing difficulty of the transition of power at the top.

Regarding the purely commercial issues, the top priority should be stepped-up encouragement of China's application for membership in the General Agreement on Tariffs and Trade (GATT), particularly with the successful conclusion of the Uruguay Round. Conclusion of the Uruguay Round will usher in a new era of multilateral trade rules, and many of the bilateral issues between the United States and China can then be handled in a multilateral forum. Outstanding differences over intellectual property, services, investment, and transparency of trade rules lend themselves especially well to multilateral consideration. One important consequence of China's accession to the GATT would be the transferal of the pressure and political friction inherent in U.S.-China bilateral talks to the multilateral level, where the United States would be joined by many other nations in negotiating China's formal legal entrance into the world trading system.

China's entry into the GATT, however, is at best several years away; in the interim, U.S.-Chinese bilateral negotiations will remain at center stage. Here the key to success is a steady persistence in applying pressure on Chinese officials to implement agreements they have already accepted. While the United States may place new issues on the table, most important for the moment is forcing China to live up to its current obligations—and for its own benefit as well as that of the United States to work to enhance a stable, efficient, and fair business climate for foreign investment and trade.

5

Influencing Human Rights in China

Andrew J. Nathan

Are China's human rights practices objectionable enough to justify strong American concern? Has China proved responsive to Western pressure on human rights issues? And does the record suggest that most-favored-nation (MFN) status has been and is likely to continue to be an effective policy instrument in influencing Chinese human rights practices? Other contributions to this volume delineate the risks and difficulties of using trade policies to influence human rights performance. This chapter does not contradict them but argues that the threat partially to revoke MFN privileges remains too legitimate and effective a policy instrument to relinquish yet.

China's Human Rights Record

China's human rights performance has vastly improved since Mao's time. Tens of millions of political victims have been rehabilitated, the caste-like "class status" *(chengfen)* system dissolved, markets and private enterprise promoted, and political and religious repression eased.

The author thanks Michael Chambers, Margot E. Landman, and James Lilley for helpful comments.

China has increased incomes and the availability of consumer goods, extended the length of compulsory education from six years to nine, and increased average life expectancy to seventy years. The government has campaigned against torture and ill-treatment of prisoners, cadre abuse of powers, and female infanticide and the kidnapping and sale of women.[1] The party has allowed legal scholars and political reformers to advocate further reforms, such as an end to the crime of counterrevolution and the establishment of a presumption of innocence in criminal trials.

But the regime's human rights record remains poor. The major problems highlighted by foreign human rights organizations are the following:

- *Political imprisonment.* Hundreds of known, and probably thousands of unknown, persons have been imprisoned for their political beliefs, although they had not used or advocated violence.[2] They include democracy movement activists, Tibetans detained for supporting independence, Mongols detained for a cultural revival movement, people detained for protesting over personal grievances, those accused of divulging state secrets, and former officials arrested for supporting Cultural Revolution–style leftism.
- *Religious repression.*[3] Hundreds, or perhaps thousands, of Catholics, Protestants, and Tibetan Buddhists are in jails and camps for rejecting Chinese government religious control. Priests, ministers, and worshipers in so-called house churches have been arrested, especially in Henan, Shandong, and Guangdong, and many Tibetans have been detained for religious practices.
- *Problems with criminal procedure.*[4] Chinese criminal procedures fail to meet international standards for fair trials; to provide adequate safeguards against police abuse, especially during the process of "shelter and investigation" *(shourong shencha);* to prevent unlimited detention without trial; to ensure independence of the judiciary; and to provide consistent sentencing standards. Under the practice of "labor reeducation," people are imprisoned at police initiative without benefit of trial.
- *Capital punishment.* As part of its worldwide campaign against capital punishment, Amnesty International has criticized China for the wide range of crimes punishable by death, the lack of adequate safeguards, the exceptionally high number of death sentences (numbering in the thousands annually, and as high as 5,000–10,000 during the anticrime campaign of 1983), and the parading and public execution of the condemned.
- *Tibet.*[5] In addition to individual cases of political and religious repression in Tibet, critics have focused on the repression of Tibetan

culture, the movement of non-Tibetan population into Tibet, and alleged nuclear dumping on the Tibetan plateau.

• *Coercive population planning.* Despite central government policy to the contrary, some local officials implement population control policies through the use of coercion, especially forced sterilization and forced abortion, sometimes including late-term abortion amounting to infanticide.

• *Prison maltreatment and labor camp exports.* These issues have been highlighted by reports from Amnesty and Asia Watch and in a book by former labor camp inmate Harry Wu, who subsequently founded the Laogai Research Foundation to keep attention focused on the issue.[6]

Other human rights problems that have so far received only passing attention in the West may have an even broader impact within China. These include denial of the right to strike (a concern of the labor movement in the West), denial of freedom of the press (raised by interest groups devoted to international press freedom), the kidnapping and abuse of women and girls, denial of the right to move one's legal residence, eugenics policies against the mentally defective, mistreatment of homosexuals, and interference with foreign journalists in China.

Some believe that trade pressures should be used as a sanction only against regimes that violate human rights in the worst way. Comparisons of human rights violations are difficult, because we lack a metric for such comparison. It would take a Jeremy Bentham to reduce to a common standard the absolute and per capita number of violations, the rights violated, and the nature of the violations, as well as their duration, painfulness, side effects, and so on. Moreover, an attempt to compare violations seems to imply the morally questionable belief that human rights violations are less objectionable if they are less extensive.

One does not need to make comparisons, however, to say that violations in China remain pervasive and systemic rather than occasional and incidental. Some of the violations affect a large proportion of the world's largest population, and government policy makers remain committed in principle to the violation rather than to the protection of certain fundamental rights. In these senses, China's human rights record remains grossly deficient, by a wide margin deficient enough to evoke urgent concern in the international community.

The fact that Western human rights concerns in China are driven by a complex interaction of public opinion, the press, nongovernmental organizations (NGOs), legislatures, and administrations—that is, that they are political—is sometimes cited to discredit them. On the contrary, this process reinforces their validity. If China seeks the benefits of full membership in the international community, asking it to behave in a way that does not offend the conscience of that community is reasonable. If human rights are a strategic rather than an altruistic interest of the West, so much stronger then is the motive to insist on their realization. Finally, the limited research available suggests that human rights are not a trade-off against economic development, political stability, responsible environmental policies, and peaceful foreign policies but are instrumental to those ends as well as being a public good in themselves.[7]

Human Rights and Sovereignty

The mainstream Western position is that the domestic human rights policies of governments are a legitimate concern of the international community under international law. Despite a widespread impression to the contrary, the Chinese position is not in principle radically different. Although China has never, to my knowledge, used trade policy as an instrument of its human rights concerns, it has energetically voiced these concerns and has participated actively in shaping and trying to apply the international human rights regime.

In the 1950s and 1960s, China often criticized South Africa, Israel, Vietnam, the United States, Japan, the USSR, and other countries for violating what China considered to be human rights, including such rights as those to development and self-determination.[8] In its first statement on the subject after joining the United Nations in 1971, China stressed the importance of the struggles against imperialism, colonialism, and racism and for national independence and sovereignty.[9] In 1979, China began to attend meetings of the UN Human Rights Commission as an observer, and in 1982 it became a member. The People's Republic of China (PRC) participated in the Subcommission on the Prevention of Discrimination and Protection of Minorities and in working groups concerned with the rights of indigenous populations, human rights aspects of communications, the rights of children, the rights of migrant workers, and the issue of torture. With other third world countries, it promoted the idea of a right to development, which the UN General Assembly enacted by resolution in 1986. China voted in favor of UN investigations into human rights violations in Afghanistan and Chile.[10] China's UN representatives denounced Israel, South Africa, Vietnam, Afghanistan, and other targets.[11]

In 1956, the PRC acceded to the 1949 Geneva Conventions relating to the treatment of wounded and sick soldiers, POWs, and civilians in wartime. Starting in 1980, China joined the Convention on the Prevention and Punishment of the Crime of Genocide, the Convention Relating to the Status of Refugees, the Protocol Relating to the Status of Refugees, the International Convention on the Elimination of All Forms of Racial Discrimination, the International Convention on the Suppression and Punishment of the Crime of Apartheid, the Convention on the Elimination of All Forms of Discrimination against Women, and the Convention against Torture and Other Cruel, Inhuman, or Degrading Treatment or Punishment.[12] The 1984 Sino-British Joint Declaration on Hong Kong committed China to allow the International Covenants on Civil and Political Rights and on Economic, Social and Cultural Rights to continue in force[13] in Hong Kong for fifty years after 1997, although China itself (like the United States) had not acceded to these covenants. By 1991, when the PRC issued a white paper on its human rights performance, it had acceded to a total of seven of the twenty-five major international human rights conventions, one more than the United States at that time.[14]

Chinese legal scholars today take the position that states, not individuals, are the subjects of international law and that human rights cannot be used as a justification to interfere in the sovereignty of a state. But within this framework, they have put forth a variety of criteria to allow the international community to protect human rights.[15] Some argue that a human right becomes of international concern when sovereign states enter into treaties or otherwise make themselves subject to international law with regard to the particular right.[16] Others have stated that violations that are particularly heinous, "large-scale, gross" and that constitute international crimes can be suppressed by the international community. Examples include genocide and apartheid.[17] A third view is that violations that threaten the peace and security of neighboring countries or the world are subject to international intervention, such as racial discrimination, genocide, international terrorism, or violations that create flows of refugees.[18]

Although proceeding from slightly different premises, these and other arguments that appear in Chinese scholarship reach roughly the same conclusions. Human rights pressures should be used against the perpetrators of fascism, hegemonism, and imperialism but not against socialism and the third world.[19] As explained in one article, China supports "the struggle of Third World countries and other justice-upholding countries against the large-scale violation of human rights by hegemonism, imperialism, colonialism and autocracy" but opposes "using alleged charges of human rights violations to vilify and attack China and to interfere in China's judicial and administrative affairs."[20]

In short, although it sometimes suits Chinese spokespersons to express a purist position on sovereignty as a bar to international pressure on human rights issues, such a view is inconsistent with Chinese legal theory and diplomatic practice.

Foreign Pressure. Although foreign human rights pressure on China started in the late 1970s with the activities of NGOs like Amnesty International and (later) Asia Watch, it began to exact a significant cost only after the Tiananmen incident of 1989.

Beginning in 1989, China suffered repeated humiliations in the UN bodies concerned with human rights. In August 1989, the UN Subcommission on the Prevention of Discrimination and Protection of Minorities adopted by secret ballot a resolution mildly critical of China, marking the first time that a permanent member of the Security Council had been censured for its human rights performance in a UN forum. In the 1990 session of the Commission on Human Rights, Chinese representatives had to sit through the presentation of a secretary general's report on human rights violations based on material complied by Amnesty International and other groups and a debate on a resolution to condemn China, although the resolution was ultimately not adopted. In 1991, Beijing came under criticism again in the subcommission, which by secret ballot voted both to request China to respect the human rights of the Tibetan people, and to ask the secretary general to prepare a report on the situation in Tibet, which he submitted in 1992.

In 1993, China managed to stave off action on a resolution presented before the full commission by the United States, Japan, and a group of other countries. Chinese problems were discussed at one time or another in reports or meetings of the UN's Special Rapporteur on Religious Intolerance, Working Group on Arbitrary Detentions, Special Rapporteur on Summary and Arbitrary Executions, Committee against Torture, Special Rapporteur on Torture, and Working Group on Enforced or Involuntary Disappearances.[21]

Each year, the meetings of UN bodies provided an opportunity for NGOs to present information disparaging of China. In 1992, for example, one report criticized China for policies undermining the independence of the judiciary and the effectiveness of lawyers; Amnesty International cited China for its "long-term pattern of serious human rights violations"; the International Fellowship of Reconciliation brought up China's exploitation of prison labor; Human Rights Advocates charged China with abuses in Tibet amounting to a "genocidal policy"; and the International Association of Educators for World Peace attacked China's policies in Tibet.[22] China had to expend diplomatic resources to respond to these attacks and to mobilize friendly countries to defeat unwelcome resolutions.

In bilateral diplomacy, human rights took a toll on Beijing's bargaining position on a host of other issues. In Sino-U.S. relations, for example, Tiananmen combined with the trade deficit and arms exports to create a synergy of anti-China sentiment that thrust China's preferred priority issue, Taiwan, so far down the agenda of bilateral issues that it was hardly discussed. The annual threat to the renewal of the

MFN status weakened Beijing's negotiating position in talks over intellectual property rights and market access; in both negotiations, China made major concessions to American demands. Likewise, the fact that China was on the defensive on the human rights issue weakened its ability to get its way in negotiations with the United States over arms transfers and in talks with Britain over Hong Kong.

In the aftermath of the massacre, some industrialized nations gave sanctuary to refugee dissidents. To avoid sending the estimated 80,000 Chinese students and scholars in the United States back to a repressive environment, President Bush extended their visas. In 1992, Congress passed the Chinese Student Protection Act, under which Chinese nationals resident in the United States before April 1990 were eligible to apply for permanent resident status in 1993. These actions symbolically tarred the PRC as unsafe for its own residents and deprived China of the services of tens of thousands of its brightest, best-educated citizens.

The massacre turned the estimated 110,000 Chinese students overseas into a potent lobby against their own government.[23] In New York, Chinese activists founded Human Rights in China, the first human rights group devoted exclusively to China and led by PRC citizens. The incident also mobilized members of the Chinese-American, Chinese-Canadian, and similar communities in other countries who had previously been politically quiescent. This process led to the April 1993 "North American Conference on U.S. Policy toward Chinese-Mainland, Taiwan, and Hong Kong: A Chinese-American/Canadian Perspective," which issued a white paper calling for U.S. promotion of human rights in China.[24]

Economically, the cost of the human rights issue is hard to measure. Many countries imposed sanctions, including diplomatic cold shoulders of one kind or another, cancellation of cultural exchanges, freezes on aid and loans, votes for suspension of World Bank and Asian Development Bank loans, and interruption of military sales and links.[25] The 1989 crackdown led to declines lasting about two years in China's credit rating, foreign investment, export orders, and tourism. Companies like Levi Strauss, Reebok, Timberland, and Sears, with corporate good-citizen policies, either imposed human rights standards on Chinese contractors or reduced or canceled their business in China. The U.S. Congress considered adopting a human rights code for American businesses in China.[26]

A still more imponderable cost was paid in the area of international and, through this, internal legitimacy. To be blackballed by advanced nations around the world undercut the prestige of the leaders, exacerbating the legitimacy crisis that had been at the root of the 1989 events. Precisely as the G-7 nations, led by Japan, moved to ease economic and political sanctions, foreign governments and politicians felt it politically necessary to maintain verbal pressure on China.[27] From 1991 onward, an endless procession of VIP visitors made public representations on human rights, including the French prime minister, the Japanese prime minister, two Australian parliamentary delegations, a U.S. House of Representatives delegation, an EC delegation, the Polish foreign minister, a Canadian parliamentary delegation, a delegation of EC ambassadors visiting Tibet, and so on. Likewise, China expended diplomatic capital denouncing the proposal for an American-funded "Radio Free Asia." If implemented, the project will have protracted negative effects on the regime's internal legitimacy. In 1993, Beijing's bid to play host to the Olympics in the year 2000 was defeated by international opposition motivated by human rights concerns, again embarrassing the government abroad and at home.

The international response to the Tiananmen incident amplified its impact in Taiwan and Hong Kong, where Beijing was trying to win friends and mollify doubters. Tiananmen may have been the most important factor persuading the British government to replace a conciliatory Hong Kong governor with one who would fight conspicuously for democratic reform. This led to a damaging political struggle, which for a time absorbed much of Beijing's diplomatic energy.

Chinese Response. Since foreign pressure had a substantial impact on Chinese interests, the Chinese government responded with a mixture of counter-initiatives and concessions. The combination of policies was designed simultaneously to rally third world support, especially in multilateral settings, to appeal to advocates of *Realpolitik* in the West, and to construct policy dilemmas for human rights advocates in the West.

China mounted a variety of ideological counterattacks on its critics. Official spokespersons pointed to a series of double standards: that China drew condemnation while other countries whose violations were in some sense worse (for example, Israel and India) were ignored; that Westerners who said nothing about Mao's violations complained about less severe violations under Deng; that prosperous Westerners insisted on immediate implementation of modern standards in a developing China; that the West itself had committed human rights violations more deplorable than those it was criticizing, such as slavery and the Holocaust; and that the West today continues to be rife with human rights problems from which it distracts attention by criticizing others. Such double standards revealed the West's bad faith, Chinese spokesmen claimed. The real motive was to deny the Chinese their own choice of political system.[28]

Second, Chinese spokesmen argued that cultural standards differ. No culture's concept of human rights has greater claim to be accepted than any other's. Thus, the West has no moral right to interfere. Third, they raised the issue of sovereignty, arguing that problems foreigners consider human rights violations are matters of domestic Chinese law, for example, counterrevolutionary crimes or the death penalty.

Finally, the government argued that China's rights record was excellent, as good at its critics'.[29] "For many years we have neglected research on and propagation of human rights issues," stated two writers. "As a result, people have misconceptions. It is as though human rights issues are a patented item of the Western world, as though only the developed capitalist countries of the West are the redeemers of human rights, whereas the socialist countries disrespect and even fear, are hostile toward, and obliterate human rights."[30] Chinese theorists argued that the most important rights are those to survival and development and that such rights are better ensured in China than in the West. Even where the painful process of achieving socialism has led to some mistakes that temporarily damaged human rights, only by forging ahead to socialism can human rights be realized.[31] A country like the United States with many human rights problems of its own "has no right whatsoever to comment on the human rights situation in other countries," said a Chinese official.[32] "I cannot see [that] those countries . . . promoting human rights have a better record than ours," stated Vice Premier Zhu Rongji on a visit to Canada in May 1993.[33]

Such arguments aimed to generate support both in the third world and in the West. Vocal endorsement on the issues of sovereignty and cultural relativism came from regional leaders such as Prime Minister Mahathir of Malaysia and Lee Kuan Yew of Singapore. The cultural relativism, double standard, and national sovereignty arguments proved congenial to Americans of the realist school, who believe that a moralistic foreign policy is neither justified nor sufficiently flexible to be useful.

Propaganda arguments dovetailed with diplomatic activity carried out with the cooperation of like-minded governments. The 1990 UN Human Rights Commission meeting, for example, decided to shelve a motion dealing with human rights in China, after China gained either support or abstentions from the Soviet Union, Ukraine, Yugoslavia, Cuba, and most participating African and Latin American countries. In 1990, China helped block a Western initiative to establish an emergency mechanism to enable the Human Rights Commission to be called into session following a major event like the Tiananmen massacre. In 1992, China joined with the Philippines and Syria, among others, to limit the mandate of the UN Special Rapporteur on Torture.[34]

Beginning in 1990, China and its allies worked to structure the agenda of the UN-sponsored World Conference on Human Rights that was to take place in Vienna in June 1993. At the regional preparatory meeting for Asia held in Bangkok, China gained the cooperation of thirty-eight of the thirty-nine countries represented to establish the concepts that UN human rights work should be guided by the principles of noninterference in the internal affairs of states; nonselectivity (that is, UN bodies should not single out specific countries for criticism); the priority of collective, economic, and social rights encompassed in the notion of a right to development; national sovereignty; and cultural particularism (the nonuniversality of human rights values across regions).[35] Indonesia, Malaysia, and Iran were especially strong allies; only Japan dissented from the regional consensus.

The Chinese government's ability to resist international human rights pressures, however, was limited by its dependency on outside sources of trade and capital and its diminished strategic importance after the end of the cold war. The government combined rhetorical rejection of human rights interference with a series of measured, timed concessions, spiced with occasional use of hard-line tactics. In 1990–1991, Beijing released three batches of Tiananmen prisoners, totaling 881 persons, at times when such releases would affect the politics of its MFN status in the U.S. Congress; lifted martial law in Beijing; and permitted Fang Lizhi to leave his refuge in the U.S. Embassy to go abroad. The government released information on prisoners who had drawn especially intense international concern, such as Wei Jingsheng, Wang Juntao, and Chen Ziming.[36] In 1992, China signed an agreement with the United States not to export products using prison labor to the United States and to allow American customs agents to make inspections to prevent this.[37] In 1993, in the week before the International Olympic Committee's decision on the 2000 Olympics, China released from jail its most famous political prisoner, Wei Jingsheng, and other prisoners.

In response to continuing international pressure as well as internal debate, China enlarged its position that human rights are a valid subject of international dialogue and within certain limits are a subject of international law, so long as there is no intervention in the internal affairs of states. China dispatched two human rights delegations to the West in 1991–1992 to engage in dialogue and gather information (a third delegation went to south Asia). In 1991, the State Council issued a white paper on human rights, followed by white papers on criminal law and the situation in Tibet.[38] Although unyielding in tone, they were significant for having been issued at all, as a sign of willingness to respond to international concern. Premier Li Peng stated at the UN Security Council "summit" on January 31, 1992, "China values human rights and stands ready to engage in discussion and cooperation with other countries on an equal footing on the question of human rights." In his government work report in March 1992, Li stated, "We believe that the human rights and fundamental freedoms of all mankind should be respected everywhere. . . . China agrees that questions concerning human rights should be the subject of normal international discussion."[39]

Less direct concessions included the release without trial or the imposition of more moderate sentences than in the past on many political prisoners, especially those of international note like Liu Xiaobo, Wang Dan, Bao Zunxin, and Bao Tong. In connection with the 1989 demonstrations, death sentences and prison terms of fifteen years or more were given exclusively to prisoners who for one reason or another had been virtually ignored by the outside world, mostly workers or intellectuals living in remote locations. The regime also responded to international pressure by giving passports to dissidents like Wang Ruowang, Wang Ruoshui, and Li Honglin and to the family members of political exiles.[40]

The most important effects of international pressure were probably measured in actions the regime did not take. Scores of dissidents were not arrested, and many detainees were released without trial. The most likely explanation was the anticipated foreign (as well as domestic) reaction.

The government structured its concessions in such a way as to divide its critics. Productive results were conspicuously tied to friendly and quiet intercessions such as those by Japanese Prime Minister Toshiki Kaifu and U.S. businessman John Kamm. Specific concessions were timed to provide cover for the resumption of World Bank lending, to reward Japan's renewal of lending under the Third Yen Loan Package, and to help George Bush beat back congressional critics who tried to revoke MFN status. Although China rewarded quiet diplomacy instead of public pressure, diplomacy would not have achieved the same results without the backing of public pressure from other sources.

At the same time, in carefully selected cases, the regime used regression on human rights issues to influence the debate in the West. Wei Jingsheng, perhaps the political prisoner given highest priority in the West, and certain other well-known prisoners were subjected to harsh prison treatment for years. China used its refusal to release Wei as a symbol of its invulnerability to Western pressure, even as it made a host of less visible concessions. Long sentences were handed out for political crimes not only to victims to whom the outside world paid little attention but also to a few exemplary cases like Wang Juntao and Chen Ziming. In November 1992, China interrupted its dialogue with the United States on human rights issues as a protest against F-16 sales to Taiwan and a warning to incoming President Bill Clinton. After rejection of its Olympic bid in September 1993, China arrested three journalists as if to signal that the rejection had not shaken the government's resolve to protect its security in any way it saw fit.

Selective use of hard-line measures created for human rights activists a moral dilemma of reverse effects, in which pressure sometimes appeared to be more damaging than beneficial to a particular victim. Such measures helped sustain the policy debate in the West over the relative effectiveness of quiet diplomacy versus public pressure. Yet in the aggregate, three and a half years of foreign pressure on human rights issues had a major impact on Chinese policy at home and abroad.

A little-noted major reason for this impact was that the West was pushing in the same direction as internal forces. In conferences and conversations and in open and internal publications, Chinese lawyers, scholars, journalists, and Communist party liberals argued for the legally binding status of the international law of human rights, the political wisdom of China's joining the world mainstream, and the practical advantages of certain revisions of Chinese law and practice.[41] In domestic law, scholars lobbied for an end to crimes of counterrevolution, for implementation of a presumption of innocence, and for reduced use of the death penalty. Indeed, it appears that Chinese legal scholars have reached a near consensus on the universality of human rights, the applicability of international conventions, and the validity of internationally recognized rights.

Liberalism has become such a strong current of thought in China that advocacy of human rights has become to some extent a tool of domestic legitimation for the regime and not merely a means of mollifying foreign critics.[42] Confluence with domestic currents makes it even more probable that future foreign pressures will exert continued or enhanced influence on the evolution of China's domestic human rights regime. Conversely, relaxation of Western pressure would weaken the ability of liberal domestic forces to influence developments. One should not be misled by the official press monopoly to believe that foreign pressure is unwelcome to all Chinese. In fact, it is desired by Chinese liberal intellectuals as ardently as it is rejected by the government, although less loudly.

MFN Status as a Policy Tool. Except for the post-Tiananmen sanctions, no policy has been as effective in achieving modifications of Chinese human rights policy as the threat of MFN withdrawal. This is not to say that MFN status works in isolation. The human rights agenda has been defined by the mixture of NGO publicity (Amnesty International reports on political imprisonment, Asia Watch reports on prison labor exports, granting the Robert F. Kennedy human rights award to Fang Lizhi, and giving the Gleitsman Foundation international activist award to Wei Jingsheng) and quiet diplomacy (State Department prisoner lists and private congressional inquiries, for example). Diplomatic defeats, the loss of the 2000 Olympics, and the impact of negative publicity on tourism and investment added to the costs of human rights abuses. Nor would foreign pressure have had more than a superficial effect without forces within China pushing for improvements in human rights. But the vigor of Chinese rhetoric and lobbying against MFN withdrawal and the timing of major Chinese concessions show that the MFN threat has been the single most important element in the effectiveness of Western policy.

Some believe that MFN conditionality is a policy asset of diminishing utility. The fact that conditions were threatened three times but imposed only once (by President Clinton) and that MFN has never been withdrawn makes it possible for China to consider the threat a bluff. Uncertainty over MFN has not staunched the growth of U.S. trade and investment with China (although it undoubtedly exacted some unmeasurable cost). The trade and investment explosion has enlarged the business lobby that is now arguing more forcefully than ever before the legitimate case that cancellation of MFN, and the Chinese response, will damage American interests.

To protect the credibility of the MFN threat, advocates of its use have reshaped it. President Clinton's executive order defining the conditions for extension of MFN status removed weapons proliferation and trade practices from consideration, leaving the issue focused exclusively on human rights. It stated conditions that the Chinese regime is considered able to fulfill. And were MFN sanctions invoked, they would be targeted only at state enterprises, thus minimizing the effect on the Chinese private sector and joint ventures and on U.S. imports from China, and leaving Beijing incentives not to retaliate.

Ultimately, the domestic political process in the United States gives the MFN threat its credibility and hence its usefulness. For proponents of MFN conditionality, the noisy annual battle is an essential opportunity to create and dramatize a political dynamic that makes partial MFN withdrawal politically possible or even inevitable under certain circumstances. In this complex process of political signaling, the Chinese government pays attention to the constituencies, the arguments, and the congressional and administrative forces at work. If past performance is a guide, they will respond with a resourceful mixture of verbal defiance and practical concessions, finely tuned and closely timed to meet the exigencies of the American political process as they analyze it.

While those who oppose MFN conditionality should fight for what they believe in, they will hurt their own interests if they contribute to a Chinese misestimation of the political, strategic, and cultural forces that make the threat of partial MFN withdrawal a real one. For miscalculation on the Chinese side could lead to the very result that many in the American business community fear.

On the whole, the Chinese government's ability to resist international human rights pressure is weak. As James D. Seymour observes, "In the early 1990s China suddenly found that most of the countries she wanted to deal with were democracies, and human rights was on their agenda."[43] Because China is so deeply involved in the world economically, culturally, and strategically, it cannot shut the door as it did under Mao. The influence of Western values and ideas is spreading, with or without governmental pressure. While a growing economic and military power, China remains weakly endowed with the ability to exert ideological and cultural influence, the assets of "soft power." The human rights issue is likely to remain a structural weakness for China's diplomacy so long as democratization and promotion of rights remain dominant world trends and China remains outside the trend.

Although human rights diplomacy is often derided as idealistic, it has proved a realistic component of China policy for the West, both for what it has achieved in influencing China's human rights performance and because it has shown itself a helpful adjunct in pursuing other goals. MFN status has been an imperfect policy tool, but in the absence of others equally effective it remains too valuable to drop.

6

American Policy and the Sentiments of the Chinese People

Anne F. Thurston

With the death of Deng Xiaoping, China will face its most serious political crisis since the passing of Mao Zedong almost twenty years ago. The question of Deng's succession will be linked to much larger issues of the legitimacy of Communist party rule and the evolution of a "socialist market economy." If a protracted power struggle at the top were to take place at the same time as popular discontent over widespread corruption, resentment over the inequality of economic opportunities and the government's handling of urban demonstrations in the spring of 1989 could spill into the streets. The specter of China's descent into chaos, coupled with the current political instability in Russia, much of Eastern Europe, and many of the states that were once part of the Soviet Union, would confront the United States with foreign policy dilemmas making the cold war look simple. While the question of continuation of most-favored-nation (MFN) status for China is only one of many uncertainties facing the Chinese people, its revocation could only further undermine an already unstable situation.[1]

The views expressed here are not necessarily representative of the organizations with which the author is affiliated.

China is a country of moods, and the mood has changed dramatically since the "people's army" turned violently against the citizens of Beijing in June 1989. Using guns, tanks, and armored personnel carriers, the army crushed the popular movement for political reform. For more than a year after the tragedy, many in China's capital—and to a lesser extent in other urban areas—suffered collectively from posttraumatic stress disorder. The events on the night of June 3–4, 1989—the incessant, inevitable, and inescapable topic of all conversations among friends—made people depressed and angry. Some were in despair. Intellectuals expressed guilt for not having prevented the violence and regretted that they had not exerted more leadership in convincing the students to leave the square. Young people clamored to go abroad.

The psychological trauma was prolonged by events in Eastern Europe and the Soviet Union. With the collapse of the Berlin Wall and the execution of Ceausescu, some hoped that the domino effect would extend to China, too. When it did not, anger and frustration turned to malaise. Political reform had failed in China, but Communist party rule had crumbled in Eastern Europe and was coming apart in the Soviet Union. Some felt betrayed that they who had been at the forefront in demanding reform were suffering new political repression, while citizens in other previously Communist-controlled countries were enjoying new political freedom.

Some were disappointed that the United States had not done more in behalf of the reformers. The revocation of most-favored-nation status was viewed by many as the most appropriate expression of American revulsion over the massacre in Beijing. Revoking MFN would both punish the regime responsible for the crackdown and, perhaps, serve as an impetus to the downfall of the political leaders behind it. Others feared a revocation would cut the ties between the United States and China, leaving the Chinese people isolated under a still harsh regime.

Deng Xiaoping's trip south in early 1992 was the catalyst that transformed the popular mood. His call for all China to emulate the freewheeling, Hong Kong-inspired model of Shenzhen unleashed a new economic energy and freed countless ordinary Chinese from the constraints of socialist economic control. State-owned enterprises at all levels of Chinese society were encouraged to establish new subsidiary companies devoted to turning a profit. Other publicly owned firms were permanently contracted to entrepreneurs who agreed to pay fixed monthly taxes in return for the freedom to manage the enterprise and maximize its profits by whatever means they could.[2] Staff members within state enterprises, long trapped in dead-end jobs with minimal salaries, were allowed to leave and work in joint ventures or establish their own money-making companies. As a result, Deng Xiaoping, who had nearly lost the Mandate of Heaven on the night of June 3–4, gained new legitimacy. "Communist party or no Communist party," said one retired engineer, "China is still Confucian. We need a father. We have to have an emperor." Deng Xiaoping is the emperor, although most believe that he will be the last. In return for new economic freedoms, the Chinese people tacitly agreed to allow him to pass his final days with face.

Deng's renewed legitimacy does not extend to the Communist party as a whole. Few in China still believe in the "four cardinal principles" that demand professions of faith in socialism, Communist party leadership, the dictatorship of the proletariat, and Marxism–Leninism–Mao Zedong thought. "We are all dissidents now," one taxi driver insisted. "It's just that we can't speak out in public." Others declare that the Chinese people have "drawn a clear line of demarcation with the party," using the Cultural Revolution jargon that once denoted verbal disavowal of sympathy for the "class enemy."

The new mood is best reflected in the popular refrain: "*Wo buyao quan; wo jiushi yao qian*" (I don't want power [or rights]; I just want money). Everyone in China, it seems, is out to strike it rich. The most confident of the new entrepreneurs have replaced the photographs of Mao that once hung from their rearview mirrors with the Chinese symbol for good fortune (*fu*). Those who still hedge their bets attach the symbol to Mao's picture.

The pursuit of wealth has been accompanied by a retreat from political concerns. In public, the Chinese people remain politically mute, and in private many confess to political apathy. The only politics in China, people say, is the behind-the-scenes power struggle over Deng's succession, which many liken to watching a play—interesting to look at but having nothing to do with them. The most thoroughly disaffected claim not to believe in democracy, either. "Even in democracies," one taxi driver insisted, "politics is nothing but struggle."

The spread of privately owned satellite dishes, particularly in the south, is bringing Hong Kong television and the BBC news into many homes, and intellectuals continue to tune in to the Voice of America and BBC (although some criticize the Voice of America for having become less objective and more a mouthpiece for the U.S. government). But only a small percentage of urban Chinese own the satellite dishes that allow access to international television, and a recent government proclamation prohibits further private sales without official permission. Less educated Chinese, and those who are busy with economic pursuits, profess little interest in the news, either domestic or international. Western "culture" is penetrating most effectively in the form of sports and popular music. Everyone knows that Michael Jordan was "number 23," and Madonna T-shirts are the rage among Chinese teenagers; but outside politically sophisticated Beijing, only a handful of the scores of ordinary people with whom I spoke—taxi drivers, shop attendants, street vendors, minor cadres, and new entrepreneurs—could name the current president of the United States. The American government is seen as an undifferentiated whole. One Chinese journalist pointed out that "more people today know the names of movie stars and the leading *qi gong* masters than that of Fang Lizhi."[3]

When pressed, most still believe that democracy is the inevitable wave of the future and that China, one day, will become democratic, too. But Chinese speak with many voices on what form democracy will take and how and when it will be achieved. The Tiananmen incident has left many wary of the political efficacy of street demonstrations; and the possibility that young and inexperienced students could lead a democratic movement, or govern China if the regime collapsed, is given little credence. Most agree that the dissidents who fled overseas in the wake of Tiananmen are irrelevant in the current political climate, although some believe they could play an important role once a new period of political reform begins. Their calls for democratization are rarely heard in China now, and some have been discredited—both because they fled and left their followers behind to suffer and because they are reputed (usually unjustifiably) to be living lives of luxury abroad.

Renewed overt demands for political reform await the death of Deng, and most agree that prospects for political reform will be tied to continued economic development. Two competing views prevail. One argues that the democratization of China will proceed Taiwan-style, with major political reforms being introduced only after long-term socioeconomic development and a dramatic rise in per capita income and the general standard of living. Only after the generation of a large middle class, the expansion of higher education, the development of a labor movement, greater pluralism, and the evolution of a civil society will democracy in China be possible. The other view argues that the popular desire for political liberalization is widespread but is now forcibly repressed. The longer the popular will is denied, the greater the likelihood of political instability, collective violence, and the disintegration of the country into chaos. One young intellectual likened the popular desire for reform to water behind a dike. The longer desires for political liberalization stay pent up, the more likely are demands to overflow into violence. Political reform must thus go hand in hand with economic development.

Both sides see economic development as vital to democratization, and both welcome "peaceful evolution," the gradual undermining of the Communist party system through the introduction of Western democratic values, that is so deeply feared by party conservatives. And the sides have similar views on the question of MFN. Everyone wants China's MFN status retained. It is one issue on which all Chinese with whom I spoke agree. Even the politically apathetic who do not know President Clinton's name are nonetheless aware that the question of most-favored-nation status remains a troublesome issue in U.S.-China relations. Popular sentiment may be based on a contradictory hybrid of economic self-interest, Chinese government propaganda, independent thought, deep-rooted patriotism, and a paucity of factual knowledge, but the time when withdrawal could have expressed American revulsion over the military crackdown and thus won support among the Chinese populace is past, many argue. To withdraw MFN now would gravely damage the process of economic development on which China's future—economic and political—depends.

Economic self-interest is a major factor in popular support for MFN. Most Chinese with whom Americans come into contact (and thus most of those with whom I spoke) believe that they gain economic advantage through most-favored-nation status. Many perceive its withdrawal as having economic effects similar to the sudden exodus of Americans following the Tiananmen tragedy. With fewer Americans in China, they reason, taxi drivers, shop attendants, restaurant owners, hotel managers, and service personnel would have fewer customers, and their own incomes would decline.

Factory managers posit a similarly deleterious effect. The manager of a garment factory that exports 60 percent of its clothes to the United States sees no way that sales to other countries could make up for the decline in exports to the United States if MFN is denied. With the cutback in factory production, workers—90–95 percent of whom are young peasant women between the ages of twenty and twenty-five, for whom factory work is an economic boon—would have to be laid off. (In this same factory, about 10 percent of the labels read "Made in India," and another 30–35 percent said "Made in Italy," suggesting sub rosa deception to avoid American textile quotas.)

The senior engineer of a Motorola cellular telephone plant pointed to similar potential effects on his factory. With increased costs for the sophisticated components that must be imported from the United States, telephone prices to his Chinese market would exceed the ability of most potential customers to pay. Production would have to be cut back, workers would be laid off, and everyone would suffer. Multiplied by thousands of factories, the ripple effect on the Chinese economy and the setbacks to the work force would be substantial, as the macroeconomic figures cited by Claude Barfield elsewhere in this volume suggest.

While most Chinese are not familiar with the specific conditions of President Clinton's executive order of May 28, 1993, they have opinions about the general issues the conditions raise. Chinese attitudes on three of those issues will be examined here: human rights, Tibet, and emigration. In addition, because many Chinese believe (mistakenly) that questions of arms control are tied to MFN and because the issue is of increasing importance in the popular Chinese perception of the United States, the question of arms control will also be explored.

Human Rights

Chinese express a variety of opinions on human rights issues and on the use of MFN to force the Chinese government to improve its record. While human rights issues were addressed only by dissidents and scholars before the Tiananmen incident, new political disaffection and the yearly MFN debate have brought the issue into popular discourse. Few repeat the official position that demands for improvement represent illegitimate interference in China's internal affairs or that the basic human right is the right to life and subsistence. One young government cadre did argue, however, that China's human rights are more extensive than those of the United States. China's current economic development, he pointed out, is taking place in the absence of legal restraints. Anything goes in China's quest to get rich. In the United States, however, all economic transactions are bound by legal controls.

More thoughtful Chinese remain troubled by the human rights question and wonder how a new respect for human rights can be introduced into Chinese society. They argue, from genuine conviction and with considerable basis in historical fact, that conceptions of human rights are rooted in national culture and traditions. Older intellectuals who received an early education in Confucianism believe that Confucian values of harmony, order, and *ren* (kindheartedness) could be revitalized to incorporate modern concepts of human rights. They hope that these Confucian values can be renewed and modernized as part of China's continuing political development.

No one outside the government argues that China's contemporary political culture embodies respect for human rights, but the younger generations who grew up under communism have had little exposure to Confucian values. Younger generations refer instead to the decline in Maoist communitarian values engendered by the new get-rich-quick mentality. Chaos (*luan*), meaning the breakdown of orderly human relations and a lack of mutual respect, has already set in, they believe: the Maoist ideal of serving the people has been lost, and civility is absent from society. People are spitting on the streets again, throwing trash at random, and picking flowers from public parks. On buses, no one offers a seat to pregnant women or to the elderly. The debilitating class struggle of the Maoist era has been superseded by a quarrelsome new economic competition. Old moral values have collapsed, and new ones have yet to replace them. Dissatisfaction with the current state of social norms has resulted in a new receptivity to human rights issues.

But Chinese struggling with how to introduce new concepts of human rights also argue that the Chinese process of socialization ensures that few adults grow up with the sense of self-respect and individual autonomy that are basic underpinnings to a society where the rights of individuals are honored. Some cite traditional Chinese child-rearing methods, which teach dependence rather than independence, and argue that the one-child-per-family policy has only exacerbated the age-old pattern. Go to any park on any Sunday, they say, and count how many fat six- and seven-year-old children are still being carried by their parents and grandparents. Chinese children are not even taught that they can walk by themselves or stand on their own two feet, let alone that every individual has inalienable rights.

Those who hope that the Chinese will learn a new respect for each other and for individual rights wonder how those changes in values might be brought about. They believe that China has much to learn from the United States, even when the goal is the reinvigoration of Confucian values through ideas from abroad. But the consensus of those with whom I spoke is that new values can best be instilled through education rather than pressure. They fault the U.S. government for not being sufficiently sympathetic to the constraints of deep-rooted Chinese values and for failing to educate the Chinese people about how new concepts might be realized.

Likewise, some Chinese argue that by focusing on political prisoners and prison labor, American policy ignores the grossest abuses of human rights in China. Political prisoners, they argue, are much better treated than ordinary criminals (though admittedly largely as a result of international pressure). Democracy Wall activist Wei Jingsheng is cited as a case in point. Outside China, Wei has long been recognized as that country's most famous and longest-serving political prisoner, while inside China, his name, until recently, has barely been mentioned in the press. Released just a few months short of his sentence and days before the decision on Beijing's bid for the 2000 Olympics, Wei emerged from nearly fifteen years of incarceration to be shown on Chinese television looking plump and smiling. In contrast, Chinese note, the conditions of ordinary, nameless prisoners are abominable. They live in tightly cramped cells, on near-starvation diets, with little opportunity for physical activity. Most of those incarcerated in Chinese jails would prefer the opportunity to work in prison-run factories, where the food is more plentiful, movement is permitted, and prisoners can see the sun.[4]

Moreover, in the periodic crackdowns against crime, youths of fifteen and sixteen have been rounded up and executed for minor crimes of theft, with no outcry from the West (or at least any protest that the Chinese people hear).

Some Chinese criticize the United States for not paying enough attention to the new abuses engendered by China's rapid economic development. As large numbers of peasants from impoverished rural areas move into the cities to take jobs in factories and on construction sites, new forms of exploitation are rising. Again, the Chinese view is complicated. The peasants work voluntarily and earn more money in a month than they would in half a year in the fields. They are learning technical skills and being introduced to a more modern way of life. Most are free to leave their work. But in some cases, particularly in China's thriving south, the working conditions of the new urban dwellers border on slavery. Working hours are long (the young women in the garment factory I visited were working fourteen hours a day), some factories are primitive and unsafe, and workers' dormitories may be crowded, decrepit, and unsanitary. Some workers are denied freedom of movement, and factories are often locked during working hours.

An example of the type of tragedy that can result from such conditions occurred recently, when eighty-one workers in southern China died in a fire from which they could not escape because managers of the toy factory had locked them in.[5] While Chinese do not blame Americans for such conditions, singling out their own entrepreneurs and businessmen from Hong Kong and Taiwan as the worst abusers, they wonder why the United States remains silent on such widespread and obvious abuses of ordinary Chinese while focusing on a minority of well-known and popular political prisoners. In short, many Chinese recognize American pressure as effective in ameliorating gross violations of the human rights of a few political prisoners but criticize American policy for ignoring the larger question of how to build a new society based on universal respect for human rights.

Emigration

Chinese naturally support efforts to allow greater freedom of emigration. Despite new economic opportunities in China, those opportunities are unequally distributed, corruption is rampant, and many believe that other countries, particularly the United States, offer better chances to seek their fortunes. The myth persists that the moon is rounder in the United States and that wealth comes quickly and easily. Letters home from students and scholars describing the high cost of living and their own modest circumstances are often ineffective in convincing their relatives and friends otherwise. Even a student fellowship is likely to be ten or fifteen times the average Chinese salary, and family members with no experience in the United States have trouble believing that such vast sums do not buy a luxurious standard of living and allow sufficient surplus funds to bring other family members to America. The recent broadcast of *Beijinger in New York,* the most widely watched television series in Chinese history, served to perpetuate the myth. The repatriation of hundreds of illegal immigrants in the summer of 1993 was not reported in the Chinese press, for example. Even taxi drivers in coastal Xiamen, ordinarily privy to unofficial news from the grapevine, claimed not to have heard about the incident, which involved illegal aliens from Fujian Province, where Xiamen is located. Few people seem to know about the impoverished and difficult conditions in which many recent Chinese emigrants in the United States live.

For most Chinese, the thought of leaving China "isn't even a dream," but many see considerable hypocrisy in the American policy promoting freedom of emigration. Some portion (approximately one-third, according to a consular official in Beijing) of Chinese who have obtained passports from their own government (allowing them the right to travel or study abroad though not ordinarily the right to emigrate) are subsequently denied visas by the U.S. consulate. The reason most frequently given is the suspicion that they intend to emigrate.[6] As one disappointed hairdresser lamented, "Your government talks about democracy, human rights, and the right to emigrate but what do your human rights mean when they refuse me a visa? False human rights!" Others claim, with considerable justification, that if the Chinese government really granted everyone the right to emigrate, tens, perhaps hundreds, of millions of Chinese would attempt to leave China immediately—and most would want to go to the United States. The lure of the United States is not likely to diminish soon, but neither is discontent over the American policy that espouses the right to emigrate while refusing to accept most of those who would exercise that right if they could.

The Question of Tibet

More than any other attitude, the popular perception of Tibet seems the product of the government "education" (or, more accurately, "propaganda") to which every Chinese schoolchild is subject. Two tenets are primary: first, that Tibet has been an integral part of China for centuries, as early as the Tang dynasty and as late as the Yuan; and second, that the Tibetan judicial system under both the current Dalai Lama and his predecessors was cruel and barbaric. Adult Chinese describe being taken as impressionable schoolchildren to photographic exhibits of

Tibetan horrors—prisoners in darkened dungeons filled with scorpions and punishment by bodily mutilations. Those images have stayed with them as adults, together with the conviction that the Tibetan culture is cruel and inhumane and that the spread of Han culture in Tibet has a civilizing effect on a backward, barbarous ethnic minority.

The State Council white paper on human rights perpetuates the widespread conviction of Tibetan atrocities, asserting that Tibetan "serfs" were subject to "cruel punishments such as gouging out eyes, cutting off feet, removing the tongue, chopping off hands and arms, pushing an offender off a cliff or drowning."[7] The philosophy of kindness, compassion, tolerance, and love that won the Dalai Lama the Nobel Peace Prize is generally denigrated in China today. "They are only words," one of my Western-educated friends insisted, "and words are cheap." The gentle Dalai Lama is seen as an undemocratic and uncivilized "splittist" who would tear the Chinese nation apart. The Han-inspired destruction of Tibetan culture and gross violation of Tibetans' human rights are unknown to most ordinary Chinese.

The extent to which popular views of Tibet are a function of party propaganda can be seen in the change of attitude once Han Chinese are exposed to unofficial sources of information. Young Chinese artists who travel to Tibet for creative inspiration return with a new respect for the Tibetan people and their culture. Some profess a faith in Buddhism. In Chongqing immediately after the Tiananmen incident, young people who had visited Lhasa and witnessed the military suppression of Tibetan demonstrators there were certain that the government account of the military crackdown in Beijing was false. They knew from first-hand experience that the government had lied about the Tibetan demonstrations and greatly underestimated the number of Tibetans killed. No doubt the government was lying about what happened in Beijing as well.[8] Similarly, while many Chinese dissidents shared the Chinese government's official stance on Tibet when they arrived in the United States, exposure to more objective historical accounts and interactions with Tibetans in exile have changed many minds. Now, many Chinese dissidents abroad assert that a democratic China would grant Tibetans the right to self-determination and assume that the majority of Tibetans would choose to be free of Chinese rule. Without exposure to alternative sources of information, however, the popular disdain of Tibetan culture is likely to remain.

Arms Control and Nuclear Proliferation

While issues of arms control and nuclear proliferation are not included in the presidential conditions for the renewal of MFN, many Chinese believe them to be. And Chinese attitudes toward arms proliferation are an important indicator of the limits of American influence.

Few Chinese view their country's sale of military weapons or continued nuclear testing in the context of international law, arms proliferation, or nuclear disarmament but rather as evidence of China's growing international power and a means to increase it further. No one, not even the most liberal, Western-oriented intellectuals, offered anything but support for their country's efforts to enhance its military might and international influence. The *Yin He* incident, during which officials boarded the Chinese ship in search of materials for chemical weapons the U.S. government believed were on board and destined for Iran (even after being assured at the highest Chinese levels that no such ingredients would be found), was a particularly galling example of American bullying. While no one echoes the official dictum that the search had "hurt the feelings of the Chinese people," even intellectuals agreed that the search had been an insult to China's sovereignty and in contravention of international law. By what legal right, they wondered, has the United States unilaterally assumed the role of world policeman?

Chinese take offense at any attempt by the United States to interfere in China's pursuit of wealth and power and see the American government's position on arms control and nuclear proliferation as hypocritical. The United States is the largest arms supplier in the world, they argue, and its nuclear arsenal is the largest. Why is the United States intervening as China tries to catch up?

This view is based on a patriotism shared by Chinese of all political stripes. Chinese people remain genuinely sensitive to any foreign slight that smacks of past "imperialism," "great power hegemony," or "looking down" on China. Until the Tiananmen incident of 1989, the Chinese Communist party was able to link patriotism effectively to unquestioning support for the party. Those who challenged party policy and demanded political reform were routinely labeled unpatriotic. When a *People's Daily* editorial in late April 1989 denounced the student demonstrators as unpatriotic, the students' response, loud and clear, was no: the demonstrators were as patriotic as any member of the Communist party. Indeed, they were demanding reform precisely because they loved their country. For the first several weeks after the accusatory editorial, entrance into the student-occupied square was contingent on verbal avowal that the students' political demands were indeed patriotic.

The popular distinction remains. Chinese who claim to have drawn a clear line of demarcation between themselves and the party nonetheless, patriotically, want China to become rich and powerful and to assume its proper position as a major force in world affairs. In 1989, Chinese political reformers praised the United States because it was democratic. Today, the United States is praised, and respected, not only because it is democratic but also because it is rich and powerful—the richest, most powerful country in the world.

Some believe that American intervention in China's efforts to extend its military power is based on fear. With the American economy on the decline as China's continues to grow at the rate of 12 or 13 percent a year, many believe that China is destined to become the dominant power of the twenty-first century. Following the November 1993 APEC meeting in Seattle between Jiang Zemin and Bill Clinton, some Chinese officials are saying that the United States needs China more than China needs the United States. The United States, by punishing China for weapons sales and criticizing nuclear testing, is seen as trying to deny China its rightful place in the world.

Conclusions

China's current drive for economic development and the widespread preoccupation with making money fast have affected the popular perception of MFN. Even those who were disappointed when President Bush refused to impose conditions as an expression of revulsion over the Beijing massacre now support the continuation of MFN. To withdraw MFN, many believe, would hinder China's economic progress and reverberate to millions of ordinary citizens who have only recently begun to benefit from economic reforms. Were China's economic advance to slow with the revocation of MFN, undermining the hopes of so many who are set on making their fortune, the United States would be blamed, and the substantial reservoir of goodwill toward Americans would be drained. Thus, one question American policy makers must ponder is whether, by withdrawing MFN, we are willing to risk alienating Chinese citizens who continue to view the United States with admiration and respect and who look to this country for long-term guidance on future political liberalization and democratic reform. This question is even more urgent since so many Chinese now regard themselves as dissidents and claim to have separated themselves decisively from the Communist party.

While opposing the withdrawal of MFN, many Chinese nonetheless agree with at least some of the goals embodied in the conditions set forth in President Clinton's executive order, particularly those concerning human rights. Many believe that the United States has influenced the Chinese government in symbolically important ways and should continue the effort, particularly in securing the release and better treatment of political prisoners. The conundrum is that while the Chinese government has responded to the threat of withdrawal of MFN, the Chinese people would be negatively affected by actual revocation.

Many Chinese, including intellectuals who listen to foreign news broadcasts, are confused over exactly what President Clinton's policy toward China is. Interested Americans have also been confused, of course, because the policy is an evolving one. In general, however, educated Chinese believe that the U.S. government can and should do more to help the Chinese people understand what U.S. policy is and how far the U.S. government is willing to go to promote democratization in China. Many wish that the United States would take a clearer stand on the side of nongovernment political reformers and assume a more activist role in educating them in Western liberal values.

Despite China's growing economic interdependence, the increasing use of privately owned satellite dishes, and the weakening of China's propaganda apparatus, most Chinese remain woefully ill informed about the world beyond their borders—and about their own society as well. (A Shanghai taxi driver who picked me up at the train station, for instance, knew that the United States is a powerful industrial state and that all Americans are wealthy and wondered whether we had come from the United States by train.) The popular view of Tibet is one example of how effectively the party's monopoly of the media controls people's minds. While many claim to believe in Chinese government propaganda no longer, they remain its victims. While many claim to be dissidents, few have a sense of what their political choices are. Thus, education and the exposure to other sources of information through radio and television broadcasts from outside are the most effective long-term tools for providing the Chinese people with alternative conceptions of reality and the means to political change. Few believe that Premier Li Peng's directive forbidding the installation of private satellite dishes without official permission will be effective in the long run, but journalists with whom I spoke are convinced that the party will continue to resist freedom of the press for as long as possible. The party, too, is well aware of the potential threats to its power of an educated, informed public. For its effect on China's domestic politics, the most important provision of President Clinton's executive order is the one calling on the Chinese government to permit international radio and television broadcasts.

The most intractable issue in U.S.-China relations is that of arms proliferation. The goal of national wealth and power is shared by all patriotic Chinese, and the current rate of economic growth has convinced many that China is destined to be the dominant world power of the twenty-first century. Any policy that would deprive China of military parity with other great powers will be resisted not only by the Chinese government but also by the Chinese people. Education and access to outside information could moderate this view, but American influence is not likely to change soon the larger Chinese goal of becoming a major world, and military, power.

Finally, while the mood in China has changed and economic concerns now take precedence over political ones, the new mood is not likely to last. The death of Deng Xiaoping will necessarily bring political concerns back to the fore, and Deng's renewed legitimacy is not likely to be extended to his successors. The popular acceptance of any new leadership will depend in large measure on how it handles the question of the Tiananmen tragedy. Most believe that the new leadership must reverse the verdict which labeled the Tiananmen incident a counterrevolutionary rebellion. But a reversal of the verdict is a double-edged sword. Many now agree with the official assessment that the Chinese government was facing a popular rebellion, but in contrast to the official view, they regard the uprising with considerable pride. Not to reverse the verdict risks the legitimacy of any new leadership but so would a reassessment recognizing the justice of the protests. Some Chinese will be satisfied if the names of the citizens, students, and soldiers who died are finally known and the citizens of Beijing are able to return to the square with wreaths of mourning. Others want revenge, and some could use the opportunity of collective mourning to unleash new political protests. The period following Deng's death will be inherently unstable. American influence over Chinese domestic politics is limited at best, but the withdrawal of MFN would alienate even those political reformers most open to that influence. To risk alienating those forces in China most worthy of our support at the period of greatest potential political instability since the death of Mao in 1976 is not in the interest of China or the United States.

The disjunction between President Clinton's executive order setting conditions on the continuation of China's most-favored-nation status and his larger foreign policy goal of expanding democracy and respect for human rights is disturbing. The process by which democracy has evolved in other parts of the world suggests that the means embodied in the presidential order are not appropriate to its ends, and the argument advanced for revoking MFN for China is at odds with the free trade argument advanced by the administration for the North American Free Trade Agreement and most other parts of the world.

Although the process of democratization is inevitably messy, the record indicates that neither economic sanctions nor policies of isolation are effective in promoting political liberalization. In parts of East Asia, such as Taiwan and South Korea, as James Lilley argues in this volume, democratization has evolved as a result of long-term socioeconomic development, the formation of new economic elites, an increasingly pluralistic and differentiated society, reformist political leadership, and continual prodding from the international community, including the United States. Scholars of the Soviet Union and Eastern Europe point to the importance of the Helsinki Accords and the Commission on Security and Cooperation in Europe (CSCE) in encouraging the development of a civil society in those Communist-controlled countries. Through a policy of carrot and stick, holding the Soviet bloc countries to the human rights provisions of the accord in return for cooperation in security, technology, and trade, the CSCE both promoted official compliance with international norms of human rights and fostered the development of civil societies.[9]

U.S. policy toward China needs to be more fully articulated for the American public, the Chinese leadership, and the Chinese people. Several principles are key:

- While the ability of the United States to influence internal events in China is significant, it is nonetheless limited. Democratization will come from within China and will be a long-term, often painful, process.
- Long-term economic development, the continuing evolution of a market economy, a marked increase in the standard of living, an expansion of educational opportunities, and a wider engagement with the outside world are the most certain routes to a more pluralistic, democratizing society in China.
- The dichotomy between rapid economic development and respect for human rights fostered by Chinese officialdom and largely accepted in public discourse in the United States is false. Rapid economic development ought to proceed with due regard to the rights and problems of the less advantaged. The availability of a huge pool of cheap labor does not necessitate denying those workers safe working conditions, reasonable hours of work, and humane accommodations. The public debate in the United States would be significantly advanced through dialogue between human rights activists and those with commercial interests in China. Business interests should be encouraged to adopt a code of ethics for their interactions with Chinese businesses, and human rights organizations should be encouraged to consider the proposition that economic development and engagement with the outside world will foster their long-term goals.
- The process of development is not undermined by humane treatment of prisoners, access to due process, or proper nourishment and medical care for those incarcerated. The release of political prisoners and the decent treatment of all prisoners should continue to be a cornerstone of U.S. policy toward China.
- The zero-sum game of MFN should be replaced by a more modulated policy similar to the terms of the Helsinki Accords. Rather

than blanket withdrawal of MFN, particularly egregious violations of international human rights norms could result in the cancellation or withdrawal of specific deals that are highly attractive to China. Conversely, progress in specific areas could be rewarded.

- U.S. policy toward China should be embedded in our general policies toward Taiwan and Hong Kong. Not only is the United States more deeply engaged in Taiwan and Hong Kong, but they, in turn, exert a growing influence over China. Support for democratization and human rights in those two places, and the promotion of a code of business ethics, would inevitably affect the mainland.

7

Leveling the Playing Field for U.S. Firms in China

Jerome A. Cohen and Matthew D. Bersani

Much has been written recently about the economic transformation occurring in China. Many U.S. companies are taking advantage of the opportunities of the China market, both as exporters and as producers in China. Yet U.S. businesses are at a significant disadvantage in competing for China's favor. Virtually every other Western country has reestablished programs for actively promoting exports to and investments in China that were suspended after Tiananmen. The U.S. government, however, has not only failed to reestablish most of its own programs to promote such interaction but also repeatedly threatened to revoke the very cornerstone of our trade relations with China, its most-favored-nation (MFN) status in the United States.

Now that President Clinton has belatedly embraced the concept of communicating with China, improvements in the U.S. government's trade and investment policies toward China can come none too soon. The stakes are enormous. Between 1980 and 1990, China's gross national product doubled in size. It will double again by the year 2000.[1] China's economy may well be the world's largest by the year 2010. According to statistics compiled

The authors would like to express their appreciation to Richard Brecher and the United States–China Business Council for providing materials and information that were essential to the preparation of this chapter.

by the United States–China Business Council, China plans to spend over $200 billion on imports between 1993 and 1995. Many of these imports will be in areas in which U.S. industries are particularly strong. China's market for imported power-generation equipment, for example, is estimated to be worth between $40 billion and $100 billion over the next twenty-five years. In the aerospace industry, China's market is estimated to be worth $40 billion over the next twenty years. In telecommunications, China's purchases should total more than $29 billion over the next five years.[2] The list goes on.

But more than dollars are at stake. As has been demonstrated in Taiwan, South Korea, and elsewhere, real and abiding political change arises from sustained domestic rather than external pressure. The most effective means of creating such pressure is economic development, which in turn creates a broad middle class and fuels demands for better education, political pluralism, and a genuine legal system. This process fosters the growth of democratic concepts and values and the protection of individual human rights. U.S. government actions that limit commercial interchange with China not only impede efforts to improve American economic competitiveness but also restrict America's ability to stimulate political and economic liberalization in China.

The current U.S. policy is partly responsible for the underachievement of American business in the China market. U.S. private direct investment in China in 1991 constituted only 4.6 percent of the total amount of such investment in China. In 1992, the U.S. portion dropped to 2.8 percent. Moreover, U.S. exports in 1991 constituted only 10 percent of the total imports of China; in 1992, this proportion dropped to 9 percent.[3] As the greatest industrial power in the world and the destination of fully one-third of China's exports, the United States has received only a paltry share of the huge China market—a cause for some concern.

Clearly, many difficulties facing foreign business in China can be more easily rectified by action of the government of the People's Republic of China (PRC) rather than by U.S. government action. Yet one should not underestimate the importance of favorable U.S. policies for promoting U.S. business interests in the PRC and for influencing the PRC government itself to adopt more favorable policies. Actions that the U.S. government can take fall into four categories: creating a stable bilateral political environment, assisting China's integration into the world economy, adopting general policies to assist American exporters, and taking specific actions to promote greater access to China's markets.

A Stable Bilateral Political Environment

Nothing is more important for creating a positive business environment than friendly relations between the two countries in question. A hostile political environment creates endless complications for addressing trade and investment issues. In this regard, the United States should take some specific steps.

Expand Communication. Until recently, the Clinton administration refused to engage the Chinese in constructive dialogue. This posture had begun to inflict devastating consequences on an already troubled relationship. Unaddressed issues simply fester.

The Clinton administration's new approach of engaging the Chinese government in talks is the most positive recent sign in U.S.-China relations. It is also likely to be the single most important factor in resolving commercial difficulties facing U.S. firms in China. Expansion and intensification of such discussions should take place at every level of government.

Depoliticize the MFN Renewal Process. A poll of U.S. businessmen would quite likely reveal that their major problem regarding China is the threat of denial of MFN status. No single aspect is more destabilizing to business with China than the annual struggle over MFN renewal.

While it is generally recognized that continued MFN status for China is the core element of commercial relations with the United States, two related points are sometimes overlooked. First, yearly continuation of MFN is a necessary but by no means sufficient prerequisite to stable U.S.-PRC business relations. What is also necessary is the predictability of such extension—the certainty that MFN will not be revoked. This element is notably lacking under our current system of judging annually whether China is worthy of this status. The uncertainty thus created leads to additional risks that constrain business investment and trade with the PRC.

Second, MFN cuts both ways. If the United States were ever to deny China MFN, China would undoubtedly retaliate by raising trade and investment barriers at least as substantially for U.S. businesses, thereby undercutting their ability to be competitive in the PRC. The impact would be felt not only by U.S. exporters but also by U.S. companies that have invested over $4 billion in China.[4] These enterprises depend on MFN status for the sale of their China-made products in the United States, and they would also find it difficult to import U.S. parts and components when the PRC retaliates against loss of MFN status.

In the past, the annual MFN debate was fueled by congressional frustration over the Bush administration's perceived lack of backbone in dealing with China and by congressional Democrats' desire to embarrass the White House. Clearly, the Clinton administration is in a different situation. Both the White House and the Congress should recognize that the highly politicized atmosphere of MFN discussions in Congress exacerbates rather than ameliorates tensions in U.S.-China relations. Finally, there is no evidence that the threat of revocation of MFN has produced any meaningful changes in China, as the PRC has mastered the art of tactical, cosmetic concessions.

It is time to reaffirm that MFN is an element of international trade relations that is in the economic and political interests of the United States to extend to all but truly outlaw states. The United States will do more for the cause of human rights in China by fostering economic development than by impeding it. This chip should be removed from the bargaining table, so that the United States can deal with China in a more constructive fashion. To do otherwise would only increase U.S. isolation from the world community in its approach to China and benefit the business communities of countries in economic competition with the United States.

China's Integration into the World Economy

As China becomes more integrated with the international economic community, the rest of the world is in a better position to encourage China to recognize and enforce international conventions and agreements. China's compliance with such international norms, among other things, benefits U.S. businesses operating in China. The United States should take the following actions.

Entry into the GATT. The United States should press for China's early entry into the General Agreement on Tariffs and Trade (GATT), provided that China's protocol of accession contains appropriate provisions. These would include tariff reductions for products and services in industries in which the United States is competitive (such as the power equipment and airline industries), greater transparency of the PRC trade regime, elimination of the foreign exchange allocation system for PRC domestic enterprises, decontrol of state foreign trade corporations to allow for more independent decision making, national treatment for foreign commercial enterprises in China, and equal treatment for foreign service industries.

Intellectual Property Protection. China has recently issued amended patent and trademark laws and promulgated copyright and software protection legislation and an unfair competition law and has strengthened other intellectual property rules. The PRC has also adhered to the principal multilateral treaties in these fields. The U.S. government should express stronger support for such actions, and at the same time it should continue to monitor China's compliance with this emerging intellectual property regime. Problems that arise should increasingly be dealt with through multilateral instrumentalities.

World Bank Programs in China. In recent years, the United States has repeatedly attempted to restrict China's access to World Bank funds. Yet since 1990, China has been the target of a larger portion of World Bank loans than any other country. As part of a more positive relationship with China, the United States should fully support the bank's efforts to assist in the reform of unproductive state enterprises in the PRC and the promotion of stable economic development.

U.S. business operations in China directly benefit from such World Bank programs. Despite post-Tiananmen restrictions, World Bank disbursements to U.S. companies working on China projects since 1988 exceed $500 million.[5] In light of the scarcity of concessionary financing available to U.S. companies in the PRC, these World Bank funds are extremely important to corporate cooperation with China.

Promotion of U.S. Trade Opportunities

The U.S. government's Trade Promotion Coordinating Committee (TPCC), an interagency group headed by the secretary of commerce, recently issued a report recommending a number of major changes in U.S. export promotion, export financing, and export control policies. The recommended actions include:

- Create one-stop shops in four major cities, consolidating all federal export promotion services in each location. Each shop would replace the many offices that exporters must now contact.
- Produce a commercial strategic plan for each country that is a key U.S. export market. These plans would consolidate and improve information now provided by numerous federal agencies.
- Provide high-level government advocacy on behalf of U.S. companies pursuing major foreign government procurement opportunities. Create an interagency advocacy network to coordinate these efforts.
- Produce an annual unified budget for all U.S. government export promotion activities.

Adoption of the TPCC suggestions would boost U.S. companies seeking to export goods to China as well as elsewhere. Relevant government entities should study the TPCC survey of export promotion efforts of foreign countries and identify the areas in which foreign companies have access to programs not now provided by the U.S. government. Steps should then be taken to level the playing field for American companies.

Creating Greater Access to China's Markets

In addition to the general actions proposed to promote U.S. exports, many specific actions could promote trade and investment with China.

Revise COCOM. Talks are now being held on the future of COCOM (Coordinating Committee). The governments involved have agreed in principle to dismantle the current system by March 31, 1994. Therefore, it is time to consider how China should be treated under a COCOM successor regime. The United States and its COCOM allies, for example, should support removal of unnecessary export controls. A system for controlling high-technology exports to China (and other destinations) is still needed. As with extension of MFN, however, disagreements over human rights or trade should be handled through more appropriate political channels and not by denying China access to American technology that presents no legitimate security concerns.

The export control regime has failed to keep pace with the rapid development of new technologies. The new COCOM regime should reflect the following:

- Ceilings on the export of telecommunications equipment to China should be raised to give U.S. companies a fair chance to obtain a portion of the estimated $29 billion worth of telecommunications business over the next five years in the PRC.
- Sales of certain equipment related to nuclear power generation should be permitted so long as such technology and equipment do not give rise to nuclear proliferation concerns.
- Prohibitions on the export of computer systems should be liberalized.

Agree on a System for Determining Trade Flows. To avoid future friction between the United States and China in determining the amount of actual exports from China to the United States, the United States and China should agree on methods of calculating and characterizing the volume of goods exported from China through Hong Kong. Resolving this issue would remove one of the principal sources of friction in U.S.-China economic relations in recent years.

Resume Favorable Programs. Following Tiananmen, a number of U.S. programs to promote exports and foreign investment were suspended for China. This has hurt U.S. businesses operating in China. The most important of these programs are those offered by the Overseas Private Investment Corporation (OPIC). OPIC provides important commercial and political risk insurance to ventures established by U.S. companies overseas. Unavailability of such insurance increases the risks that must be borne by U.S.-invested enterprises in China and thereby increases the interest rates that such enterprises must pay to obtain necessary financing.

As with OPIC, the financial and other assistance provided by the Trade and Development Agency is vital for American enterprises to compete effectively against foreign companies whose governments back them with concessionary financing and other forms of trade assistance.

The U.S. government should also permit Agency for International Development (AID) funding in China. AID funds would be useful in building relationships that strengthen the commitment to a free market. In addition, AID funds could be used by the United States-Asia Environmental Partnership to promote exports of U.S. environmental goods and services to China. China's environmental needs are enormous, and, with AID backing, U.S. companies would be able to compete in this market.

Finally, the Export-Import Bank should broaden the availability of financing of sales to and investments in the PRC. Currently, the Export-Import Bank is prohibited from extending individual loans to China in excess of $50 million unless the president waives such prohibition on a case-by-case basis. The requirement for the presidential waiver should be dropped.

Monitor the Market Access Agreement. The United States recently made considerable progress with the PRC through the successful negotiation of a market access Section 301 agreement. The agreement addressed such nontariff barriers to trade as import licenses, quotas, and testing restrictions. The United States should closely monitor these arrangements and should press the PRC in other areas such as excessively high tariffs, foreign exchange controls that restrict imports, and direct and indirect restrictions on the operation of U.S. service companies, such as banks, engineering companies, and law firms that seek greater access to the China market.

Business and Political Goals

Much is at stake in U.S. business involvement with China. Although the focus of this chapter has been actions the government can take to promote American business in China, we firmly believe that the growth of Western business interests in China plays a vital role in other respects, such as the development of a market economy, the protection of human rights, and the emergence of political pluralism. Thus, adoption of these policies favoring U.S. businesses also promotes the most basic political goals of the United States in the PRC.

8

Why Does MFN Dominate America's China Policy?

Wendell L. Willkie II

Shortly before 2 a.m., on June 6, 1993, two New York City police officers were on a routine beach patrol in the Rockaway peninsula of Queens. They saw in the moonlight a decrepit steamer, bearing the name Golden Venture *and flying a Honduran flag, run aground offshore. As the officers looked on in amazement, and as the boat's ancient hull creaked and groaned, more than 200 destitute Chinese immigrants rushed up out of holds and hatches to the deck.*

Standing at the rails, these huddled masses—who had traveled four months, 17,000 miles, with little food, in a stinking hold of appalling conditions—saw in the distance the beckoning lights of the city representing all of their hopes for a better life. Immediately, scores plunged into the thundering and frigid surf, where they flailed and struggled frantically, desperate to reach the shore. One of the first rescuers on the scene, firefighter Michael Penna, recounted, "The current kept pulling them toward the jetties. . . . They didn't

The author is very grateful to the following individuals whose comments were enormously helpful in the preparation of this chapter: Richard Bush, Seth Cropsey, Charles Horner, Kenneth Juster, James Lilley, Warren Maruyama, Richard Perle, and Norman Ornstein.

have . . . [many] clothes on, just short-sleeved shirts and pants. Hypothermia set in. By the time they got to shore, they couldn't even stand."[1] Indeed, eight of them died in the fifty-three–degree waters.

America's Ambivalence about Chinese Emigration

The Clinton administration has moved quickly to address the rising tide of illegal immigration from China, powerfully symbolized by the *Golden Venture*'s ill-fated landing. Previously, Chinese claiming asylum have been released, pending the outcome of legal proceedings, allowing many poor immigrants simply to disappear in large cities like New York. But in a dramatic departure from past practice, the White House ordered the *Golden Venture*'s unfortunate passengers to be held in prisons indefinitely, awaiting deportation proceedings.[2]

As further evidence of the Clinton administration's get-tough approach, Vice President Al Gore telephoned President Salinas of Mexico five weeks later to persuade an unwilling Mexican government to accept custody of three vessels bearing 650 Chinese peasants, detained by the U.S. Coast Guard in international waters off San Diego. Mexico, unlike the United States, has no procedure for appealing or delaying a deportation decision and gave no consideration to doing so in this instance. Instead, the miserable Chinese immigrants were led from the boats in handcuffs and promptly dispatched by charter jet to the People's Republic of China.[3]

In cracking down on Chinese immigration, the Clinton administration has clearly reversed the policy of its predecessor, which in the wake of the violent suppression of the Tiananmen Square demonstrations in 1989 had accommodated virtually all immigrants from China claiming asylum. Responding in part to congressional and public outrage over Tiananmen Square, President Bush had directed officials of the Immigration and Naturalization Service to give special consideration to the concerns of Chinese dissidents and students.

But the Bush administration as a practical matter also afforded asylum to any Chinese, not just the educated elite, claiming any form of persecution, specifically including China's draconian birth control policy. As word spread in China's coastal provinces of the Bush administration's lenient policy, tens of thousands of Chinese peasants departed by sea and air to surge through America's porous borders.[4] While some of these boat people may have sought greater political or religious freedom, most were simply in search of economic opportunity and a better life in America. The ability of these peasants to leave at all reveals not only the enormously enhanced individual mobility but also the radically diminished authority of the Communist party in today's China.

After all, in Mao's time, peasants had neither the means nor the permission needed to leave their villages.

The Clinton administration's clampdown, with the help of Chinese authorities, has produced results. By the fall of 1993, the flood of illegal Chinese immigration had slowed to a trickle. In the past, provincial authorities had facilitated illicit emigration for a fee. Now, the Chinese central government is not only discouraging this practice but also intercepting the ships and jailing the ringleaders of these human smuggling operations. Furthermore, Beijing state television is broadcasting films from the U.S. Information Agency, showing recent Chinese immigrants being hauled off to jail and threatening the same of viewers contemplating illegal entry into the United States. Thus, it is hardly surprising, given the considerable tension between the two countries on human rights, weapons proliferation, and trade issues, that one U.S. official in the fall of 1993 characterized Chinese assistance on immigration control as the "one bright spot" in the relationship.[5]

America has been ambivalent about Chinese immigration for some time. In 1979, Deng Xiaoping made a historic visit to the United States to further the normalization of relations between the two countries. At a White House meeting, President Carter raised the issue of human rights and asked whether Deng was willing formally to permit freedom of emigration from China. Deng responded: "If you want me to release ten million Chinese to come to the United States, I'd be glad to do so." Everyone, of course, laughed.[6]

As unwelcome as such a mass migration from China might be to Americans, Carter's inquiry was not an idle one. On the contrary, it was legally required by certain provisions of the Jackson-Vanik amendment to the Trade Act of 1974, which specifically conditions normal trade relations with a Communist country on one cardinal principle: the right of its people to emigrate freely.

China has dramatically liberalized its emigration policies and practices since 1979. It has also permitted tens of thousands of its citizens to study, travel, and work abroad at any one time. This has remained true since the Tiananmen Square crisis of 1989. The U.S. government, however, is now enlisting the cooperation of Chinese authorities (as well as the governments of Mexico, Taiwan, and other countries) to stem the flow of Chinese masses to this country.[7]

As President Clinton reported to Congress on May 28, 1993: "The principal restraint on increased emigration [from China] continues to be the capacity and willingness of other nations to absorb Chinese immigrants, *not* Chinese policy" (emphasis added).[8] Clinton's statement was submitted under the Jackson-Vanik amendment, which requires the president to certify each year that a continuation of normal trade relations—so-called most-favored-nation, or MFN, trading status with any "nonmarket economy [that is, Communist] country" will advance the objective of freedom of emigration from that country.[9]

President Clinton's observation, echoing that of George Bush in previous years, raises the question whether the framework of Jackson-Vanik—enacted at the height of the cold war to facilitate emigration from the Soviet Union—should continue to dominate policy deliberations about our relationship with China. For the most important issue today in that bilateral relationship is the retention of MFN, which the United States currently grants without any serious policy debate to every other economy of any consequence in the world. Proponents of conditioning or withdrawing MFN for China contend that the legal foundation of Jackson-Vanik, providing for annual review and renewal of MFN for Communist countries, affords the leverage for advancing universally recognized human rights. They argue that new conditions beyond the principle of free emigration should be written into law or imposed by executive order as indeed was undertaken by President Clinton on May 28, 1993.[10]

Other contributors to this volume have addressed the question of whether withdrawal of MFN would in fact undermine, rather than advance, the realization of American ideals and interests. This chapter examines whether withdrawal of MFN would even be consistent with the underlying motivation of Jackson-Vanik. For without that statutory framework, withdrawal of MFN after the events of Tiananmen Square would never have even been seriously considered in this country.

International Trade and MFN in the Postwar Era

What is MFN? It lies in international commercial agreements, whereby signatory nations extend to one another treatment in trade matters no less favorable than that extended to any other nation. Thus all countries to which MFN applies are "the most favored" ones; hence, all are treated equally.[11]

Today, nearly every country (182, to be exact), however repressive, and whether friend or foe, routinely gets MFN status from the United States, including the illiberal regimes of Saudi Arabia, Syria, Libya, and Burma, countries not particularly noted for their respect of human rights. Even during the height of multilateral sanctions against South Africa, withdrawal of MFN from that apartheid regime was never seriously considered in the United States.[12] In earlier times, other repugnant regimes have received MFN without substantial public debate, including Haiti under "Papa Doc" Duvalier and Argentina under its military dictatorship in the 1970s, when thousands of dissidents "disappeared."[13] In fact, most developing countries—including a number that are no better than China in recognizing fundamental civil liberties—receive from the United States without controversy *duty-free* treatment for eligible articles under the general system of preferences (GSP), known to trade specialists, oxymoronically, as "better-than-MFN."[14] Therefore, while proponents of conditioning or withdrawing MFN argue they are seeking to advance universal human rights, they are in fact uniquely applying these standards to one country.

Withdrawal of MFN from China, a major U.S. trading partner, would constitute an unprecedented and radical departure from what are now viewed as fundamental, universally accepted, principles of international commerce. It would also be viewed as an unjustified as well as a counterproductive act by the governments of every other major nation in the world.

This is a very different question, however, from the unwillingness of the United States during the cold war to extend normal trading privileges to our global adversary, the Soviet Union, and its client states. The Jackson-Vanik amendment itself, while controversial at the time of its enactment in 1974, was fully consistent with U.S. government postwar policies toward the Soviet Union.[15] In the years after World War II, free trade was a fundamental goal of our international economic policy. But there was always a significant, well-recognized exception in the case of the Soviet empire.

What were the origins of MFN and of the exception for Communist countries? At the end of World War II, the consensus among American policy makers was that a principal cause of the worldwide depression had been the extremely protectionist Smoot-Hawley tariff of 1930. This tariff had driven average rates from 26 to 50 percent.[16] More than any other factor, Smoot-Hawley, by denying European exporters American markets, had spread America's depression to Europe. By the summer of 1931, European banks were collapsing from the business failures, forcing countries to withdraw from the gold standard and to repudiate national debt obligations. America's exports to Europe dried up in the sudden collapse of European purchasing power.[17]

The sheer depth of the depression that followed led to the rise of fascism and the catastrophe of the Second World War. This produced extraordinary agreement among the world's postwar leadership that free trade among nations was essential to international peace and prosperity. To pursue this lofty objective, they established the General Agreement on Tariffs and Trade, or GATT. From the outset, the GATT was committed to a radical multilateral reduction in tariffs.

Under the GATT, which the United States joined in 1948, all signatory nations must accord every other signatory nation MFN. At that time, GATT had twenty-three member countries, including all the major Western powers. Given the global tensions between East and West, membership in the GATT for the Soviet Union, however, was not seriously contemplated.

Today the GATT includes 113 member countries as well as several more acting as members. Although their membership is now actively being considered, Russia, the other republics of the former Soviet Union, and China do not yet belong. Notwithstanding their radical economic reforms, these post-Communist economies are not yet fully prepared to subscribe to today's far-reaching obligations for GATT membership regarding the organization of a member state's economy. These obligations, as reflected in the broad range of commitments agreed to by member nations in the Uruguay Round negotiations completed in December 1993, are far more comprehensive now than they were in the late 1940s. Although Russia and China are not yet GATT members, all major economies have already accorded them MFN.[18]

But at the outset of the cold war, free trade was quite deliberately withheld from Communist regimes to avoid facilitating the proclaimed expansionist objectives of the Soviet empire. In 1951, Congress enacted legislation requiring the president to withhold MFN status from the Soviet Union and all other Communist countries except Yugoslavia. Poland was exempted from this trade restriction in 1960 by President Eisenhower.[19]

Additional legislation in 1963 confirmed the principle of denying MFN to Communist countries and removed the exceptions for Poland and Yugoslavia—unless the president were to determine that waiving the ban was in the national interest, a determination President Johnson made for these two countries in 1964.[20] Thus, before the enactment of the Jackson-Vanik amendment in 1974, Congress had twice clearly endorsed the general principle of prohibiting normal trade with Communist countries, granting the president only limited authority to do so in individual cases. Of course, in retrospect, except for natural resources, the Soviets and their satellite countries would have had little to offer American markets in any event.

Realpolitik and the Soviet-American Trade Agreement of 1972

In initialing an unprecedented trade agreement with the USSR on October 18, 1972, President Richard Nixon demonstrated, as he had in his historic visit to China a few months earlier, a willingness to move beyond the reflexive, ideological anticommunism that had previously typified his personal views, as well as the nation's cold war policies. Nixon and his National Security Adviser Henry Kissinger saw themselves as rescuing American foreign policy from the excessive idealism and dangerous naiveté they believed had characterized the tenures of

Presidents Kennedy and Johnson. In the wake of the profound frustrations of the Vietnam War, in an era of enormous national self-doubt, of extraordinary skepticism about America's role in the world, Nixon and Kissinger believed that America's foreign policy should be guided less by its traditional lofty moralism and more by a realistic, sophisticated cold-blooded assessment of the nation's interests as a great power. This policy, known as *Realpolitik,* was designed largely to restrain the global ambitions of the Soviet Union through a complex linkage of incentives and deterrents, or "carrots and sticks." "By acquiring a stake in this network of relationships with the West," Kissinger told the Senate, "the Soviet Union may become more conscious of what it would lose by a return to confrontation."[21]

The 1972 trade agreement was an essential component of this strategy to achieve détente between the superpowers. Negotiated by Commerce Secretary Pete Peterson, the agreement promised to extend to the USSR not only MFN but also Export-Import Bank credits, a concession of enormous interest to the cash-strapped Soviets. Indeed, Henry Kissinger was later to suggest that the Soviets were far more interested in the Export-Import Bank credits than in MFN itself.[22]

While the Soviets promised to repay a portion of their World War II lend-lease debt to the United States, the agreement as a whole was explicitly conceived by the Nixon administration as a major incentive for the Soviets to cooperate in areas such as arms control and regional conflict—especially Vietnam. Although American critics argued that the agreement, taken alone, benefited the Soviet Union disproportionately, that was in fact Nixon's intent: in an era of American retreat the economic benefits conferred by the agreement were designed to encourage Soviet military restraint.[23]

In simultaneously pursuing rapprochement with the Soviets and collaborating closely with authoritarian anti-Communist regimes in the developing world, the Nixon administration deliberately deemphasized human rights concerns. "What is important is not a nation's internal political philosophy," Nixon told Mao at their first meeting in 1972. "What is important is its policy toward the rest of the world and toward us."[24]

In the context of the cold war rivalry between two nuclear superpowers, Nixon believed that the search for international peace and stability necessarily ruled out interference in the internal affairs of other nations. "The United States cannot gear our foreign policy to the transformation of other societies," he argued: "Peace between nations with totally different systems is also a high moral objective."[25] Kissinger went further, questioning even the desirability of American efforts to influence the internal developments of other societies and arguing that a proper respect for the legitimacy and national sovereignty of other countries should preclude such meddling.[26]

Anticommunism, American Idealism, and the Jackson-Vanik Amendment

But Kissinger's Old World balance of power approach to foreign affairs encountered grave political problems at home. In spite of the dramatic success of President Nixon in his diplomatic forays to Moscow and Beijing, a panoply of opposition emerged to *Realpolitik* and its perceived amoral assumptions. These critics, including many conservatives, liberals, and trade unions, have been described as strange bedfellows, but they evoked deep and diverse chords within the American memory: staunch anticommunism, passionate internationalist idealism, and intense sympathy for underdogs and victims of persecution. One man was to unite these disparate elements into a powerful engine that shook the foundations of détente and the entire Nixon-Kissinger geopolitical strategy—the Democratic senator from Washington State, Henry "Scoop" Jackson.

Beginning in 1972, the focus of Jackson's efforts and the hinge on which the public critique of détente turned was emigration, specifically Jewish emigration, from the Soviet Union. Kissinger—himself a Jewish refugee from persecution in Germany—has argued that he and the Nixon administration had been highly successful in persuading the Soviets, without publicity, to permit Jews to leave. In 1968, fewer than 400 Soviet Jews had been permitted to emigrate; by 1972, Jewish emigration was averaging more than 2,500 a month.[27]

But in August 1972, shortly after the conclusion of negotiations on the bilateral trade agreement, the USSR imposed a prohibitively expensive "exit tax" on emigration. While this tax was ostensibly to reimburse the Soviet government for the cost of a departing individual's education, it made emigration from the Soviet Union all but impossible.

In October, Senator Jackson, with energetic support from Democratic Congressman Charles Vanik of the House Ways and Means Committee, sponsored the bill that eventually became known as the Jackson-Vanik amendment. It blocked the granting of most-favored-nation status to any "nonmarket economy" (that is, Communist country) restricting emigration. The Soviets quickly withdrew the "exit tax," but it was too late; the battle had already been engaged. And by the time Nixon submitted the trade agreement conferring MFN and trade credits on the USSR for ratification to Congress in April 1973, Jackson and his assistant Richard Perle, and Vanik and his assistant Mark Talisman, had already enlisted overwhelming, bipartisan support in both houses of Congress for their legislation.[28]

As Kissinger himself acknowledged, Jackson was admired in Congress and the administration for his dedication to principle, his personal integrity, and his extraordinarily capable staff. Although Jackson was fairly liberal on most domestic issues, Richard Nixon in 1968 offered him the position of secretary of defense. In 1969, Nixon suggested to Jackson that he serve as secretary of state. Jackson, however, declined each time.[29]

The son of Norwegian immigrants, Jackson was a fearless cold warrior from the beginning and remained one long after being a hard-liner went out of fashion. Like Ronald Reagan, in whose administration several Jackson staffers were later to serve, Jackson believed the Soviet Union to be an evil empire. "I regard the Soviet Union," Jackson said, "as an opportunistic hotel burglar who walks down the corridors to see which door is open."[30] He viewed the trade agreement—with its hard currency credits for a hostile superpower—as a one-sided giveaway. And how could tariff concessions truly be reciprocal with a command economy? Furthermore, in Jackson's view, the Soviets simply could not be trusted to make the accommodations Kissinger claimed in other areas. No, such a major reward to an adversary called for a more fundamental concession in return. To Jackson, principled and uncompromising positions were not only ethically imperative but also politically attainable.

It was Jackson himself, not any political constituency, that drove this issue forward. Indeed, when Jackson introduced this bill, the Jewish community in the United States was relatively quiescent about Soviet emigration. Prominent Jewish organizations initially opposed the idea of linking Soviet trade with Jewish emigration, thinking it could prove counterproductive. Jackson and Perle convinced them otherwise through the intensity of their arguments and the force of their convictions.[31]

It has been suggested that Jackson was posturing before a constituency critical to his 1976 presidential bid. But Jackson's legislation was utterly consistent with his life-long practices and beliefs, old-fashioned beliefs that otherwise hurt him politically in the Democratic party as it moved to the Left. Indeed, the steadfastness of his convictions distinguished him from many of his political colleagues. Others, for example, largely because of their distrust of Nixon's motives, supported Jackson's legislation, even though they had previously backed unconditional trade liberalization with the Soviets. Several of these individuals later recanted their support for Jackson-Vanik after its enactment led to the Soviet withdrawal from the trade agreement.[32]

But Jackson would have preferred no agreement rather than an agreement without conditions that he considered contrary to the national security interests of the United States. He was willing to support Nixon on the agreement, however, if it were redeemed through Soviet recognition of the right of emigration.

The beauty of this demand was that it did not appear to dictate to another country how it governed itself. It merely insisted that people be permitted to leave if they chose. Yet the senator considered this right to be the "mother of all liberties" in any nation: if people were free to leave their country, after all, their government would in time be forced to liberalize in response to a steady drain of individual talent.[33] This liberalization in turn would be a far more likely guarantor of improved international conduct by the Soviets than the "linkage" of various international commitments negotiated by Kissinger.[34]

Separately, Jackson and Democratic Senator Adlai Stevenson of Illinois introduced amendments allowing for congressional review of any Export-Import Bank loan above $50 million and placing a straight ceiling of $300 million on *all* loans to the USSR. "They arranged that whatever happened to MFN in the trade bill," Kissinger complained, "U.S.-Soviet commerce could be throttled by turning off credits from the Export-Import Bank."[35]

Kissinger was caught off guard by the relentless intensity of Jackson and his staff in promoting the legislation over a two-year period, through Watergate and the succession of Gerald Ford as president. "We did not believe that Jackson was going to drive matters to such an extreme," Kissinger commented later. "Too slowly did it dawn on us that Jackson's whole crusade depended on proving that our sense of what was attainable was flawed; he did not want a compromise."[36]

But Kissinger, characteristically, sought to broker a deal so that Jackson could have his legislation and the Soviets could have the trade agreement on terms acceptable to them. In October 1974, Jackson and his legislative coalition agreed to an executive waiver provision that would extend MFN to the Soviets, based on Kissinger's representation that they had agreed to an emigration quota that "may . . . exceed 60,000 per annum." Kissinger had thus played "good cop" to Jackson's "bad cop," with Kissinger acting as the succor to the Soviets and Jackson as their mighty scourge.

Jackson, however, was uncomfortable with relying on private assurances and went public with the Soviet commitment. Soviet Foreign Minister Andrei Gromyko complained of the publicity and also alleged certain misrepresentations by Kissinger, in a letter that Kissinger kept secret—fearing it would unravel the arrangement he had negotiated. In December 1974, Congress enacted omnibus trade legislation, including the U.S.-USSR trade agreement, the Stevenson limitations on credit, and the Jackson-Vanik amendment, allowing the president to extend MFN to a "nonmarket economy" country if it had provided appropriate assurances about its emigration policies.[37]

Shortly thereafter, in January 1975, the Soviets informed the United States that they were rejecting the entire trade package negotiated and agreed to in 1972. They would no longer seek MFN status. Emigration was sharply curtailed.[38] Kissinger's vision of détente was seriously jeopardized—all the more so when major Communist military offensives that spring resulted in the collapse of American-supported governments in Cambodia, Laos, and South Vietnam.

Public disillusionment with *Realpolitik* grew and was much in evidence in the following year's presidential campaign. Ronald Reagan nearly denied President Ford the Republican nomination by attacking détente and the entire Kissinger model of diplomacy. And the Democratic nominee Jimmy Carter was elected president, pledging to restore the emphasis on human rights in U.S. foreign policy. Interestingly, Senator Jackson had enlisted the support of both Carter and Reagan for the provisions of the Jackson-Vanik legislation.[39]

When Reagan succeeded Carter as president, he appointed Jackson staffers, including Perle, to significant foreign policy positions. After Jackson's death in 1983, President Reagan bestowed on him the nation's highest award, the Presidential Medal of Freedom, describing him as "the great bipartisan patriot of our time."[40] In challenging intellectually fashionable notions of moral equivalence between the superpowers and envisioning the ultimate demise of the Soviet totalitarian state when many sophisticated observers considered this prescription self-righteous and foolhardy, Reagan continued to evoke the anti-Communist idealism of Henry Jackson.

With the Gorbachev era, of course, came extraordinary reform to the Soviet Union. The world was changed forever. In June 1990, the Gorbachev government, desperate for credits and Western investment, signed a trade agreement with the United States that finally granted MFN. In the later Gorbachev years, freedom of emigration from the USSR was realized as hundreds of thousands of Jews, Christians, dissidents, and others were at last permitted to leave.[41] This was truly a hallmark development in the dismantling of the Soviet regime.

To ensure against any subsequent Soviet backsliding, however, President Bush informed the Soviets that he would not submit the new trade agreement to Congress until the Supreme Soviet had passed a law guaranteeing the right of emigration, which, after a year's hesitation, it did in June 1991. President Bush, proceeding under Jackson-Vanik, then asked Congress to approve the trade agreement, which it did six months later, on November 25, 1991.[42] Within weeks, the Soviet Union officially ceased to exist.

Seventeen years had elapsed since the enactment of Jackson-Vanik and the collapse of the 1972 trade agreement, a long and frustrating time for those in the United States who favored trade relations with the USSR. But in recent years, as the Soviets grew desperate for Western assistance, they finally proved willing to release their own citizens, knowing the Americans would withhold trade and credit benefits until Jackson's simple, enduring requirement was met.

Jackson, China, and MFN

The violent suppression of Chinese prodemocracy demonstrators in Tiananmen Square on June 4, 1989, shocked the world and brought immediate American sanctions. President Bush promptly criticized the Chinese and immediately discontinued all military sales. He also suspended high-level civilian and military personnel exchanges. Furthermore, he announced that the United States would act to block Chinese loan applications to international lending institutions.[43] There was broad congressional and public support for these initial sanctions, but there was also widespread consternation across the American political spectrum about Bush's public unwillingness to condemn the Chinese leadership more forcefully.

As months passed, congressional frustration and anger grew toward the president, whose limited rhetoric, existing sanctions, and more conciliatory posture toward the Chinese were blamed for failing to prevent a widespread crackdown on dissent in China. To strengthen congressional authority in U.S.-China policy, calls grew for legislation supplementing Jackson-Vanik, to condition or withdraw China's MFN status. President Bush strongly resisted, and thus began the heated and emotional debate over MFN for China that lasts to this day.[44]

Ironically, Senator Jackson, staunch anti-Communist and leading proponent of human rights though he was, had also been a strong proponent of normalized relations with China. He supported MFN for China at a time when Chinese society was far more repressive than it has been in the aftermath of Tiananmen Square. Indeed, in November 1969, when relations between the two countries were virtually nonexistent, Jackson was advocating full normalization of relations with mainland China, including comprehensive political, cultural, and trade ties.[45]

Through four trips to China between 1971 and 1983, Jackson deepened his commitment to the realization of a dynamic and prosperous China with close ties to the United States. In particular, he was instrumental in the passage of the Carter administration's trade agreement with China in late 1979, providing for access to official credits and the extension of MFN.[46]

While Jackson believed that closer ties between the United States and China could be helpful in containing Soviet imperialism, geopolitical considerations were by no means his sole motivation. Jackson's communications with four presidents repeatedly indicated his fear of America's using China for short-term tactical maneuvers against Moscow.[47] He had a longer-term vision. China was a huge, developing, potentially powerful nation, with whom America had a compelling interest in establishing a "constructive, enduring . . . relationship."[48]

Should China's developmental aspirations be disappointed, Jackson opined, the likely political instability would be unsettling to the entire region, potentially embroiling the United States. The more likely outcome, as he correctly foresaw, was extraordinary economic progress, in which event American interests and ideals were best served by extensive involvement rather than isolation. How could the United States extend MFN to China and not to the Soviet Union? Jackson said in 1979:

> China and the Soviet Union are two very different countries at different stages of development, with different interests and ambitions, different associates and allies, and different relations with this country. They should be treated on separate tracks and, in our own national interest, they cannot be treated alike.[49]

Although it was opposed by the AFL-CIO and certain human rights organizations, granting China MFN did not stir up much controversy in 1979.[50] Nor was there any congressional debate about MFN for China for the next ten years, during which time relations with the United States grew closer, China's economy boomed, and political controls under Deng Xiaoping were substantially relaxed. Indeed, from the time of Nixon's opening to China in 1972, through Carter's extension of diplomatic recognition in 1979, through periodic crackdowns on dissent in the 1980s, human rights in China never became a significant political issue in the United States. This changed forever in the spring of 1989, when American television viewers looked on in horror as the tanks of the People's Liberation Army rolled into Tiananmen Square.

America Responds to Tiananmen Square

As the repression intensified in China, the Soviet Union and Eastern Europe were undergoing the most extraordinary evolution in modern times toward the civilized norms of liberal democracy. These dramatic developments in the crumbling Soviet empire, for a host of reasons, greatly reinforced the negative reactions in the United States to China's bloody imposition of martial law.[51]

First, the relaxation of tensions between the United States and the Soviet Union under Gorbachev undermined the national security rationale for continuing strategic coordination between the United States and China. As the Soviet threat diminished, so did the justification, to many Americans, for close relations with the Chinese government. Thus many influential members of Congress, for example, considered themselves free for the first time to criticize Chinese abuses of human rights.

Second, at a time when quintessentially American ideals were acquiring unprecedented recognition across the globe, the brutal suppression of dissent in China appeared in contrast especially heinous. Whereas in the years since normalization of relations with the United States China had seemed to be the most reform-minded and progressive of the Communist countries, it was now, as a consequence of Tiananmen Square, suddenly transformed in the American imagination into the world's most despotic regime.

Finally, the rapid advance of Western concepts of liberal democracy into previously authoritarian societies led Americans to believe that the United States had both the capacity and the moral authority to transform the world in its own image. The national self-doubt engendered by the Vietnam War had previously rendered American opinion leaders silent during the bloody mass terror of the Cultural Revolution. The repression of dissidents in 1989, while appalling, was clearly limited in comparison. But 1989, a year that saw free elections ousting Communist officials in Moscow, the display of a Chinese version of the Statue of Liberty in Tiananmen Square, and the destruction of the Berlin Wall, was a year in which all things seemed possible. The euphoria induced by the end of the cold war encouraged influential Americans to believe that if only the government imposed the proper sanctions, it could compel the Chinese government to lift martial law, reverse course, and permit wholesale political liberalization.

China, however, is governed by tough Communist party autocrats. This regime had just experienced a serious challenge to its legitimacy and had drawn lessons of its own from the global collapse of communism. Indeed, China's old-guard leadership now believed that a tough crackdown on dissent was the only way to resist the ideological advances of the West, to retain power, and to prevent chaos, which the Chinese most fear, from once again engulfing their country.[52]

After Western sanctions were implemented, the arrest of dissidents nonetheless continued and executions occurred, prompting further expressions of outrage as well as frustration with President Bush. Bush consistently avoided idealistic or emotional rhetoric and relied largely on his personal relationships with foreign heads of state to advance America's interests in the world. Even as relations warmed with the

Soviet Union, Bush was ever mindful of the continuing American national security interest in constructive relations with China. He had served as America's envoy to China under President Ford, and he believed that personal criticism of the Chinese leadership would only strengthen reactionary elements seeking justification for tightening political controls and curtailing relations with the West. He also believed that continued dialogue was required to encourage moderation in Beijing.[53]

Bush was tough with the Chinese in private, but his publicly conciliatory posture was increasingly out of step with much of America's opinion elite. When the repression continued congressional leaders of both parties, as well as the nation's newspapers, called on the president to condemn the Chinese leadership and to impose additional sanctions.[54]

In the fall of 1989, Democratic Representative Nancy Pelosi of California sponsored legislation with overwhelming bipartisan congressional support, granting the tens of thousands of Chinese students in the United States extended terms to stay, with permission to work in the interim.[55] The Chinese government threatened to curtail educational exchanges if the legislation passed. President Bush vetoed the legislation in November as counterproductive and also an unwarranted legislative intrusion on the president's authority in foreign affairs.[56] While he simultaneously issued an order with provisions similar to the Pelosi bill, his veto strained his relations with Congress over China policy.

The following month, December 1989, President Bush dispatched National Security Adviser Brent Scowcroft and Deputy Secretary of State Larry Eagleburger to Beijing to explore steps by each country to improve the relationship. Shortly after their mission, the administration modified sanctions imposed after Tiananmen: export licenses were granted for communications satellites to be launched by the Chinese, Export-Import Bank lending was resumed, and the administration announced that World Bank loans to China for humanitarian projects would now be considered.[57] For their part, the Chinese publicly committed for the first time not to export missiles to the Middle East and eased their restrictions on educational and cultural exchanges. In January 1990, martial law was lifted in Beijing and 600 political prisoners were released.[58] The Chinese, however, continued to deny permission to leave the country to Fang Lizhi, their most prominent dissident, who had been given refuge by the American Embassy.

China specialists generally endorsed Bush's initiative, but most public commentary was extremely critical of the Scowcroft mission. The *Washington Post*, for example, characterized it as a "placatory concession to a repressive and bloodstained Chinese government," and the *New York Times* as "hailing the butchers of Beijing."[59]

In short, the trip, whatever its substantive merits, had been a public relations nightmare. Announced in the middle of the night, Washington time, just as Scowcroft arrived in Beijing, it aroused suspicion about "secret diplomacy," and fueled a perception that the mission violated the president's own sanction against high-level exchanges. Scowcroft's photograph subsequently appeared in newspapers across America, toasting his Chinese hosts with champagne. And his banquet remarks seemed in part to blame the deterioration in relations on human rights advocates and congressional leaders, thus generating a firestorm of criticism at home.[60] Shortly thereafter, Chinese sources revealed that Scowcroft and Eagleburger had also visited Beijing in July 1989, just weeks after Tiananmen. This revelation reinforced the perception that the Bush administration was "kowtowing" to the Chinese, while deceiving Congress and the American people. Henceforth, the President had limited political capital with the Congress on China policy. [61]

MFN Legislation—Congress Challenges the President

In the spring of 1990, congressional critics seized on the annual Jackson-Vanik review of MFN for China as a convenient legislative vehicle for repudiation of the president. It is important to note that withdrawal of MFN had *not* been seriously considered by Congress in 1989 in the especially emotional months after Tiananmen. It was not, for example, included in the comprehensive sanctions legislation of 1989.[62] But in May 1990, when Bush announced that he would renew MFN for China for another year, his decision was roundly denounced on Capitol Hill. This criticism came even though the simple requirements of Jackson-Vanik provided no basis for denying MFN. Legislation was immediately introduced to overturn Bush's decision.[63]

The continuing dialogue with the Bush administration, as well as the prospect of congressional removal of MFN, encouraged the Chinese in the spring of 1990 to release several hundred more dissidents, to increase the purchase of American goods (including a $2 billion purchase of commercial aircraft from Boeing), and to permit Fang Lizhi, after thirteen months in the American Embassy, to leave the country.[64]

But at a time when democratization was proceeding at breathtaking speed in a collapsing Soviet empire, congressional critics of China and the administration's policy were not easily appeased. They pointed to the continued detention of countless political prisoners, China's repressive political atmosphere, and various offensive aspects of China's foreign policy, including the sale of missiles and other dangerous technology to the Middle East.[65] Over time, China's growing trade surplus with the United States, as well as the difficulties U.S. firms encountered in gaining access to that country's markets, provided yet another grievance to the Congress.[66]

Proponents of MFN argued that withdrawal of MFN would seriously harm American exporters, investors, and consumers; devastate Hong Kong; and do the gravest damage in China itself, not to the reactionary old guard but rather to the rapidly developing private economy, which many Americans otherwise wished to encourage as the greatest internal force for the progressive evolution of Chinese society.[67] In addition, prominent individuals in China supporting political reform argued for retention of MFN, arguing that withdrawal would only encourage further repression by their own government.[68]

These arguments impelled many members of Congress, led by Representative Pelosi and later Senate Majority Leader George Mitchell, to support annual legislation requiring not revocation but rather conditional extension of MFN. Thus the Chinese would have until the following year to meet the new terms required by legislation.[69] The sponsors argued withdrawal of MFN would not in the end be necessary, because the Chinese would eventually accede to the threat of withdrawal and comply with the new legislative requirements.[70] Other members also supported this legislation, identifying themselves with worthy objectives, knowing of a certain presidential veto. Absolved of real responsibility for ever actually compelling withdrawal of MFN, they could ignore with impunity the president's arguments against the legislation.

The conditions Congress proposed were vastly more comprehensive than the original, simple requirement of Jackson-Vanik, that MFN be certified annually by the president as advancing freedom of emigration. From 1990 through the end of the Bush administration in 1992, the House and the Senate easily passed legislation to require the president to certify in the following year that "overall significant progress" had been made in human rights, trade practices, and weapons proliferation. Specific conditions included, for example, the release of all 1989 prodemocracy demonstrators, freedom of the press, the termination of all prison labor imports, and the cessation of all religious persecution. The legislation also mandated that China protect intellectual property rights, cease "unfair" trading practices, and discontinue any activities "inconsistent with international control standards" on missile technology and nuclear, biological, and chemical weapons.[71] To diminish pressure for such legislation during this period, China strategically timed certain concessions in trade relations, purchased additional American goods, and released political prisoners.[72]

President Bush vetoed the legislation on the two occasions it reached his desk, in March and September of 1992. While expressing full support for its goals, Bush stated that comprehensive engagement was the best method for promoting political reform in China over the long term. The ultimatum mandated by Congress, Bush argued, would in fact weaken ties with the United States and lead to further repression.[73]

In 1991 and 1992, Bush toughened his policies toward the Chinese. He was the first president to meet with the Dalai Lama, thus demonstrating U.S. support for human rights in Tibet.[74] His threat of U.S. trade sanctions under Section 301 of the Trade Act of 1974 led to new trade agreements in market access and the protection of intellectual property rights.[75] The denial of certain high-tech export licenses encouraged the Chinese to sign the Nuclear Proliferation Treaty and to adhere to the Missile Technology Control Regime. Finally, he strengthened Taiwan, an old ally, and directly confronted the Chinese leadership in authorizing the sale of F-16s.[76]

But the prospect of achieving bipartisan support for the Bush policy toward China had long since vanished. And in the 1992 campaign, Bill Clinton found political advantage in claiming that Bush's policy was to "coddle tyrants" in Beijing.[77]

Given the widespread respect for President Bush's skill in foreign policy among opinion leaders and the public, why did his policy toward China remain a source of continuing political vulnerability throughout his administration? This question is especially troubling because of the recognition by scholars and independent observers that normal trade with China has been a very effective means for promoting not only vast economic liberalization but also greater understanding of Western values.[78]

With America triumphant at the end of the cold war, many Americans had greatly enhanced, if not exaggerated, expectations about this country's ability to promote its interests and ideals abroad. These expectations and the corresponding frustrations when they were not realized were evident in Senator Mitchell's remarks in 1991. When he proposed legislation conditioning MFN he said: "Clearly, the Bush Administration's China policy has failed. It hasn't improved human rights conditions in China. It hasn't improved China's trade record with the U.S. And it has not made China a more responsible world citizen with respect to weapons proliferation."[79]

Of course, Senator Mitchell was hardly an objective observer. He sought partisan political advantage against President Bush whenever and wherever possible. And MFN had become a partisan political issue: the Democratic Congress, knowing of certain veto by Bush, enacted MFN legislation not once but twice in 1992, on the second occasion a mere six weeks before the presidential election. With a Democrat in the White House, congressional passion for legislated conditions on MFN has cooled.

But why did MFN become such a political issue? Why did Democrats pursue it so aggressively? Indeed, why did two of every three House Republicans vote against Bush on this question in 1992, an election year? Why did conservative Republicans in the Senate join liberal Democrats in supporting this legislation?

After a decade of politically divided government in Washington, relations between the Democratic Congress and Republican administrations regarding the conduct of foreign policy had become deeply strained. As disputes over such issues as the War Powers Act and the doctrine of executive privilege illustrate, each branch of government had grown extremely sensitive about its institutional prerogatives. And as the controversy over the Iran-contra episode demonstrated, tensions were often greatest over the responsibilities of each branch, with respect to the *process* of making policy as much as its substance.

Thus, many in Congress were offended when Bush implemented the provisions of the Pelosi student visa bill by executive order while vetoing the legislation. Bush argued, "I want to keep control of managing the foreign policy of this country as much as I can."[80] His desire to retain executive discretion in the conduct of foreign policy was eminently reasonable, especially in light of his conviction that the legislation would lead to new restrictions by the Chinese on educational exchanges.[81] But his veto also reinforced the sense of members of Congress that they were simply being excluded from the decision-making process.

A few weeks later, congressional antagonism increased because of the Scowcroft missions to Beijing. There had been no advance notice to or consultation with congressional leadership regarding the missions. Members of Congress were especially irritated to learn of the first mission six months after it occurred from CNN, quoting *Chinese* sources.[82] Nixon and Carter, of course, had also engaged in extensive secret diplomacy with the Chinese, but they were acting at a time when Congress was less jealous of its institutional prerogatives.

Thus many members of Congress came to view the statutory procedure governing annual renewal of MFN as the most effective vehicle for ensuring congressional participation in policy making on China. In passing legislation not to withdraw MFN but rather to impose conditions beyond emigration on renewal of MFN in the following year, Congress was seeking to enhance its authority in an important area of foreign affairs and to circumscribe the president's discretion. Congress could also reasonably assume that enacting the legislation, notwithstanding the certain veto, would itself influence the policy of both the Bush administration and the Chinese government. At the same time, MFN would, at least for the time being, be retained.

Idealism in American Foreign Policy

The struggle between the executive and the legislative branches over China policy occurred in the context of a larger debate about America's foreign policy objectives. As with Jackson-Vanik in the early 1970s, broad bipartisan support had emerged for legislation to limit the prerogatives of a president whose foreign policy was widely perceived, fairly or otherwise, to lack an adequate moral foundation. Liberals and conservatives alike had supported Jackson-Vanik because of a fundamental discomfort in the American body politic with the assumption that a foreign regime's treatment of its own people should not be a factor in calculating the national security interests of the United States.

Similarly, George Bush's policy toward China became so politically controversial because he allowed the perception to take hold, incorrect though it may have been, that he was indifferent to the suppression of thousands of individuals who aspired to American ideals of freedom. As Jeane Kirkpatrick has observed:

> No significant number of people in the United States in our history has ever argued that our foreign policy should be oriented toward anything except moral ends. . . . The notion that foreign policy should be oriented toward balance of power politics, or *Realpolitik*, is totally foreign to the American tradition and, in fact, to the American scene today.[83]

Like President Nixon and Henry Kissinger twenty years earlier, President Bush and Secretary of State James Baker approached foreign policy with considerable sophistication and pragmatism. They relied substantially on the development of confidential relationships with the leaders of both authoritarian and democratic governments. While pursuing human rights they deliberately avoided the use of idealistic rhetoric.[84] For all these reasons, the Bush and Nixon administrations, notwithstanding their extraordinary success in the conduct of foreign affairs, encountered serious political opposition from ideological conservatives as well as from liberals and the American labor movement.

The image of Bush's foreign policy as unduly pragmatic was strongly reinforced by the contrast with his predecessor, Ronald Reagan. President Reagan had argued with great conviction and eloquence that America should aggressively promote the cause of freedom and democracy abroad, even or especially when it unsettled existing Communist regimes. Reagan had shocked the Soviet leadership, not to mention polite society at home, when he condemned the Soviet Union as the "evil empire."[85] Bush, in contrast, who did not wish to "gloat" or needlessly offend the Gorbachev regime, consistently avoided suggesting that the disintegration of the Soviet empire constituted a great triumph for Western democratic ideals.[86]

Reagan had deeply influenced public opinion about America's role in the world when he argued that American foreign policy should be based explicitly on the moral superiority of liberal democracy. Bush's obvious skepticism about the role of ideology in foreign affairs, on the other hand, made him vulnerable politically to the bipartisan allegation that his policies lacked what he himself described as "the vision thing."

This contrast between the bold, soaring idealism of Reagan and the prudent, studied pragmatism of Bush encouraged Kirkpatrick and a number of other Reagan conservatives to abandon Bush on such questions as MFN for China. It may also help explain why Bush, like Nixon, sustained legislative defeat and political embarrassment in supporting MFN for a major Communist power whose abuse of human rights, it was argued, he had overlooked.

Of course, the enactment of Jackson-Vanik led the USSR to withdraw from the trade agreement negotiated by the Nixon administration. It was not to receive MFN from the United States for another seventeen years.

China, in contrast, promised to permit freedom of emigration when it entered into a trade agreement with the United States in 1979. It therefore has had MFN continuously since 1980. The legislation, vetoed by Bush, and the executive order, issued by Clinton, imposing new, far broader conditions on the existing trade relationship, have to this date only threatened MFN's revocation. Withdrawing MFN from China today, radically disrupting current bilateral trade of vast proportions, could have a far more profound adverse effect on an existing relationship than did the Soviet withdrawal from the U.S.-USSR trade agreement in 1975.

There are other distinctions worth noting. Both Nixon and Kissinger on the one hand and Jackson on the other viewed the 1972 trade agreement as a cold war concession to America's global adversary. Although there were some liberals and businessmen who were wildly optimistic about the prospects for trade with the Soviets, both Jackson and Nixon clearly understood that the benefits to the American economy of trade with the Soviets would be extremely limited in the foreseeable future.

The same cannot be said of trade with China today. American companies, workers, and consumers would suffer substantially if MFN were withdrawn. Furthermore, extraordinary economic possibilities in the world's third largest and fastest-growing economy of considerable future benefit to Americans would be seriously jeopardized, if not lost. In purely economic terms, therefore, MFN for China, while quite unlike MFN for the Soviet Union in the 1970s, is indisputably in America's interests.[87]

Furthermore, the Soviet agreement provided for trade with a command economy, with Soviet state enterprises. Neither Jackson nor Nixon and Kissinger believed that such trade was likely to help establish the preconditions of a market economy in the Soviet Union or otherwise contribute to the opening of that society.[88] The same cannot be said about China, which over the past fifteen years has undertaken a series of radical, market-oriented reforms simply inconceivable under the traditional Soviet model.[89] Trade with the United States, the market for 30 percent of China's exports, has certainly furthered the development of Chinese private enterprise, resulting not only in greater prosperity but also in greater personal liberty for millions of Chinese.[90]

Unlike the trade contemplated with the Soviet Union in the 1970s, U.S. trade with China today is trade with the *people* of China, thus enhancing their individual autonomy at the expense of the authority traditionally exercised by the Communist party. There is, therefore, a very strong moral argument for normal trade relations with China that could not be made regarding trade with the Soviet Union twenty years ago. Trade with the Soviet Union a generation ago would have strengthened communism, whereas trade with China today undermines communism. U.S. trade with China substantially contributes to the development of a vibrant private sector, a growing middle class, greater pluralism, and a diminished role for the state and the Communist party.[91] Trade with the United States by no means makes real political freedom inevitable in China, but it does make it more likely over time than would a return to a policy of attempted isolation. This more idealistic argument was one that President Bush, true to character, shied away from making too publicly.

Of course, there are those who would argue that a market economy can go hand in hand with authoritarianism, and that is certainly true. It is true in China today. Obviously, much of China's leadership hopes this remains true in the future. But the emergence of an exploding market economy in China has given individuals personal liberty, prosperity, and independence that were unimaginable a mere decade and a half ago. Free market forces in China today are unquestionably eroding the historical and theoretical underpinnings of Communist oppression. The emergence of freely negotiated contracts and the development of property rights are laying the foundations of a civil society and creating irreversible pressures for the establishment of a rule of law.

Finally, the Chinese, unlike the Soviets, did accede to the U.S. requirement that freedom of emigration be recognized. This is more than a legalistic point. Not unrelated, after all, is the fact that the Chinese government has permitted thousands of Chinese scholars and students to study, to work, and to travel in the United States, a remarkable phenomenon that itself has radically increased the understanding of Western values and advanced the opening of Chinese society.[92] Just as elements of the Chinese leadership believe repressive Communist party rule can survive extensive economic engagement with the West, so Deng Xiaoping believed, incorrectly, that Chinese students coming to the United States would not be "corrupted" by American political values.

But Henry Jackson knew better. He well understood the powerful corrosive effect on totalitarian regimes when their citizens develop relationships with Americans. His reasons for questioning the Soviet trade agreement in 1973 are relevant today:

> We will have moved from the appearance to the reality of détente when East Europeans can freely visit the West, when Soviet students in significant numbers can come to American universities, and when American students in significant numbers can study in Russia. When reading the Western press and listening to Western broadcasts is no longer an act of treason, when families can be reunited across borders, when emigration is free—then we shall have a genuine détente between peoples.[93]

Chinese practice today, though hardly perfect, largely satisfies these conditions. And because of China's opening to the outside world, as Jackson predicted in supporting normalized relations, millions of Chinese understand the United States and its ideals today in ways they never did before. This understanding of Western ideals is still very crude.[94] But the glimpse of a better life they now have, in large measure as a result of American economic engagement, is clearly a subversive force in a politically repressive environment.[95]

The American idea has proved far more powerful than the Chinese leadership had assumed. Today, owing largely to U.S.-China trade, the American idea is conveyed to the people of China, like others around the world, in countless ways—from a satellite dish or a securities transaction to a pair of sneakers—communication increasingly beyond the reach of Mao's heirs.[96]

No wonder then, that untold thousands of indigent Chinese, like the *Golden Venture*'s unhappy passengers, have fled to the United States. Countless millions more would surely follow if they could only find the means to do so. The United States, of course, cannot begin to absorb them. But our foreign policy should, for idealistic as well as for pragmatic considerations, take full cognizance of the extraordinary fascination with America of the Chinese people. We need to consider how we can advance their hopes and aspirations for a better life in a manner that also serves our own interests. No other American policy is sustainable.

As the history of Jackson-Vanik and the debate over MFN for China reveal, the American people understand the power of the American idea abroad, and they expect their government to give it voice. As Henry Jackson taught us, America's leaders in foreign affairs most effectively pursue the national interest through a tough-minded realism—one that includes the power of American ideals.

9

MFN in the Spring of 1994

Wendell L. Willkie II

On February 1, 1994, the State Department released its annual report on human rights practices, describing the continuing denial of human rights in numerous countries. Regarding China, the report observed:

> The [Chinese] Government's overall human rights record in 1993 fell far short of internationally accepted norms as it continued to repress domestic critics and failed to control abuses by its own security forces.[1]

In China, Mexico, Saudi Arabia, and other countries, the report said, widespread human rights abuses occurred in the past year, including arbitrary detentions, the denial of meaningful due process, and the use of torture by security forces. The report did take note of "some positive steps" by China during 1993. The Chinese released a few political prisoners, granted permission to certain dissidents to leave the country, and indicated they would soon permit the Red Cross to visit prisons holding political detainees.

These initiatives, however, according to senior American officials in the winter of 1994, failed to meet the standards articulated by President Clinton in his executive order of May 28, 1993. That order specifically conditioned the renewal of most-favored-nation trading status (MFN) for China in June 1994 on a presidential determination that China had "made overall, significant progress" in respecting the human rights of its people.

Offering little evidence that the Chinese were making substantial human rights concessions in response to Clinton's demands, the State Department nonetheless described longer-term trends that were more promising. Indeed, it offered persuasive testimony that China's booming market economy had greatly increased individual freedom, while substantially eroding the authority of a once all-powerful state:

> A decade of rapid economic growth, spurred by market incentives and foreign investment, has reduced party and government control over the economy and permitted ever larger numbers of Chinese to have more control over their lives and livelihood.

Significantly, the report attributed the increased freedom of the Chinese news media to comment on nonpolitical issues to the development of a thriving private sector in China's economy. It stated that the emergence of a substantial middle class and the growing diversity of employment opportunities have effectively terminated the role of ideology in the economy, with corresponding benefits for freedom of expression.

The report also provided specific evidence that China's increasing engagement with the West since the years of Mao has created strong internal pressures to limit state tyranny. By international standards, the treatment of individuals in China's criminal justice system remains appalling. Today, however, in a departure from past practice, the government is making an effort to punish those who engage in torture and other mistreatment of prisoners. And while the Chinese government continues to insist that human rights are a purely internal affair, it has been far more willing in recent years to discuss its human rights practices with foreign governments.

More encouraging news came from U.S. Ambassador to China J. Stapleton Roy. In an interview with the *New York Times* appearing on January 1, 1994, Roy commented that in the history of modern China,

> The last two years are the best in terms of prosperity, individual choice, access to outside sources of information, freedom of movement within the country and stable domestic conditions.[2]

Roy pointed to the government's limited but increasing tolerance of criticism. He also referred to the growing recognition of the rights of individuals in the legal system as evidence of a "radical transformation" of Chinese society. At the same time, he said, it must be remembered that the Communist party fundamentally depends on repression to retain political control.

Roy's last observation regarding the inherently authoritarian nature of China's government raises a critical question regarding the Clinton administration's threat to withdraw MFN. The exercise of this threat would, as most contributors to this volume have argued, seriously damage America's national interests. They are hardly alone in this view. Tom Friedman of the *New York Times* reflected the thoughts of many observers when he wrote that this tactic is "the diplomatic equivalent of the United States holding a gun to its own head and threatening to pull the trigger."[3]

The credibility of the threat, therefore, is somewhat suspect. Indeed, as Winston Lord, assistant secretary of state for East Asian and Pacific affairs, was compelled to acknowledge in congressional testimony on February 24, 1994: "We frankly are not certain that the Chinese take seriously the requirement for more significant progress on human rights before June."[4]

Under these circumstances, it must be asked, can the proclaimed "conditionality" of MFN really be expected to yield more than modest gestures—such as a few prearranged prison visits or the well-orchestrated release of a handful of political prisoners—from a government that relies on repression to survive? Can this American demand be expected to produce any truly meaningful reform, which by definition might jeopardize the Communist grip on power?

Or is not systemic change in China far more likely to occur over time as a result of the inexorably increasing internal pressures—rising out of an exploding market economy and the growing exposure to Western values—for greater personal liberty and the establishment of a rule of law? Can the United States most effectively advance economic and political liberalization in China through normalized, indeed enhanced, commercial and cultural engagement?

Through the winter of 1994, the Clinton administration appeared to come down on both sides of this fundamental issue. On the one hand, Secretary of State Warren Christopher and other State Department officials admonished the Chinese that they were failing to meet the terms of President Clinton's executive order. If there was not real improvement in China's human rights practices before June 1994, they warned, the president was prepared to revoke MFN.[5]

On the other hand, Treasury Secretary Lloyd Bentsen and Robert Rubin, chairman of the National Economic Council, stressed the compelling American interest in normal trade relations with China. They publicly suggested that if the Chinese could satisfy only the president's relatively modest conditions this one time, then MFN should no longer be linked to America's human rights objectives.[6]

By June 3, 1994, the Clinton administration will be forced to choose between the retention and the withdrawal of MFN. Of course, the very existence of the issue can only be considered a historical accident. Virtually every country in the world today receives at least MFN status from the United States, irrespective of its human rights policies. In the especially emotional months after Tiananmen Square in 1989, there was no serious debate about withdrawing from normal trade relations. MFN became a real issue in 1990, only as a manifestation of congressional displeasure with President Bush, whose policies were portrayed by political opponents as too conciliatory to the Chinese.

In 1990, the provisions of the Jackson-Vanik amendment became a convenient vehicle for congressional criticism of Bush's China policy as inadequately committed to human rights. This cold war statute, enacted in 1974, was designed simply to promote freedom of emigration from America's global adversary, the Soviet Union. It requires the president to report annually to Congress on the extension of MFN to any Communist country. The annual extension of MFN to China was uncontroversial in the decade following normalization of trade relations with China in 1980, notwithstanding the continuing denial of human rights.

But beginning in 1990, Congress sought to expand on the requirements of Jackson-Vanik through legislation to impose new conditions on MFN in trade, security, and human rights. Revocation would occur only if the Chinese failed to meet the specified conditions in the following year. In Congress, to vote for conditional MFN was to go on record in support of important American objectives in China. For Democrats, the vote was also an opportunity to embarrass a Republican president and to limit his discretion in a significant area of foreign affairs. In arguing that the Chinese could meet the conditions, members of Congress furthermore claimed MFN would be retained. Finally, as China each year took certain palliative measures to address the concerns of its congressional critics, members of Congress believed they were playing "bad cop" to Bush's "good cop."

In issuing the executive order, Clinton essentially adopted the congressional position on the conditionality of MFN. U.S. government policy now alternates between ritual invocation of the MFN threat and frequent high-level meetings with the Chinese, seeking to establish justification not to use this weapon. The administration therefore finds itself in the awkward and untenable position of attempting to play "bad cop" and "good cop" at the same time.

In the Bush years, Congress, the "bad cop," could enact MFN conditions knowing that the president, the "good cop," would veto the legislation, thus relieving Congress of responsibility for the implementation of such conditions. President Clinton, however, having imposed conditions on MFN by executive order, does not enjoy that luxury.

Before Secretary Christopher's scheduled visit to Beijing in March 1994, there were indications that the Chinese government would make limited human rights "concessions" by June 1994. In January, China's President Jiang Zemin advised visiting American congressmen that China was "going to make an effort" to address President Clinton's requirements.[7]

U.S. officials, for their part, while calling for more than cosmetic improvements, nonetheless signaled to the Chinese that modest additional measures might be sufficient to fulfill the conditions of the executive order. Thus, Winston Lord "welcomed" as "concrete steps" the early release of a handful of political prisoners, specifically mentioning the prominent Democracy Wall dissident Wei Jingsheng. (Wei was released in September 1993, days before the decision of the International Olympic Committee on Beijing's bid to host the 2000 Olympics, after having served fourteen and a half years of a fifteen-year jail term.)[8] It has been reported that four of seven specific human rights demands recently conveyed by the United States to China involved the rights of fewer than twenty Chinese dissidents.[9]

Of course, given the disastrous implications for American interests of withdrawal of MFN, the Clinton administration now has a tremendous incentive to characterize any Chinese initiatives in human rights as meaningful progress. Furthermore, a determination by President Clinton in June 1994 that the Chinese had minimally satisfied his conditions would largely be spared the intense criticism from a Democratic Congress that George Bush had received for extending MFN. But in diplomacy as elsewhere, it is generally unwise to engage in threats unless one is prepared to act on them. Brandishing a mutually destructive and therefore dubious weapon—in pursuit of worthy but very limited objectives—does little to enhance America's standing in the world. This has indeed been a policy that gives every appearance of having been dictated by yesterday's battles in Washington, not today's challenges in China.

It is no wonder that Treasury Secretary Bentsen and White House adviser Robert Rubin have publicly suggested that America's human rights concerns should be "delinked" from MFN. If the president accepts this advice, however, he should, to preserve credibility, be explicit about his reversal in policy. Claiming predictable, modest concessions by the Chinese in the spring of 1994 as "significant progress" in human rights may well project weakness and hypocrisy. An eloquent, forthright admission, on the other hand, that a policy is being discarded as unwise and ineffective can demonstrate real leadership and thus win respect at home and abroad. Franklin Roosevelt and John Kennedy, for instance, became more presidential in abandoning earlier positions. In foreign affairs, there is an honorable tradition of presidents explaining to the American people why it has become necessary to depart from campaign rhetoric.

There are other, more credible ways the administration can diligently promote human rights. The United States, for example, should take greater advantage of its leverage in multilateral organizations, such as the UN Human Rights Commission and the international lending institutions. The administration could demonstrate support for Chinese democracy by establishing official contact with the government of Taiwan. And the president can speak out, when circumstances warrant, in support of the cause of freedom. In the final analysis, the inspiration of American ideals is far more powerful in advancing human rights than the threat of economic sanctions.

We hope the contributions to this volume have not only shed light on the MFN decision but also offered a deeper understanding of America's increasingly important relationship with China. There are remarkable changes under way in that great country, presenting extraordinary opportunities for the realization of American objectives. Our contributors have brought to bear different perspectives, experiences, and beliefs. Yet each has identified dynamic forces now undermining the pillars of repression and offering the promise of a real liberalization of Chinese society.

The United States has a vital interest in the further development of a stable, prosperous, and more humane China, one that plays a constructive role in international affairs. The future of that country will primarily be decided by the Chinese themselves. The most sensible American policy will be one that takes full cognizance of the progress that has already occurred, moves beyond earlier political debates in Washington, and effectively pursues the opportunities that China now presents for the advancement of American ideals and interests.

Appendix

Public Attitudes toward the People's Republic of China

Karlyn H. Bowman

China scholar Harry Harding has argued that the U.S. relationship with China is likely to be "less central" for the United States than in the past, "more complex," and possibly "more contentious." What role will American public opinion play in defining that new relationship? The polling summary that follows provides a basis for answering that question. As we will see, the role public opinion plays in whatever new relationship emerges will be very much like the role it has played in the past.

Public opinion pollsters in the United States began taking the public's pulse on a range of foreign policy issues more than half a century ago, providing analysts insights on American attitudes toward foreign affairs in general and on feelings for specific countries. This large compendium of survey data reveals that Americans provide their leaders broad general guidance about foreign policy ends, but very little specific guidance about how those ends should be achieved. This understanding of American opinion fits comfortably with Americans' predispositions about international involvement. Americans are today, as they have long been, reluctant internationalists, aware of their global responsibilities but cautious about active involvement abroad. They are often inattentive to foreign affairs, giving their leaders significant latitude in the conduct of foreign policy once a basic level of trust has been established.

While the polling business has grown substantially over the past fifty years and thousands of questions are now asked yearly, pollsters still concentrate overwhelmingly on domestic and not foreign policy attitudes. In foreign policy, the pollsters' searchlight moves restlessly from crisis to crisis. A few questions may be asked, for example, about granting most-favored-nation (MFN) status for China when the subject is in the news, but the issue is soon dropped from the pollsters' agenda when other events overtake it. The pollsters' sporadic interest in foreign policy issues and general American inattentiveness to the details of foreign policy often make interpretation of the results difficult.

Attitudes toward China—A Historical Perspective

Table A–1 provides a look at attitudes toward China over time. In 1954, Gallup first asked Americans to rate their feelings about China on a scale of +5 to –5. Given Americans' concerns about Communist expansion, it is not surprising that negative feelings overwhelmed positive ones in 1954, with only 13 percent of Americans giving China a positive rating and 74 percent a negative one.

Other questions from the period help elucidate the negative feelings. In 1948, the National Opinion Research Center (NORC) asked Americans if it would make much difference to the United States if China became Communist. Seventy-one percent said it would. In another question asked in 1952 by NORC, 54 percent said the United States should send military supplies to help Asian countries threatened by communism. As table A–1 shows, feelings toward China warmed considerably in 1973 after President Nixon's opening to China, and they improved continuously from 1982 through 1988. The Tiananmen incident halted that improvement, as once again, in 1990, a bare majority expressed more negative than positive feelings about China. In 1993, positive and negative feelings about the People's Republic of China were almost evenly split (see table A–1).

Another perspective on U.S. feelings toward China comes from a question asked by the Roper Organization. Roper has asked Americans a number of times over the past decade whether a specified country has acted as a "close ally" of the United States, "a friend but not a close ally," "more or less neutral," "mainly unfriendly but not an enemy," or "an enemy." In 1993, 2 percent described mainland China as a close ally; 12 percent, a friend; 33 percent neutral; 26 percent, mainly unfriendly; and 9 percent, an enemy. Seventeen percent had no opinion. Table A–2 shows how Americans rank a number of different countries on the "close ally/friend" dimension of the question. Not surprisingly, neighbors and long-time allies are most highly regarded.

TABLE A–1
U.S. FEELING TOWARD CHINA, SELECTED YEARS, 1954–1993

Question: How far up the scale or how far down the scale would you rate . . . China?

Year	*Positive (+1 to +5)*	*Negative (–1 to –5)*
1954	13	74
1972	24	70
1973	47	43
1974	42	52
1975	36	56
1977	36	54
1982	52	42
1983	53	47
1985	61	32
1986	64	33
1988	65	28
1989	58	34
1990	49	51
1991	55	44
1993	52	49

NOTE: Percentages may not add to 100 because of rounding.
SOURCE: 1954–1973, Gallup. 1974–1993, National Opinion Research Center. In Richard G. Niemi, John Mueller, and Tom W. Smith, *Trends in Public Opinion.*

Countries that have had less involvement and share less history with the United States are ranked lower on this dimension. The findings in table A–2 generally mirror those in table A–1. Americans ranked China as more friendly during the early 1980s, but the Tiananmen incident caused perceptions to deteriorate.

The data in table A–3 reinforce the point made in table A–2. Unfavorable ratings about mainland China rose after 1989. Again, a neighboring country and long-time ally, Canada, got much better ratings than mainland China.

Trade and Most-Favored-Nation Status

A handful of questions have been asked over the past decade about trade with the People's Republic of China. These questions may shed more light, however, on America's unease about its competitive position in the world than on its specific feelings about trade with China. The Roper Organization has asked Americans whether we are trading "too much," "about the right amount," or "too little" with a handful of countries, including China. The question has been posed four times

TABLE A–2
U.S. RATINGS OF FOREIGN NATIONS' ATTITUDES TOWARD THE UNITED STATES, 1982–1993
(percent)

Question: Turning to another subject, I'd like to have your impressions about the overall position that some countries have taken toward the U.S. [card shown respondent]. Would you read down that list and for each country, tell me if you believe that country has acted as a close ally of the U.S., has acted as a friend but not a close ally, has been more or less neutral toward the U.S., has been mainly unfriendly toward the U.S. but not an enemy, or has acted as an enemy of the U.S.?

	"Close Ally/Friend Combined"							
	1982 June	1985 Dec.	1987 June	1988 May	1989 July	1990 July	1991 Nov.	1993 July
Great Britain	85	83	85	83	84	80	81	78
Canada	83	*	87	87	*	79	81	81
Mexico	46	*	57	53	56	51	53	47
Israel	60	50	51	49	47	38	52	45
France	54	*	*	*	*	51	49	50
Germany**	59	60	*	54	48	53	49	46
Japan	64	68	66	61	62	54	43	38
Kuwait	*	*	*	*	*	*	36	*
Poland	33	*	*	*	35	35	35	30
Soviet Union***	4	3	3	7	16	22	35	33
Saudi Arabia	27	25	25	24	*	21	33	*
Philippines	*	41	47	43	*	33	33	*
Egypt	51	33	36	32	*	24	26	29
Mainland China	24	31	26	26	16	16	13	14
Haiti	7	4	*	*	*	2	13	16
Syria	*	*	8	6	*	6	6	*
Iran	*	*	2	1	3	1	6	2
Iraq	*	10	5	6	*	4	5	1

* = Not asked.
** = Trend data prior to 1991 is for West Germany.
*** = Trend data prior to 1993 is for Soviet Union.
NOTE: All countries except Great Britain and Soviet Union evaluated by half sample. Items ranked according to "close ally" and "friend" combined.
SOURCE: Surveys by the Roper Organization, latest that of 1993.

TABLE A–3
U.S. RATINGS OF SELECTED COUNTRIES, 1989–1991
(percent)

	Total Favorable			*Total Unfavorable*		
	1989	1990	1991	1989	1990	1991
Canada	92	89	91	3	3	3
Japan	69	61	65	23	29	26
China	72	39	35	13	47	53

SOURCE: Surveys by the Gallup Organization, latest that of 1991.

since 1975, and the results are shown in table A–4. In 1992, 42 percent of Americans said the United States was trading too much with mainland China, 25 percent said the level of trade was about right, and 10 percent felt it was not enough. Significantly, about a quarter (23 percent) responded that they did not know enough to have an opinion. The numbers in this table also suggest that Americans are more skeptical about expanding trade in times of recession. Not surprisingly, concerns appear to be greatest about the level of trade with Japan, a country Americans see as a very aggressive competitor (see table A–4).

In 1990, 60 percent of Americans told Gallup pollsters that the time had come to resume normal economic and trade relations with the People's Republic of China, while approximately a third disagreed. Support specifically for granting China's MFN status is lower, however, perhaps reflecting lingering concerns about the Tiananmen incident or unease about granting any nation what appears to be special trading privileges in a competitive trading environment. In May 1990 and June 1991, CBS News and the *New York Times* asked whether the United States should give the same trade privileges to China that it gives to other countries. A bare majority in 1990 (52 percent) and a strong plurality in 1991 (47 percent) said it should. In both years, nearly four in ten disagreed.

Another question, posed by NBC News and the *Wall Street Journal* in late June 1991, found that 44 percent of Americans wanted to give China MFN trading status—that is, in the words of the pollsters, "allow them the same privileges and ability to trade with the United States that most other countries have"; 49 percent disagreed. In June of 1993, Americans were asked by NBC/*Wall Street Journal* pollsters whether they supported or opposed President Clinton's approval of a one-year renewal of MFN status for China. Americans were split, with 41 percent in favor and 42 percent opposed, but the response may reflect either views about MFN status for China or views about President Clinton, who was then suffering low approval ratings in the polls.

TABLE A–4
U.S. RATING OF FOREIGN TRADE LEVEL, 1992
(percent)

Question: We'd like to find out how much you think the United States should be trading with certain specific foreign countries. At the present time do you think we are trading too much with Japan, about the right amount, or not enough with Japan? How about (Russia, China, South Africa, Mexico, Canada, the Western European countries)—do you think we are trading too much, about the right amount, or not enough?

Trading Too Much with . . .

	1975 June	*1981 May/June*	*1985 Feb.*	*1987 June*	*1992 June*
Japan	37	50	48	55	60
China	21	22	21	19	42
Mexico	*	12	16	18	27
South Africa	*	15	20	33	25
Russia	27	42	31	28	21
West European countries	*	*	*	*	19
Canada	6	6	8	8	14

* = Not asked.
SOURCE: Surveys by the Roper Organization, latest that of 1992.

In December 1993, NBC News and the *Wall Street Journal* tapped sentiments about trade with China again, asking Americans which of two statements came closer to their view about our relationship with China. Nearly three in ten (29 percent) said "we should maintain good trade relations with China, despite disagreements we might have with its human rights policies"; but a substantial 65 percent favored the statement "we should demand that China improve its human rights policies if China wants to continue to enjoy its current trade status with the United States."

What are we to make of the different responses to questions recently asked about most-favored-nation status for China? First, different question wordings produce different responses, depending on the particular nuance the question conveys to the person answering it. Second, there is some resistance to granting China MFN status, driven either by concerns about China's posture or by anxiety about the world trading environment. The December 1993 question asked by NBC News and the *Wall Street Journal* reveals something more. Respect for human rights is one of the underlying values Americans bring to their thinking about what U.S. foreign policy should be. It is one of the foreign policy "ends" referred to at the beginning of this appendix that Americans want their leaders to pursue. Americans clearly want China to make progress on human rights. On questions that speak to a basic foreign policy value as the NBC News/*Wall Street Journal* one does, Americans respond strongly. They want their leaders to reiterate that concern to Chinese leaders. Their responses to the questions cited here suggest that they are not giving specific guidance beyond that point.

As a general proposition, Americans believe expanding trade is in their interest, although they are often anxious about our trade dealings with particular countries. Questions about trade with Japan today reveal this anxiety, as did questions asked during consideration of the North American Free Trade Agreement in the fall of 1993. Still, they see the U.S.-Chinese relationship as a consequential one. In the December 1993 NBC News/*Wall Street Journal* poll cited above, Americans were asked: "Thinking about U.S. relations with foreign countries, with which of the following five countries or regions do you think our relationship will be most important over the next five years?" China and the Middle East tied for first place. Russia, Japan, and Latin America trailed in the poll rankings. Americans give their leaders in the White House and Congress flexibility in devising the means by which the broader ends they endorse can be accomplished.

In defining the new U.S. relationship with China, Americans will, as they have in the past, provide broad general guidance to policy makers about the ends that U.S. policy should serve. They will continue to be inattentive to the details or complexities of specific negotiations with China and are likely to be drawn into debates only when an issue commands center stage in Washington and, therefore, the pollsters' interest.

Notes

Chapter 2: Clinton's First Year, *David M. Lampton*

1. Cited in Foster Rhea Dulles, *American Policy toward Communist China, 1949–1969* (New York: Thomas Y. Crowell Company, 1972), p. 20.

2. U.S. Congress, House of Representatives, Subcommittee on Trade of the Committee on Ways and Means, *Hearing on U.S.-China Trade Relations,* 103d Congress, 1st session, June 8, 1993.

3. Edward Walsh, "Clinton Indicts Bush's World Leadership," *Washington Post,* October 2, 1992.

4. Nancy Benac, "Clinton Says He Will Extend Favorable Trade Status to China," Associated Press, May 27, 1993.

5. Robert Jervis, *Perception and Misperception in International Politics* (Princeton, N.J.: Princeton University Press, 1976), pp. 22–23.

6. U.S. Congress, House of Representatives, Subcommittee on Trade of the Committee on Ways and Means, *Hearing on U.S.-China Trade Relations.*

7. Letter of Barber B. Conable, Jr., to Representative Sam Gibbons, July 1, 1992, in *Additional Requirements in the Extension of China's Most-Favored-Nation Trade Status in 1993: Hearing before the Subcommittee on Trade, House Committee on Ways and Means,* 102d Cong., 2d sess., June 29, 1992, pp. 149–50.

8. "Economic Scene," *New York Times,* June 3, 1993.

9. Don Oberdorfer, "How Washington and Beijing Avoided Diplomatic Disaster," *Washington Post,* November 7, 1993.

10. This contingency was given some life when, in early November 1993, Vice Premier Qian Qichen said that Beijing would give "positive consideration" to any request it might receive from the International Committee of the Red Cross to visit Chinese prisons. The Chinese, it appears, took this initiative to prepare the way for productive talks between President Clinton and President Jiang Zemin in Seattle on November 19, 1993. Patrick E. Tyler, "China May Allow Red Cross to Visit Dissidents in Jail," *New York Times,* November 10, 1993.

11. David M. Lampton, "Breaking Down China's Ruling Clichés," *Asian Wall Street Journal*, October 20, 1993.

12. Anthony Lake, "From Containment to Enlargement," Address at Johns Hopkins University, School of Advanced International Studies, Washington, D.C., September 21, 1993.

13. "In His Own Words: Clinton on China MFN," *China Business Review* (January-February 1993), p. 18.

14. Ibid.

15. Ibid.

16. Ibid; see also, Thomas L. Friedman, "Clinton Says Bush Made China Gains," *New York Times*, November 20, 1992.

17. Three documents were issued as a package on May 28, and they must be considered as a whole: (1) "Executive Order," Conditions for Renewal of Most Favored Nation Status for the People's Republic of China in 1994, May 28, 1993; Office of the Press Secretary, "Report to Congress concerning Extension of Waiver Authority for the People's Republic of China," May 28, 1993; and President Bill Clinton, "Statement by the President on Most Favored Nation Status for China, " May 28, 1993 (issued by Office of the Press Secretary).

18. Conversation with academic in China, April 1993.

19. In this section, I draw heavily on interviews with persons involved in the policy process in the executive branch, in the legislative branch, and in private sector organizations, including lobbyists. Because this is a continuing policy issue, interviews were conducted with the understanding that some details would not be made public nor respondents identified.

20. Winston Lord, "China Policy under the Clinton Administration," Speech to the U.S.-China Business Council, Washington, D.C., June 9, 1993 (unpublished transcript).

21. Hearing transcript, Senate Appropriations Subcommittee on Foreign Operations, March 30, 1993, "Christopher: U.S. Will Try to Use MFN to Curb China Abuses," pp. 1–2.

22. One of the essential things we need to know about the policy process in the Clinton administration is how key principals (for example, the secretaries of defense and state, the NSC adviser, and the head of the Central Intelligence Agency) interact. There were informal patterns of regular interaction in the Carter administration that proved very important, and there are indications that some of those patterns have been replicated by Secretary Christopher and the president's national security adviser, Anthony Lake, who spent earlier periods of their careers in Jimmy Carter's government. Gwen Ifill, "Security Official Guides U.S. Aims at Conference," *New York Times*, July 5, 1993, reports, "Every Wednesday, three men gather around the conference table in a spacious corner office in the West Wing of the White House to share sandwiches and talk. . . . They are the backbone of President Clinton's foreign policy team." They are Anthony Lake, Warren Christopher, and Les Aspin.

23. Business influence was important in its effects on both the administration and Congress. In relative terms, however, the impact of business was most obvious *vis-à-vis* Congress. See, Michael Weisskopf, "Backbone of the New China Lobby: U.S. Firms," *Washington Post*, June 14, 1993. Notably, however, the

groups acting on their interests and concerns in China policy have multiplied since June 1989—this activation of interest groups has occurred because of the human rights problems in the PRC revealed on global television, a rapidly mounting trade deficit with the PRC, and increased popular and elite concern about proliferation of weapons of mass destruction. Many of the interest groups formerly preoccupied with the Soviet Union in these problem areas turned their attention to China after the cold war. Such groups include human rights organizations, labor unions, disarmament and arms control organizations, and the like.

24. Business Coalition for U.S.-China Trade, "Letter to the Honorable Bill Clinton," May 12, 1993. Six major corporations also wrote separately to the president on May 17, 1993, asking for a meeting and saying that "for our respective firms, we project exports to China in excess of $105 billion between now and the year 2010. Those exports to China by our companies will mean sustaining and creating more than 2 million man-years of U.S. high-wage, high-technology employment over this period."

25. See, for example, leaks of satellite intelligence in May 1993 that could have come only from the intelligence community. These leaks indicated that China was in clear violation of promises made in November 1991 to Secretary Baker concerning missile transfers to Pakistan. See Douglas Jehl, "China Breaking Missile Pledge, U.S. Aides Say," *New York Times,* May 6, 1993; see also Associated Press, "China Still Shipping Missiles, Official Says," *Washington Post,* May 6, 1993.

26. Oberdorfer, "How Washington and Beijing Avoided Diplomatic Disaster."

27. Ibid.

28. Lo Ping and Li Tzu-ching, "One Hundred and Sixteen Generals Write to Deng Xiaoping on Policy toward the United States," *Cheng Ming* (Hong Kong), no. 188, June 1, 1993, pp. 14–16, in Foreign Broadcast Information Service (*FBIS*), no. 104 (1993), p. 35.

29. Oberdorfer, "How Washington and Beijing Avoided Diplomatic Disaster."

30. James McGregor, "Talks on China's Trade Status Begin, Made Trickier by Human-Rights Issues," *Wall Street Journal,* May 12, 1993.

31. Ibid.

32. David H. Zhu, "Dealing with the One and Only Superpower: Recent Trends in China's America Policy," *China Monitor* (Bethesda, Md.: U.S. China Research Associates, May/June 1993).

33. Conversation with senior Chinese official in Beijing, April 1993.

34. Zhu, "Dealing with the One and Only Superpower," p. 5.

35. See "PRC-DPRK Relations Growing Worse," *Ching Pao* (Hong Kong), no. 6, June 5, 1993, p. 46. This is confirmed by conversations with Chinese officials.

36. "Report to Congress concerning Extension of Waiver Authority for the People's Republic of China," p. 2.

37. Meeting with senior Chinese leader, April 1993, Beijing. In files of the National Committee on United States–China Relations, New York.

38. It is important to note that when Vice Premier and Foreign Minister Qian Qichen announced in early November that China would allow the inspection of Chinese prisons by the International Committee of the Red Cross, he was careful to say that China would look favorably on a request from the international body, were such a request made.

39. See Hedrick Smith, *The Power Game: How Washington Works* (New York: Random House, 1988), especially chapters 2, 7, and 15, for a fine exposition concerning how the reforms of Congress, the breakdown of the political parties, and the increased role of the mass media have interacted to produce a Congress that is more responsive to external constituencies than to internal discipline.

40. Lee Hamilton, "A New U.S. Policy for China," Speech to the Business Coalition for U.S.-China Trade, April 1, 1993, p. 1.

41. Ibid., p. 2.

42. John Whitehead and Barber B. Conable, Jr., cochairmen, and David M. Lampton and Alfred Wilhelm, rapporteurs, *United States and China Relations at a Crossroads* (Washington, D.C.: Atlantic Council of the United States and the National Committee on United States–China Relations, February 8, 1993).

43. In this context, congressional staff was key, and no one was more important than Richard Bush on the House Foreign Affairs Committee staff. When the definitive history of U.S.-China relations is written, he will be seen to have played an important role.

44. In May, a "dear colleague" letter was circulating over the signatures of representatives Lee Hamilton, Robert Matsui, Michael Kopetski, Jim McDermott, and Jim Leach. U.S. Congress, House of Representatives, Subcommittees on Economic Policy, Trade and Environment, International Security, International Organizations, and Human Rights and Asia and the Pacific, of the Committee on Foreign Affairs, *Statement of Donald M. Anderson,* 103d Cong., 1st sess., May 20, 1993.

45. Hamilton, "A New U.S. Policy for China," pp. 4–5. The chairman of the Subcommittee on Asia and the Pacific, Gary Ackerman (D-N.Y.), aligned himself with Hamilton, saying, "I agree with Chairman Hamilton's contention that we must look beyond only the MFN issue as we work to formulate a cogent foreign policy toward the People's Republic of China. To neglect other aspects of the relationship, particularly the potentially constructive role China can play in resolving such disputes as the North Korean nuclear problem, is sophomoric and near-sighted." Gary L. Ackerman, "Opening Statement," ibid., p. 1.

46. Gary Milhollin, "Prepared Statement," ibid. See also, Jehl, "China Breaking Missile Pledge, U.S. Aides Say"; see also, Associated Press, "China Still Shipping Missiles, Official Says."

47. Senator Biden apparently wrote Secretary of State Christopher a letter about this time on the subject of China's MFN status, but that letter has not been publicly released.

48. John B. Judis, "The Foreign Unpolicy," *New Republic,* July 12, 1993, pp. 16–20.

49. Steven A. Holmes, "Christopher Reaffirms Leading U.S. Role in World," *Wall Street Journal,* May 28, 1993; see also, Holmes, "Backing Away Again, Christopher Says Bosnia Is Not a Vital Interest," *New York Times,* June 4, 1993.

50. David M. Lampton, "The U.S. Image of Peking in Three International Crises," *Western Political Quarterly,* vol. 26, no. 1 (March 1973), pp. 28–50.

51. Benac, "Clinton Says He Will Extend Favorable Trade Status to China."

52. Sidney Jones, cited in *Notes from the National Committee,* vol. 22, no. 2 (Summer 1993), p. 3.

53. James MacGregor Burns, *Leadership* (New York: Harper & Row, Publishers, 1978).

54. Indeed, in an October 1993 interview, the president's national security adviser, Anthony Lake, so much as said that the president was insufficiently involved in many foreign policy decisions that later turned out to be important: "Mr. Lake said that in an effort to conserve the time of the President, he might not have been brought into enough of 'the larger contemplative discussions' on issues that were not of the highest rank, including Somalia." Thomas L. Friedman, "Clinton's Foreign Policy: Top Adviser Speaks Up," *New York Times,* October 31, 1993. For a more hostile, partisan analysis that makes the same point, see Rowland Evans and Robert Novak, "Adm. Crowe to the Rescue?" *Washington Post,* October 25, 1993.

55. Smith, *The Power Game,* chap. 15.

56. Ibid., p. 568.

57. Patrick E. Tyler, "China May Allow Red Cross to Visit Dissidents in Jail," *New York Times,* November 10, 1993.

58. Even issues beyond trade, the proliferation of weapons of mass destruction, and human rights can be linked to MFN status in the Congress. Senator Joseph Biden, for instance, is not only very concerned about weapons and technology sales by China, but he is also committed to the creation of Radio Free Asia. He and like-minded individuals in Congress can link their priority concerns to MFN status to prevail. See, for example, David Binder, "Senators Battle over Foreign Broadcast Cuts," *New York Times,* October 31, 1993.

59. See, for example, Lo and Li, "One Hundred and Sixteen Generals Write to Deng Xiaoping," p. 35. This report asserts,

> At a routine meeting of the Politburo on 14 May, Jiang Zemin made a strongly worded summary of the one-and-a-half day talks between Lord, assistant U.S. secretary of state, and Chinese Vice Foreign Minister Liu Huaqiu. He said: This is the coercive ultimatum resorted to by U.S. hegemonists. We should plan our policy toward the United States. Our basic stance is: We want cooperation and not confrontation. We will develop Sino-U.S. ties based on the principle of the Three Joint Communiques. We will not yield to hegemonism and power politics. We are not afraid of their confrontation and challenge. For the motherland's sovereignty, independence, and dignity, we are ready to pay a price.

Other articles reflecting the military's dissatisfaction with Radio Free Asia, U.S. military sales to Taiwan, and support for the Dalai Lama, among other issues, have appeared. One report (Meimei Chan, "PRC 'Aware' of U.S. Hegemonism Offensive," *Standard* [Hong Kong], June 4, 1993, p. 6; in FBIS, June 4, 1993, no. 106, p. 2), says, "The Chinese government and military produced a four-part documentary in April attacking the U.S. as a 'world hegemony' and blaming its meddling for leading to communism's downfall." See also, Chen Shao-pin, "United States Plots Strategic Encirclement against China," *Ching Pao,* no. 6, June 5, 1993, p. 44; in *FBIS,* no. 106 (1993), p. 2.

60. Jen Hui-wen, "Background to China's 'Four Nots' Policy toward the United States," *Hsin Pao* (Hong Kong), September 17, 1993; in *FBIS,* no. 179 (1993), pp. 1–3.

61. In the near future, Taiwan is undertaking what may amount to a U.S. $35 billion military modernization procurement effort, holding out the promise of substantial purchases from the United States. Taipei is calling on Washington to make policy adjustments to facilitate the effort. In Congress, one again hears calls such as the following from Representative Sam Gejdenson, chairman of the Subcommittee on Economic Policy, Trade and Environment, who said on May 20, 1993: "The U.S. should immediately upgrade its relations with Taiwan. . . . We should stop treating Taiwan like a second-class country." In "Opening Statement," Joint Subcommittee Hearings of the Committee on Foreign Affairs, May 20, 1993, p. 2.

CHAPTER 3: TRADE AND THE WAKING GIANT, *James R. Lilley*

1. Paul Johnson, *Modern Times: The World from the Twenties to the Eighties* (New York: Harper & Row, Publishers, 1983), pp. 544–45.
2. Ibid.
3. Lu Ya-li, "Political Developments in the Republic of China," in Thomas W. Robinson, ed., *Democracy and Development in East Asia: Taiwan, South Korea, and the Philippines* (Washington, D.C.: AEI Press, 1991), p. 36.
4. Ibid., pp. 35–36.
5. Jonathan D. Spence, *The Search for Modern China* (New York: W.W. Norton, 1990), p. 529.
6. Jan S. Prybyla, "Economic Developments in the Republic of China," in Robinson, *Democracy and Development*, pp. 62–63.
7. Ibid., pp. 49–50.
8. Hung-Mao Tien and Chyuan-Jeng Shiau, "Taiwan's Democratization: A Summary," *World Affairs*, vol. 155, no. 2 (Fall 1992), pp. 60–61.
9. Cecilia Sun, Laura Lee-Chin, and Alfred Ritter, "Chronology," *World Affairs*, vol. 155, no. 2 (Fall 1992), pp. 54–57; and ibid.
10. Sung-joo Han and Yung Chul Park, "South Korea: Democratization at Last," in James W. Morely, ed., *Driven by Growth: Political Change in the Asia-Pacific Region* (Armonk, New York: M.E. Sharpe, 1993), p. 166.
11. Ahn Byung-joon, "Korea's International Environment," in Robinson, *Democracy and Development*, p. 162.
12. Robert B. Oxnam, "Asia/Pacific Challenges," *Foreign Affairs*, vol. 72, no. 1 (1992–1993), p. 70.
13. Han and Park, "South Korea," p. 168.
14. Ibid., p. 169.
15. Ibid., pp. 170–71.
16. Ibid., p. 173.
17. Andrew Nagorski, "East Asia in 1980," *Foreign Affairs*, vol. 59, no. 3 (1980), p. 670.
18. Kim Kyong-dong, "Sociocultural Developments in the Republic of Korea," in Robinson, *Democracy and Development*, p. 147.
19. Nagorski, "East Asia," p. 671.
20. Ibid., pp. 671–72.

21. Ibid., p. 673.
22. Elaine P. Adam, "Chronology 1981," *Foreign Affairs*, vol. 60, no. 3 (1981), p. 742.
23. Daryl M. Plunk, "Political Developments in the Republic of Korea," in Robinson, *Democracy and Development*, p. 107.
24. Ibid., p. 118.
25. Kenneth B. Pyle, *The Japanese Question: Power and Purpose in a New Era* (Washington, D.C.: AEI Press, 1992), p. 25.
26. Kenneth B. Pyle, "How Japan Sees Itself," *The American Enterprise*, November-December 1991, p. 31.
27. Ibid., p. 34.
28. Oxnam, "Asia/Pacific Challenges," p. 67.
29. Karel van Wolferen, "Japan's Non-Revolution," *Foreign Affairs*, September-October 1993, p. 55.
30. Ikuo Kabashima, "Japan: There May Be a Choice," in Morely, *Driven by Growth*, p. 271.
31. Van Wolferen, "Japan's Non-Revolution," p. 55.
32. Ibid., p. 58.
33. Ibid., p. 62.
34. "Japan's New Wave of Politicians," *Economist*, July 31, 1993, p. 31.
35. "Japan's New Dawn," *Economist*, August 28, 1993, p. 31.
36. "Japan's New Wave of Politicians," *Economist*, p. 31.
37. David E. Sanger, "New Japan Premier Offers Political Reform Plan," *New York Times*, September 18, 1993.
38. Gary Clyde Hufbauer and Jeffrey J. Schott, *Economic Sanctions Reconsidered: History and Current Policy* (Washington, D.C.: Institute for International Economics, 1985), p. 254.
39. Ibid., p. 258.
40. Michael C. Williams, *Vietnam at the Crossroads* (New York: Council on Foreign Relations Press, 1992), p. 26.
41. Ibid., p. 44.
42. Ibid., pp. 50–51.
43. Ibid., pp. 52–58.
44. Johnson, *Modern Times*, p. 546.
45. Ibid., p. 548.
46. Spence, *The Search for Modern China*, p. 539.
47. Johnson, *Modern Times*, pp. 548–49.
48. Ibid., p. 549.
49. Spence, *The Search for Modern China*, p. 579.
50. Ibid., pp. 582–83.
51. Johnson, *Modern Times*, pp. 556–57.
52. Spence, *The Search for Modern China*, pp. 605–6.
53. Ibid.
54. Johnson, *Modern Times*, pp. 557–58.
55. Thomas P. Bernstein, "China: Change in a Marxist-Leninist State," in Morely, *Driven by Growth*, p. 49.
56. "A Survey of China," *Economist*, November 28, 1992, p. 6.

57. David K. Li, "Behind the China Miracle," *International Economy*, May-June 1993, p. 61.
58. "A Survey of China," *Economist*, p. 11.
59. Lawrence Zuckerman, "That Hum You Hear Is Asia Growing," *Wall Street Journal*, October 18, 1993.
60. David C. Morrison, "Capitalist Roaders," *National Journal*, May 29, 1993, p. 1282.
61. Seth Cropsey, "Renew China's Trade Status," *Backgrounder*, no. 191, May 20, 1993, p. 2.
62. Conversation with Zhiling Lin, AEI research associate.
63. Elizabeth J. Perry, "China in 1992: An Experiment in Neo-Authoritarianism," *Asian Survey*, January 1993, p. 17.
64. "A Survey of China," *Economist*, p. 5.
65. Ibid., p. 4.
66. Central Intelligence Agency, paper, "China's Economy in 1992 and 1993: Grappling with the Risks of Rapid Growth," July 30, 1993, pp. 11–12; and Cropsey, "Renew China's Trade," p. 2.
67. Ibid.
68. Murray Weidenbaum, "Greater China: A New Economic Colossus?" *Washington Quarterly* (Autumn 1993), p. 71.
69. Ibid. p. 74.

CHAPTER 4: TRADE AND INVESTMENT, *Claude E. Barfield*

1. *Financial Times*, November 15, 1993.
2. Thomas J. Duesterberg, "Trade, Investment and Engagement in the U.S.-Asian Relationship," *Washington Quarterly* (Winter 1994), p. 7. For the best general analysis of the growth of the East Asian economies, see World Bank, *The East Asian Miracle: Economic Growth and Public Policy* (Washington, D.C.: World Bank, 1993).
3. Ibid, p. 10.
4. *Financial Times*, November 18, 1993; See also Central Intelligence Agency, "China's Economy in 1992 and 1993: Grappling with the Risks of Growth" (paper submitted to the Subcommittee on Technology and National Security of the Joint Economic Committee, July 30, 1993); and "When China Wakes: A Survey," *Economist*, November 28, 1992.
5. *Wall Street Journal*, December 10, 1993; see also *Journal of Commerce*, November 16 and December 2, 1993.
6. *Journal of Commerce*, December 4, 1993.
7. "China's Economy in 1992 and 1993," p. 1.
8. Ibid., p. 4.
9. *Financial Times*, November 30 and December 2, 1993; *Journal of Commerce*, November 23, 1993; *Economist*, November 20, 1993.
10. *Economist*, November 28, 1992.
11. "China's Economy in 1992 and 1993," pp. 29–30; see also, American Embassy, "Foreign Economic Trends and Their Economic Implications for the United States" (American Embassy, Beijing, China, May 1992, mimeographed).

12. Ibid.
13. Ibid.
14. Murray Weidenbaum, "Greater China: A New Economic Colossus?" *Washington Quarterly* (Autumn 1993), pp. 71–83.
15. *Financial Times*, November 18, 1993.
16. Lee M. Sands and Deborah M. Lehr, "Expanding Trade and Opening Markets in China" (memorandum to Clinton administration, undated). See also, "Foreign Economic Trends and Their Economic Implications," pp. 13–14; "The Case for China's MFN Status," U.S.-China Business Council (mimeographed, May 1992), pp. 1–3.
17. Ibid.
18. Zhiling Lin, "MFN and Its Implications" (speech before the Annual Hong Kong/China Forum, March 27, 1993), pp. 3–4.
19. Sands and Lehr, "Expanding Trade and Opening Markets in China," pp. 4–5.
20. Ibid., p. 7.
21. *Journal of Commerce*, November 17, 1993.

CHAPTER 5: INFLUENCING HUMAN RIGHTS, *Andrew J. Nathan*

1. James D. Seymour, "Cadre Accountability to the Law," *Australian Journal of Chinese Affairs*, vol. 21 (January 1989), pp. 1–28; James D. Seymour, ed., *Cadre Accountability to the Law*, special issue of *Chinese Law and Government*, vol. 21, no. 3 (Fall 1988). Of course, it is another question whether these campaigns were adequately effective.
2. See, for example, *China: Violations of Human Rights: Prisoners of Conscience and the Death Penalty in the People's Republic of China* (London: Amnesty International, 1984); *Punishment Season: Human Rights in China after Martial Law* (New York: Asia Watch, 1990); *Anthems of Defeat: Crackdown in Hunan Province 1989–1992* (New York: Asia Watch, 1992).
3. Asia Watch, "Continuing Religious Repression in China," June 1993.
4. *China: Punishment without Crime: Administrative Detention* (New York: Amnesty International USA, 1991); Timothy A. Gelatt, *Criminal Justice with Chinese Characteristics: China's Criminal Process and Violations of Human Rights* (New York: Lawyers Committee for Human Rights, 1993).
5. See, for example, Amnesty International, "People's Republic of China: Repression in Tibet 1987–1992," May 1992; *Merciless Repression: Human Rights in Tibet* (New York: Asia Watch, 1990).
6. *China: Torture and Ill-Treatment of Prisoners* (London: Amnesty International, 1987); Amnesty International, "Torture in China," December 1992; Asia Watch, "Prison Labor in China," April 19, 1991; Hongda Harry Wu, *Laogai: The Chinese Gulag*, trans. Ted Slingerland (Boulder, Colo.: Westview Press, 1992).
7. Asia Watch, "Indivisible Human Rights," September 1, 1992.
8. Examples are cited in my article, "Human Rights in Chinese Foreign Policy," forthcoming in *China Quarterly*.

9. Samuel S. Kim, *China, the United Nations, and World Order* (Princeton: Princeton University Press, 1979), pp. 484–86.

10. Roberta Cohen, "People's Republic of China: The Human Rights Exception," *Human Rights Quarterly*, vol. 9, no. 4 (November 1987), pp. 536–40.

11. For example, speech by Chinese representative at the 38th session of the UN Commission on Human Rights, *Foreign Affairs China* (Ministry of Foreign Affairs), vol. 2, no. 1 (March 1982), pp. 44–47; "UN Envoy Condemns Human Rights Violations," Beijing Xinhua in English May 23, 1985 in Foreign Broadcast Information Service (*FBIS*) May 23, 1985, p. A1.

12. Hongdah Chiu, "Chinese Attitudes toward International Law of Human Rights in the Post-Mao Era," in Victor C. Falkenheim, ed., *Chinese Politics from Mao to Deng* (New York: Paragon House, 1989), pp. 255–56.

13. Partially, as James Seymour points out in a paper for Samuel Kim's forthcoming *China and the World*, third edition, because they are to be enjoyed only insofar as they are already in force, which excludes representative democracy and the right to self-determination.

14. Information Office of the State Council, "Human Rights in China," *Beijing Review* (hereafter BR), vol. 44 (1991), p. 43.

15. From Chiu, "Chinese Attitudes," pp. 252–54, unless otherwise noted, who cites two textbooks, one by Wei Min and one by Wang Tieya and Wei Min. See also Wei Min, "An Examination of Some Problems on Human Rights, *Renmin ribao*, December 3, 1988, p. 44, in FBIS-CHI-88-237, December 9, 1988, pp. 4–6.

16. For example, Fu Xuezhe, "The Principle of Noninterference in the Internal Affairs of Other Countries and the Question of Human Rights," *Renmin ribao*, December 8, 1989, p. 7, in FBIS-CHI-89-237, December 12, 1989, p. 3.

17. Besides Chiu, "Chinese Attitudes," also see Tian Jin, "The Development of International Human Rights Activities and Some Controversial Issues," *Guoji wenti yanjiu*, January 13, 1989, pp. 4–7, in FBIS-CHI-89-045, March 9, 1989, p. 5.

18. Gu Yan, "On Human Rights in International Relationships," *International Strategic Studies* (Beijing Institute for International Strategic Studies), no. 3 (September 1991), p. 10.

19. Xin Chunying, "Xiandai guoji zhengzhi douzhengzhong de renquan wenti" (Human rights issues in the contemporary international political struggle), *Xuexi yu sikao* (Study and reflection), (Graduate School, Chinese Academy of Social Sciences), vol. 1 (1981), pp. 49–52.

20. Shen Baoxiang, Wang Chengquan, and Li Zerui, "Guanyu guoji lingyu de renquan wenti" (The human rights issue in the international arena), in *Hongqi*, April 16, 1982, pp. 46–47, trans. in *Beijing Review*, vol. 30 (1982), pp. 15, 17.

21. Felice Gaer, "Human Rights and Social Issues: Human Rights," in John Tessitore and Susan Woolfson, eds., *Issues 45: Issues before the 45th General Assembly of the United Nations* (Lexington, Mass.: Lexington Books, 1991), pp. 121–33, 153–55; Felice Gaer, "Human Rights and Social Issues: Human Rights," in Tessitore and Woolfson, eds., *A Global Agenda: Issues before the 46th General Assembly of the United Nations* (Lanham, Md.: University Press of America, 1991), pp. 171–83, 197–98, 200; Felice Gaer, "Human Rights and Social Issues: Human Rights," in Tessitore and Woolfson, eds., *A Global Agenda: Issues before the 47th General Assembly of the United Nations* (Lanham, Md.: University Press

of America, 1992), pp. 224, 226–29, 232; *Yearbook of the United Nations, 1991* (Dordrecht, The Netherlands: Martinus Nijhoff, 1992), p. 606; UN Economic and Social Council, Commission on Human Rights, Document E/CN.4/1993/L.104 (March 8, 1993).

22. See, respectively, E/CN.4/Sub.2/1992/25, pp. 27–29, 30–31 (although not an NGO report, this report by Louis Joinet, chairman and rapporteur of the Working Group on Arbitrary Detention, was based on material supplied by the International Federation of Human Rights); E/CN.4/Sub.2/1992/SR.13, p. 15; E/CN.4/Sub.2/1992/SR.7, pp. 11–12; E/CN.4/Sub.2/1992/SR.17, pp. 7–8; and E/CN.4/Sub.2/1992/SR.25, pp. 3–5.

23. The number 110,000, which is probably an underestimate, comes from *Liaowang* overseas edition, no. 4–5, January 25, 1993, pp. 11–13, in JPRS-CAR-93-022, April 8, 1993, p. 26. Also see Deng Ziduan, "China's Brain-Drain Problem: Causes, Consequences and Policy Options," *Journal of Contemporary China*, vol. 1, no. 1 (Fall 1992), pp. 6–33.

24. "On U.S. Policy towards Chinese Mainland, Taiwan and Hong Kong: A Chinese-American/Canadian Perspective," a position paper endorsed by Tiananmen Memorial Foundation and eleven other groups, May 25, 1993.

25. James D. Seymour, "Human Rights and the World Response to the 1989 Crackdown in China," *China Information*, vol. 4, no. 4 (Spring 1990), pp. 1–14.

26. International League for Human Rights, "Getting Down to Business: The Human Rights Responsibilities of China's Investors and Trade Partners" (July 1992), pp. 15–17, 35–36; *Newsweek*, May 17, 1993, p. 46.

27. For example, for the United States, see Lawyers Committee for Human Rights, "Human Rights Diplomacy and Strategies: A Country Case Study of China," November 1991, pp. 23–27.

28. Citations are too numerous to list, but see, for example, Jiang Zemin's interview with Borchgrave in BR, vol. 46 (1991), p. 15. Many of these themes are outlined in a purported Propaganda Department document, "Confidential Document on Study of Human Rights Issue (part one)," published in Hong Kong, *Tangtai*, no. 15, June 15, 1992, pp. 67–70, in FBIS-CHI-92-121, June 23, 1992, pp. 32–36.

29. Information Office of the State Council, "Human Rights in China," BR, vol. 44 (1991), pp. 8–45.

30. Gu Zhaoji and Zhang Jun, "Renquan wenti dayi yu bobian" (Ideas and debates on human rights issues), *Xuexi yu yanjiu* (Study and research), November 5, 1990, p. 18.

31. Among others, Gu Yan, "On Human Rights," p. 11; and Tian Jin, "Development," p. 5.

32. Zhang Yishan, Chinese representative to the UN Commission on Human Rights, quoted by BR, vol. 9 (1992), p. 27; after the 1992 Los Angeles riots, there was a rush of commentary making this point in specific reference to the riots.

33. *South China Morning Post*, May 25, 1993.

34. 1989, Gaer in *Issues 45*, pp. 153–54; 1990, Gaer in *46th General Assembly*, p. 121; 1992, Gaer in *47th General Assembly*, pp. 237–38.

35. For example, Kong Youzhen, "The Right to Develop Is an Extended Human Right," *Zhen Di*, no. 1, January 10, 1993, pp. 54–56, in JPRS-CAR-93-029,

May 6, 1993, pp. 2–4; Gaer in *46th General Assembly*, pp. 171, 197, and in *47th General Assembly*, pp. 240–41; Alan Riding, "A Rights Meeting, but Don't Mention the Wronged," *New York Times*, June 14, 1993.

36. For example, "Justice Officials: Dissident 'Refuses to Repent,'" Hong Kong AFP, April 8, 1992, in FBIS-CHI-92-070, April 10, 1992, pp. 21–22; Nicholas D. Kristof, "China Offers Peek at Famed Prisoner," *New York Times*, April 8, 1992; Kristof, "China Is Reported to Plan Release of Some Political Prisoners Soon," *New York Times*, May 6, 1992.

37. BR, vol. 42 (1991), p. 10.

38. "Human Rights in China"; "Tibet: Its Ownership and Human Rights Situation," BR, vol. 39 (1992), pp. 10–43; "Criminal Reform in China," BR, vol. 33 (1992), pp. 10–25.

39. UN Statement in PRC Mission to the UN Press Release, New York, January 31, 1992, p. 4; work report statement in BR, vol. 15 (1992), p. xvi.

40. A passport has yet to be given to Yu Haocheng, who has an invitation from Columbia University and has not been convicted of any crime.

41. See, for example, *Waiguo wenti yangjiu* (Research on foreign questions), special issue on human rights, 1990, no. 2 (March 15, 1990), *neibu;* Gu Yan, "On Human Rights"; Sun Zhe, *Xin renquan lun* (A new discussion of human rights) (Zhengzhou: Henan renmin chubanshe [Henan people's publishing house], 1992); and numerous publications of Yu Haocheng.

42. Jeremy T. Paltiel, "Self and Authority in Contemporary China: The End of Ideology?" *Institute Reports*, East Asian Institute, Columbia University, April 1993, p. 19; Baogang He, "Three Models of Democracy: Intellectual and Moral Foundations of Liberal Democracy and Preconditions for Its Establishment in Contemporary China" (Ph.D. diss., Australian National University, 1993), pp. 3, 257.

43. Seymour, "Human Rights," forthcoming.

Chapter 6: Sentiments of the Chinese, *Anne F. Thurston*

1. The interviews and conversations on which this essay is based were conducted while the author was living in Beijing and traveling to other parts of China from May 1989 to June 1990 and in five visits to China from August 1992 to October 1993. In 1989–1990, I had a grant from the National Endowment for the Humanities to study dissent in China. Of the five visits in 1992–1993, one was sponsored by the Committee to Protect Journalists, one by the Committee on Scholarly Communication with China, one by the U.S. Institute of Peace, and two were private. While my sampling technique is hardly scientific, I have been conducting extensive interviews in China since 1981 and have known many of the intellectuals whose views are expressed here (and whose attitudes toward MFN have changed since 1989) since then. From 1986 to 1990, during which I spent two and a half years in Beijing, I was interviewing ordinary, less educated citizens, returning to meet with them over the years. In addition to Beijing, my visits to China in 1992–1993 included Shenzhen, Xiamen, Guangzhou, Hangzhou, Suzhou, and Shanghai, where I interviewed both intellectuals and

ordinary Chinese. This article thus represents a distillation of conversations with well over 100 people in relatively prosperous urban areas of the People's Republic of China.

2. The complicated system of ownership whereby state-owned enterprises are forming new companies that behave like private firms or state-owned enterprises are contracted to individuals suggests that the public-private distinction that some would like to make in granting MFN would be difficult. Many firms that appear to be private are in fact owned by the state.

3. *Qi gong* is a set of breathing, exercise, and meditation techniques, and some *qi gong* masters claim to have the power to cure a wide range of illnesses, including cancer and AIDS. Fang Lizhi is the astrophysicist and leading dissident who found refuge in the American Embassy following the military crackdown.

4. For a description of the abominable conditions in a Shanghai detention center in the late 1970s, see my *Chinese Odyssey: The Life and Times of a Chinese Dissident* (Scribners: New York, 1991), pp. 310–50.

5. *New York Times*, November 20, 1993.

6. One particularly distressing case in point is that of the daughter of Ge Yang, the feisty seventy-seven-year-old former editor of the reformist *New Observer*, who was labeled a "black hand" behind the 1989 protests and who is currently living in the United States, unable to return to China. Her daughter has repeatedly been denied a visa to visit her aged mother on the grounds that she might emigrate.

7. "Human Rights in China," Information Office of the State Council, *Beijing Review*, November 4–10, 1991, p. 33.

8. I arrived in Chongqing on the night of June 4, 1989.

9. See, for instance, Neil J. Kritz, "The CSCE in the New Era," *Journal of Democracy*, vol. 4, no. 3, July 1993, pp. 17–29. I am grateful to Fen Hampson for pointing to the importance of the CSCE.

CHAPTER 7: A LEVEL PLAYING FIELD, *Jerome A. Cohen and Matthew D. Bersani*

1. *China Statistical Yearbook 1991* (State Statistical Bureau of the People's Republic of China), p. 27.

2. These statistics were derived by the United States–China Business Council from a variety of sources.

3. Verbal confirmation of these statistics provided by the Ministry of Foreign Trade and Economic Cooperation of the People's Republic of China.

4. Ibid.

5. Verbal confirmation provided by the World Bank.

CHAPTER 8: WHY DOES MFN DOMINATE? *Wendell L. Willkie II*

1. Robert D. McFadden, "Crew and 263 Illegal Aliens Are Seized," *New York Times*, June 7, 1993; N.R. Kleinfield, "Immigrant Dream of Heaven Chokes in Journey of Misery," *New York Times*, June 8, 1993.

2. Ibid.

3. Ted Robberson, "Mexico Flies Immigrants Back to China," *Washington Post*, July 18, 1993.

4. Tim Weiner, "Fixing Immigration," *New York Times*, June 8, 1993.

5. Al Kamen, "China Helping Stem Flow of Illegal Immigrants," *Washington Post*, November 1, 1993.

6. Jimmy Carter, *Keeping Faith: Memoirs of a President* (New York: Bantam Books, 1982), p. 209.

7. Kamen, "China Helping Stem Flow of Illegal Immigrants."

8. President, "Report to Congress concerning Extension of Waiver Authority for the People's Republic of China," May 28, 1993.

9. *Trade Act of 1974*, U.S. Code, vol. 19, sec. 2432 (1974).

10. Executive Order no. 12850, "Conditions for Renewal of Most Favored Nation Status for the People's Republic of China in 1994," May 28, 1993.

11. House Committee on Ways and Means, *Overview and Compilation of U.S. Trade Statutes*, 102d Cong., 1st sess., March 25, 1991, p. 168.

12. Confirmed by conversation with J. Daniel O'Flaherty, executive director, U.S.–South Africa Business Council, Washington, D.C., January 1994.

13. A review of congressional debate and legislation introduced during the time in question reveals no significant discussion of withdrawing most-favored-nation status from either Argentina or Haiti.

14. Title V of the *Trade Act of 1974*, sec. 2461, as amended.

15. House Committee, *Overview and Compilation of U.S. Trade Statutes*, p. 169.

16. *Encyclopaedia Britannica*, 15th ed., S.V. "The United States from 1920 to 1945."

17. Paul Johnson, *Modern Times* (New York: Harper & Row, 1983), p. 246.

18. Oral confirmation concerning the GATT, Office of the U.S. Trade Representative. See also House Committee, *Overview and Compilation of U.S. Trade Statutes*, p. 169. Oral confirmation regarding MFN for Russia from the Delegation of the European Commission, Washington, D.C.; also, oral confirmation regarding MFN for Russia from Chancellor Kodera, head of the Trade Section of the Japanese Embassy, Washington, D.C. Oral confirmation on countries granting China MFN from Richard Bercher of the United States–China Business Council, Washington, D.C.

19. House Committee, *Overview and Compilation of U.S. Trade Statutes*, p. 169.

20. Ibid.

21. Kissinger testimony, September 19, 1974, before the Senate Foreign Relations Committee, quoted in Walter Isaacson, *Kissinger* (New York: Simon & Schuster, 1992), p. 610.

22. *Washington Post*, January 3, 1975. Quoted in Paula Stern, *Water's Edge: Domestic Politics and the Making of American Foreign Policy* (Westport, Conn: Greenwood Press, 1979), p. 181.

23. John Sinclair Petifer Robson, "Henry Jackson, The Jackson Amendment and Detente: Ideology, Ideas and United States Foreign Policy in the Nixon Era" (Ph.D. diss., University of Texas, Austin, 1989), pp. 166–68.

24. *RN*, p. 562, quoted in Isaacson, *Kissinger* (New York: Gosset & Dunlap, 1978), p. 611.

25. Richard Nixon, *Public Papers of the Presidents of the United States: Richard Nixon*, "Remarks at Commencement Ceremonies at the United States Naval Academy, Annapolis, Maryland," June 5, 1974, no. 165 (Washington, D.C.: GPO, 1974), p. 467.

26. Isaacson, *Kissinger*, p. 614.

27. Stern, *Water's Edge*, pp. 5–6. See also Henry Kissinger, *Years of Upheaval* (Boston: Little, Brown, 1982), p. 249.

28. Henry Kissinger, *The White House Years* (Boston: Little, Brown, 1979), p. 1272.

29. Kissinger, *Years of Upheaval*, p. 987. See also *Congressional Quarterly*, May 19, 1990, p. 1538; and Richard Reeves, "The Inevitability of Scoop Jackson," *New York*, December 17, 1973.

30. Reeves, "Inevitability of Scoop Jackson."

31. Stern, *Water's Edge*, pp. 21–22.

32. Robson, *Henry Jackson*, pp. 132–33, 254–56; Kissinger, *The White House Years*, p. 1272; and Adlai E. Stevenson and Alton Frye, "Trading with the Communists," *Foreign Affairs*, vol. 68, no. 2 (Spring 1989), pp. 54–55, 57.

33. Conversation of the author with Richard Perle, November 1993.

34. Ibid.; and Isaacson, *Kissinger*, pp. 610–11.

35. Kissinger, *Years of Upheaval*, p. 997.

36. Ibid., p. 987.

37. *Trade Act of 1974*, sec. 2432.

38. Kissinger, *Years of Upheaval*, p. 998.

39. Robson, *Henry Jackson*, pp. 140–41. See also Charles Horner, "Human Rights and the Jackson Amendment," in Dorothy Fosdick, ed., *Staying the Course: Henry M. Jackson and National Security* (Seattle: University of Washington Press, 1987), p. 127. See also Michel Oksenberg and Dwight H. Perkins, "The China Policy of Henry Jackson," in Fosdick, *Staying the Course*, pp. 153, 162–63.

40. Ronald Reagan, *Public Papers of the Presidents of the United States: Ronald Reagan*, "Remarks on Presenting the Presidential Medal of Freedom to the Family of the Late Senator Henry M. Jackson of Washington," June 26, 1984 (Washington, D.C.: GPO,), p. 915.

41. "Emigration Holdup Snags Soviet Pact," *Congressional Quarterly*, May 26, 1990, p. 1640. See also "Trade Barriers Lifted for Soviets, Others," *Congressional Quarterly Almanac*, vol. 47, 1991, p. 125.

42. "Trade Barriers Lifted for Soviets, Others," p. 126.

43. Robert S. Ross, "National Security, Human Rights, and Domestic Politics: The Bush Administration and China," in Kenneth A. Clye, Robert J. Lober, and Donald Rothchild, eds., *Eagle in a New World: American Grand Strategy in the Post–Cold War Era* (New York: Harper Collins, 1992), pp. 293–95.

44. Ibid., p. 298.

45. Oksenberg and Perkins, "China Policy of Henry Jackson."

46. Ibid., p. 155.

47. Henry Jackson, "The United States, China, and the 1980s" (Speech given at the School of International Studies, University of Washington, Seattle, February 9, 1980); reprinted in *Henry Jackson and World Affairs, Selected Speeches,*

1953–1983, Dorothy Fosdick, ed. (Seattle: University of Washington Press, 1990), p. 283.

48. Oksenberg and Perkins, "China Policy of Henry Jackson," p. 161 (the phrase is the authors').

49. U.S. Senate Committee on Armed Services and Committee on Energy and Natural Resources, *China and United States Policy: Report of Senator Henry M. Jackson,* 96th Cong., 1st sess., 1983. Quoted in ibid., p. 165.

50. *Congressional Quarterly Almanac,* vol. 36, Congressional Quarterly Inc., Washington, D.C., pp. 356–57.

51. The following analysis reflects contemporaneous news accounts, discussions with former administration officials and congressional staff, and my own recollections as general counsel of the Department of Commerce during the period in question. Especially helpful was the analysis of post-Tiananmen relations between Washington and Beijing found in Harry Harding, *A Fragile Relationship: The United States and China since 1972* (Washington, D.C.: Brookings Institution, 1992).

52. Harding, *A Fragile Relationship,* pp. 221–24.

53. Ibid., pp. 224–29; also conversation of author with James Lilley, January 1994.

54. Thomas Friedman, "Congress, Angry at China, Moves to Impose Sanctions," *New York Times,* June 23, 1989. See also *Congressional Record,* daily ed., June 22, 1989, p. 57250, and June 23, 1989, p. 57504.

55. Harding, *A Fragile Relationship,* p. 234.

56. George Bush, *Public Papers of the Presidents of the United States: George Bush,* 1989, vol. 2 (Washington, D.C.: GPO, 1990), pp. 1612–13. See also "Veto on Chinese Students in U.S. Sustained," *Congressional Quarterly Almanac,* 1990, p. 767.

57. "Repression in China Leads to Sanctions," *Congressional Quarterly Almanac,* 1989, pp. 519, 525–26.

58. Harding, *A Fragile Relationship,* p. 257.

59. "The China Mission," *Washington Post,* December 11, 1989; and "Hailing the Butchers of Beijing," *New York Times,* December 12, 1989.

60. See, for example, George J. Church, "Bush the Riverboat Gambler," *Time,* December 25, 1989. See also Meg Greenfield, "Beware of Geobaloney," *Newsweek,* December 25, 1989, p. 84; George J. Church, "Showing Muscle," *Time,* January 1, 1990, p. 20; Strobe Talbott, "Rethinking the Red Menace," *Time,* January 1, 1990, p. 66; Jack W. Germond and Jules Witcover, "Bush Seems Out of Touch with World Affairs," *National Journal,* February 17, 1990, p. 409.

61. Ibid. See also "Repression in China Leads to Sanctions," p. 518.

62. See H.R. 3792—Public Law 101-246.

63. John R. Cranford, "House Passes Bills to Punish China for Tiananmen Action," *Congressional Quarterly,* October 20, 1990, vol. 48, no. 42, p. 3490.

64. Harding, *A Fragile Relationship,* p. 264. See also Thomas Friedman, "Turmoil in China; U.S. and Chinese Seek to Resolve Rift on Dissident," *New York Times,* June 18, 1989; and Adi Ignatius, "Beijing Permits Fang Lizhi to Leave U.S. Embassy and Travel to Britain," *Wall Street Journal,* June 26, 1990.

65. See, for example, the *Congressional Record,* Senate, "MFN Status for China," report by Senator Dennis DeConcini, June 13, 1990, p. 57869; and Harding, *A Fragile Relationship,* pp. 276–77.

66. See, for example, "Extensions of Remarks: Six Month Extension for MFN Status for the PRC," *Congressional Record,* report by the Hon. Benjamin A. Gilman, June 20, 1990, p. E2050.

67. Hearing, Senate Committee on Finance, *Statement of John Kamm,* 101st Cong., 2d sess., June 20, 1990, pp. 71–72. See also *Statement of Senator John Chafee,* pp. 51–52, in same document.

68. Harding, *A Fragile Relationship,* p. 267.

69. See H.R. 2212—H. Rept. 102-392.

70. Hearing, House Committee on Ways and Means, *Statement of Hon. Nancy Pelosi,* 102d Cong., 1st sess., June 12, 1991, pp. 106–7.

71. See, for example, H.R. 2212 (1991) and H.R. 5318 (1992).

72. Harding, *A Fragile Relationship,* pp. 264–65.

73. Bush, "Message to the House of Representatives Returning without Approval the United States–China Act of 1991," March 2, 1992, vol. 1, 1992–1993, p. 363. See also Bush, "Message to the House of Representatives Returning without Approval the United States-China Act of 1992," September 28, 1992, vol. 2, 1992–1993, p. 1689.

74. Harding, *A Fragile Relationship,* p. 281.

75. Keith Bradsher, "U.S. and China Reach Accord on Copying," *New York Times,* January 17, 1992; and Stephen Greenhouse, "China Will Lower Barriers to Trade in Accord with U.S.," *New York Times,* October 10, 1992.

76. Sheryl Wu Dunn, "For Taiwan, New Access to Western Arms," *New York Times,* September 24, 1991. See also John Kohut, "F-16 Sale Attacked by Trade Minister," *South China Morning Post,* October 16, 1992.

77. Bill Clinton, "Speech Accepting the Democratic Presidential Nomination," *Facts on File,* July 16, 1992, p. 579.

78. See David C. Morrison, "Capitalist Roaders," *National Journal,* May 29, 1993, p. 1282–84. See also Paul Theroux, "Going to See the Dragon," *Harper's,* October 1993, p. 33.

79. George Mitchell, Speech of May 16, 1991, quoted in *Congressional Quarterly Almanac,* vol. 47 (1991), p. 122.

80. Bush, "Memorandum of Disapproval for the Emergency Chinese Immigration Relief Act of 1989," vol. 2, November 30, 1989, pp. 1853–54. See also Bush, "Remarks and a Question and Answer Session with Editorial Page Editors," vol. 2, December 11, 1989, p. 1933.

81. Harding, *A Fragile Relationship,* pp. 223–34.

82. "Repression in China Leads to Sanctions," *Congressional Quarterly Almanac,* 1989, pp. 524–25. See also Harding, *A Fragile Relationship,* p. 258.

83. Jeane Kirkpatrick, "Human Rights and Foreign Policy," in Jeane Kirkpatrick, *Legitimacy and Force,* vol. 1 (New Brunswick, New Jersey: Transaction Books, 1988), p. 147.

84. For a trenchant discussion of this approach, see George Weigel, "On the Road to Isolationism?" *Commentary,* January 1992, pp. 36–42.

85. Ronald Reagan, "Remarks at the Annual Convention of the National Association of Evangelicals in Orlando, Florida," vol. 1, March 8, 1983, p. 359. See also Ronnie Dugger, *On Reagan, the Man and His Presidency* (New York: McGraw-Hill, 1983), p. 353.

86. See, for example, Bush, "Address to the 46th Session of the United Nations General Assembly in New York, New York," vol. 2, September 23, 1991, pp. 1199–1203.

87. As one journalist put it, "China's economy is now the third largest in the world . . ., those who want to use trade as a weapon to pressure China on human rights and other issues threaten to damage what will probably be the world's single most important bilateral relationship by early next century" (William A. Schreyer, *Roll Call,* June 21, 1993, p. 5).

Further, as an article in the *Wall Street Journal* stated, in China,

> Exports are a driving force and the U.S. is the main market, taking 26% of the total. China provides 60% of U.S. shoes, plus, among other things, many of its toys, textiles, and simple appliances . . .
>
> Americans would lose. They would have to pay more for consumer goods from jogging gear to hair driers to Barbie dolls" (Robert Keatley, "Clinton Administration Is Seen Facing Difficult Decisions on Trade with China," *Wall Street Journal,* November 6, 1992).

88. As Patrick Glynn writes: "Nixon's hope at the time of the summit was to dangle the carrot of trade to get further help from the Soviets on political issues, especially Vietnam." (Patrick Glynn, *Closing Pandora's Box* [New York: Basic Books, 1992], p. 265).

89. David C. Morrison, "Capitalist Roaders," *National Journal,* May 29, 1993, p. 1284.

90. See Patrick E. Tyler, "Rights in China Improve, Envoy Says," *New York Times,* January 1, 1994.

91. See Marcus W. Brauchli, "Beijing's Grip Weakens as Free Enterprise Turns into Free-for-All," *Wall Street Journal,* August 8, 1993.

92. House Ways and Means Committee, Subcommittee on Trade, *Statement of Arnold Kanter,* June 29, 1992, 102d Cong., 2d sess., p. 7. Note also the statement of Lawrence S. Eagleburger before the same committee on June 12, 1992, p. 4.

93. Henry Jackson, "Speech of October 11, 1973," in Dorothy Fosdick, ed., *Henry Jackson and World Affairs: Selected Speeches 1953–1983* (Seattle: University of Washington Press, 1990), p. 191.

94. See Anne Thurston, "The Dragon Stirs," *Wilson Quarterly* (Spring 1993), pp. 10–37.

95. See Lena Sun, "China's New Ideology: Make Money, Not Marxism," *Washington Post,* July 27, 1993. See also "China: The Emerging Economic Powerhouse of the 21st Century," *Business Week,* May 17, 1993, pp. 55–69.

96. Ibid.

CHAPTER 9: MFN IN THE SPRING OF 1994, *Wendell L. Willkie II*

1. U.S. Department of State, *Country Reports on Human Rights Practices for 1993,* Report submitted to the Committee on Foreign Relations, U.S. Senate, and the Committee on Foreign Affairs, U.S. House of Representatives, February 1, 1994.

2. Patrick Tyler, "Rights in China Improve, Envoy Says," *New York Times*, January 1, 1994.

3. Thomas Friedman, "With a Close Embrace, U.S. Seeks to Budge China," *New York Times*, January 23, 1994.

4. *Mid-Term Review on China*, Statement of Assistant Secretary of State for East Asian and Pacific Affairs Winston Lord, before the House Ways and Means Committee, Subcommittee on Trade, February 24, 1994.

5. Thomas Lippman, "U.S. Says China Lagging on Human Rights Issue," *New York Times*, January 25, 1994.

6. Peter Behr, "Offering China a Carrot on Trade," *Washington Post*, January 29, 1994. Remarks of Treasury Secretary Lloyd Bentsen, U.S. Chamber of Commerce, January 27, 1994.

7. Patrick Tyler, "China Promises U.S. to Try to Improve Its Human Rights," *New York Times*, January 16, 1994.

8. Lord, *Mid-Term Review on China*, February 24, 1994. See also Patrick Tyler, "Chinese Dissident Emerges, Still Unbowed," *New York Times*, September 21, 1993.

9. Susan V. Lawrence, "How Not to Pressure China," *U.S. News and World Report*, January 31, 1994.

The American Enterprise Institute for Public Policy Research

Founded in 1943, AEI is a nonpartisan, nonprofit, research and educational organization based in Washington, D.C. The Institute sponsors research, conducts seminars and conferences, and publishes books and periodicals.

AEI's research is carried out under three major programs: Economic Policy Studies; Foreign Policy and Defense Studies; and Social and Political Studies. The resident scholars and fellows listed in these pages are part of a network that also includes ninety adjunct scholars at leading universities throughout the United States and in several foreign countries.

The views expressed in AEI publications are those of the authors and do not necessarily reflect the views of the staff, advisory panels, officers, or trustees.

A Note on the Book

*This book was edited by Dana Lane of the AEI Press.
The text was set in Palatino, a typeface designed by
the twentieth-century Swiss designer Hermann Zapf.
Publication Technology Corporation of Fairfax, Virginia,
set the type, and Data Reproductions Corporation,
of Rochester Hills, Michigan, printed and bound the book,
using permanent acid-free paper.*

The AEI Press is the publisher for the American Enterprise Institute for Public Policy Research, 1150 17th Street, N.W., Washington, D.C. 20036; *Christopher C. DeMuth,* publisher; *Dana Lane,* director; *Ann Petty,* editor; *Cheryl Weissman,* editor; *Lisa Roman,* editorial assistant (rights and permissions).

www.ingramcontent.com/pod-product-compliance
Lightning Source LLC
Jackson TN
JSHW061756151224
75386JS00041BA/1420
9780844738574